Web Caching

Web Caching

Duane Wessels

O'REILLY®

Beijing · Cambridge · Farnham · Köln · Paris · Sebastopol · Taipei · Tokyo

Web Caching
by Duane Wessels

Published by O'Reilly & Associates, Inc., 101 Morris Street, Sebastopol, CA 95472.

Editors: Nathan Torkington and Paula Ferguson

Production Editor: Leanne Clarke Soylemez

Cover Designer: Edie Freedman

Printing History:

>   June 2001:   First Edition.

Library of Congress Cataloging-in-Publication Data

Wessels, Duane.
    Web Caching/Duane Wessels
        p. cm.
    ISBN 1-56592-536-X
    1. Cache memory. 2. Browsers (Computer programs) 3. Software configuration
        management. 4. World Wide Web. I. Title.
TK7895.M4 W45 2001
004.5'3--dc21   2001033173

ISBN: 1-56592-536-X
[C]

Table of Contents

Preface

When I first started using the Internet in 1986, my friends and I were obsessed with anonymous FTP servers. What a wonderful concept! We could download all sorts of interesting files, such as FAQs, source code, GIF images, and PC shareware. Of course, downloading could be slow, especially from the busy sites like the famous *WSMR-SIMTEL20.ARMY.MIL* archive.

In order to download files to my PC, I would first *ftp* them to my Unix account and then use Zmodem to transfer them to my PC through my 1200 bps modem. Usually, I deleted a file after downloading it, but there were certain files—like *HOSTS.TXT* and the "Anonymous FTP List"—that I kept on the Unix system. After a while, I had some scripts to automatically locate and retrieve a list of files for later download. Since our accounts had disk quotas, I had to carefully remove old, unused files and keep the useful ones. Also, I knew that if I had to delete a useful file, Mark, Mark, Ed, Jay, or Wim probably had a copy in their account.

Although I didn't realize it at the time, I was *caching* the FTP files. My Unix account provided temporary storage for the files I was downloading. Frequently referenced files were kept as long as possible, subject to disk space limitations. Before retrieving a file from an FTP server, I often checked my friend's "caches" to see if they already had what I was looking for.

Nowadays, the World Wide Web is where it's at, and caching is here too. Caching makes the Web feel faster, especially for popular pages. Requests for cached information come back much faster than requests sent to the content provider. Furthermore, caching reduces network bandwidth, which translates directly into cost savings for many organizations.

In many ways, web caching is similar to the way it was in the Good Ol' Days. The basic ideas are the same: retrieve and store files for the user. When the cache becomes full, some files must be deleted. Web caches can cooperate and talk to each other when looking for a particular file before retrieving it from the source.

Of course, web caching is significantly more sophisticated and complicated than my early Internet years. Caches are tightly integrated into the web architecture, often without the user's knowledge. The Hypertext Transfer Protocol was designed with caching in mind. This gives users and content providers more control (perhaps too much) over the treatment of cached data.

In this book, you'll learn how caches work, how clients and servers can take advantage of caching, what issues are important, how to design a caching service for your organization, and more.

Audience

The material in this book is relevant to the following groups of people:

Administrators

This book is primarily written for those of you who are, or will be, responsible for the day-to-day operation of one or more web caches. You might work for an ISP, a corporation, or an educational institution. Or perhaps you'd like to set up a web cache for your home computer.

Content providers

I sincerely hope that content providers take a look at this book, and especially Chapter 6, to see how making their content more "cache aware" can improve their users' surfing experiences.

Web developers

Anyone developing an application that uses HTTP needs to understand how web caching works. Many users today are behind firewalls and caching proxies. A significant amount of HTTP traffic is automatically intercepted and sent to web caches. Failure to take caching issues into consideration may adversely affect the operation of your application.

Web users

Usually, the people who deploy caches want them to be transparent to the end user. Indeed, users are often unaware that they are using a web cache. Even so, if you are "only" a user, I hope that you find this book useful and interesting. It can help you understand why you sometimes see stale web pages and what you can do about it. If you are concerned about your privacy on the Internet, be sure to read Chapter 3. If you want to know how to configure your browser for caching, see Chapter 4.

To benefit from this book, you need to have only a user-level understanding of the Web. You should know that Netscape Navigator and Internet Explorer are web browsers, that Apache is a web server, and that *http://www.oreilly.com* is a URL. If you have some Unix system administration experience, you can use some of the examples in later chapters.

What You Will and Won't Find Here

Chapter 1 introduces caching and provides some background material to help the rest of the book make sense. In addition, companies that provide caching products are listed here. In Chapter 2, we'll dive into the Hypertext Transfer Protocol and explore its features for caching. Chapter 3 is relatively nontechnical and discusses some of the controversies that surround web caching, such as copyrights and privacy.

In Chapter 4, you'll see the various ways to configure user agents (browsers) for caching, with a focus on Netscape Navigator and Microsoft Internet Explorer. Many administrators prefer to automatically intercept and divert HTTP connections to a cache. We'll talk about that in Chapter 5. Then, in Chapter 6, we'll turn to servers and see how content providers can make their information cache-friendly.

Chapter 7 and Chapter 8 are about cache hierarchies. First we'll talk about them in general, including why you should or should not participate in a hierarchy. Then you'll learn about the protocols caches use to communicate with each other. Chapter 9 is a short chapter about cache clusters. Although clusters have some things in common with cache hierarchies, it is easier to understand some of the nuances after you've learned about the intercache protocols.

In Chapter 10, I'll walk you through some of the decisions you'll face in procuring and building a caching service for your organization. Following that, Chapter 11 offers advice on monitoring the health of your caches once they are operational. For the Unix-savvy, I'll show how to set up UCD-SNMPD and RRDTool for this purpose. Chapter 12 is about benchmarking the performance of caches.

I analyze some logfiles from production caches in Appendix A. Here you can see some sample file size distributions, content types, HTTP headers, and hit ratio simulations. The next four appendixes are about intercache protocols. Appendix B describes the technical details of ICP. Appendix D does the same for HTCP, Appendix C for CARP, and Appendix E for cache digests. Appendix F is a list of HTTP status codes from RFC 2616. Appendix G contains the text of a U.S. copyright statute that mentions caching. Finally, in Appendix H, you'll find definitions for many of the acronyms I use in this book.

The new, hot topics in the caching industry are streaming media and content distribution networks. This book focuses on HTTP and FTP caching techniques with proven results, eschewing technology that is still evolving.

Caching Resources

Here are a few resources you can use to find additional information about caching. Caching vendors' web sites are listed in Section 1.8, "Products."

Web Sites

See the following web sites for more information about web caching:

http://www.web-caching.com

> This well-designed site contains a lot of up-to-date information, including product information, press releases, links to magazine articles online, industry events, and job postings. The site also has a bulletin board discussion forum. The banner ads at the top of every page are mildly annoying.

http://www.caching.com

> This professional site is full of web caching information in the form of press releases, upcoming events, vendor white papers, online magazine articles, and analyst commentaries. The site is apparently sponosred by a number of the caching companies.

http://www.web-cache.com

> At my own site for caching information, you'll find mostly links to other web sites, including caching vendors and caching-related services. I also try to keep up with relevant technical documents (e.g., RFCs) and research papers.

http://dmoz.org/Computers/Software/Internet/Servers/Proxy/Caching/

> The Open Directory Project has a decent-sized collection of web caching links at the above URL.

http://www.wrec.org

> The Web Replication and Caching (WREC) working group of the IETF is officially dead, but this site still has some useful information.

http://www.iwcw.org

> This site provides information about the series of annual International Web Caching Workshops.

Mailing Lists

The following mailing lists discuss various aspects of web caching:

isp-caching

> Currently the most active caching-related mailing list. Averages about 2–3 messages per day. Posting here is likely to result in a number of salespeople knocking on your mailbox. One of the great things about this list is that replies automatically go back to the list unless the message composer is

careful. On many occasions people have posted messages that they wish they could take back! For more information, visit *http://www.isp-caching.com*.

WEBI

WEBI (Web Intermediaries) is a new IETF working group, replacing WREC. The discussion is bursty, averaging about 1–2 messages per day. This is not an appropriate forum for discussion of web caching in general; topics should be related to the working group charter. Currently the group is addressing inter-mediary discovery (a la WPAD) and the resource update protocol. For additional information, including the charter and subscription instructions, visit *http://www.ietf.org/html.charters/webi-charter.html*.

HTTP working group

Although the HTTP working group is officially dead, the mailing list still receives a small amount of traffic. Messages are typically from somebody asking for clarification about the RFC. For subscription information and access to the archives, visit *http://www.ics.uci.edu/pub/ietf/http/hypermail/*.

loadbalancing

The people on this list discuss all aspects of load balancing, including hints for configuring specific hardware, performance issues, and security alerts. Traffic averages about 3–4 messages per day. For more more information, visit *http://www.lbdigest.com*.

Conventions Used in This Book

I use the following typesetting conventions in this book:

Italic

Used for emphasis and to signify the first use of a term. Italic is also used for URLs, host names, email addresses, FTP sites, file and directory names, and commands.

`Constant width`

Used for HTTP header names and directives, such as `If-modified-since` and `no-cache`.

How To Contact Us

You can contact the author at *wessels@packet-pushers.com*.

Please address comments and questions concerning this book to the publisher:

O'Reilly & Associates, Inc.
101 Morris Street
Sebastopol, CA 95472
(800) 998-9938 (in the United States or Canada)

(707) 829-0515 (international or local)
(707) 829-0104 (fax)

We have a web page for this book, where we list examples, errata, or any additional information. You can access this page at:

http://www.oreilly.com/catalog/webcaching/

To comment or ask technical questions about this book, send email to:

bookquestions@oreilly.com

For more information about our books, conferences, software, Resource Centers, and the O'Reilly Network, see our web site at:

http://www.oreilly.com

Acknowledgments

I am extremely lucky to have been put in the position to write this book. There are so many people who have helped me along the way. First, I want to thank Dr. Jon Sauer and Dr. Ken Klingenstein at the University of Colorado for supporting my graduate work in this field. Huge thanks to Michael Schwartz, Peter Danzig, and other members of the Harvest project for the most enjoyable job I'll probably ever have. I don't think I can ever thank k claffy and Hans-Werner Braun of NLANR enough for taking me in and allowing me to work on the IRCache project. I am also in karma-debt to all of my CAIDA friends (Tracie, Amy, Rochell, Jenniffer, Jambi) for taking care of business in San Diego so I could stay in Boulder. Thanks to Marla Meehl and the National Center for Atmospheric Research for a place to sit and an OC-3 connection.

This book has benefited immensely from the attentive eyes of the folks who reviewed the manuscript: Ittai Gilat (Microsoft), Lee Beaumont (Lucent), Jeff Boote (NCAR), Reuben Farrelley, and Valery Soloviev (Inktomi). Special thanks also to Andy Cervantes of The Privacy Foundation.

As usual, the folks at O'Reilly have done a fantastic job. Nat, Paula, Lenny, Erik: Let's do it again sometime!

Since I've been working on web caching, I have been very fortunate to work with many wonderful people. I truly appreciate the support and friendship of Jay Adelson, Kostas Anagnostakis, Pei Cao, Glenn Chisholm, Ian Cooper, Steve Feldman, Henry Guillen, Martin Hamilton, Ted Hardie, Solom Heddaya, Ron Lee, Ulana Legedza, Carlos Maltzahn, John Martin, Ingrid Melve, Wojtek Sylwestrzak, Bill Woodcock, and Lixia Zhang.

Thanks to my family (Karen, John, Theresa, Roy) for their constant support and understanding. Despite the efforts of my good friends Ken, Scott, Bronwyn, Gennevive, and Brian, who tried to tie up all my free time, I finished anyway! My coworkers, Alex Rousskov and Matthew Weaver, are champs for putting up an endless barrage of questions, and for tolerating my odd working hours. A big thank you to everyone who writes free software, especially the FreeBSD hackers. But most of all, thanks to all the Squid users and developers out there!

1

Introduction

The term *cache* has French roots and means, literally, *to store*. As a data processing term, caching refers to the storage of recently retrieved computer information for future reference. The stored information may or may not be used again, so caches are beneficial only when the cost of storing the information is less than the cost of retrieving or computing the information again.

The concept of caching has found its way into almost every aspect of computing and networking systems. Computer processors have both data and instruction caches. Computer operating systems have buffer caches for disk drives and filesystems. Distributed (networked) filesystems such as NFS and AFS rely heavily on caching for good performance. Internet routers cache recently used routes. The Domain Name System (DNS) servers cache hostname-to-address and other lookups.

Caches work well because of a principle known as *locality of reference*. There are two flavors of locality: temporal and spatial. Temporal locality means that some pieces of data are more popular than others. CNN's home page is more popular than mine. Within a given period of time, somebody is more likely to request the CNN page than my page. Spatial locality means that requests for certain pieces of data are likely to occur together. A request for the CNN home page is usually followed by requests for all of the page's embedded graphics. Caches use locality of reference to predict future accesses based on previous ones. When the prediction is correct, there is a significant performance improvement. In practice, this technique works so well that we would find computer systems unbearably slow without memory and disk caches. Almost all data processing tasks exhibit locality of reference and therefore benefit from caching.

When requested data is found in the cache, we call it a *hit*. Similarly, referenced data that is not cached is known as a *miss*. The performance improvement that a cache provides is based mostly on the difference in service times for cache hits compared to misses. The percentage of all requests that are hits is called the *hit ratio.*

Any system that utilizes caching must have mechanisms for maintaining *cache consistency.* This is the process by which cached copies are kept up-to-date with the originals. We say that cached data is either *fresh* or *stale.* Caches can reuse fresh copies immediately, but stale data usually requires validation. The algorithms that are to maintain consistency may be either weak or strong. Weak consistency means that the cache sometimes returns outdated information. Strong consistency, on the other hand, means that cached data is always validated before it is used. CPU and filesystem caches require strong consistency. However, some types of caches, such as those in routers and DNS resolvers, are effective even if they return stale information.

We know that caching plays an important role in modern computer memory and disk systems. Can it be applied to the Web with equal success? Ask different people and you're likely to get different answers. For some, caching is critical to making the Web usable. Others view caching as a necessary evil. A fraction probably consider it just plain evil [Tewksbury, 1998].

In this book, I'll talk about applying caching techniques to the World Wide Web and try to convince you that web caching is a worthwhile endeavor. We'll see how web caches work, how they interact with clients and servers, and the role that HTTP plays. You'll learn about a number of protocols that are used to build cache clusters and hierarchies. In addition to talking about the technical aspects, I also spend a lot of time on the issues and politics. The Web presents some interesting problems due to its highly distributed nature.

After you've read this book, you should be able to design and evaluate a caching proxy solution for your organization. Perhaps you'll install a single caching proxy on your firewall, or maybe you need many caches located throughout your network. Furthermore, you should be well prepared to understand and diagnose any problems that may arise from the operation or failure of your caches. If you're a content provider, then I hope I'll have convinced you to increase the cachability of the information you serve.

1.1 *Web Architecture*

Before we can talk more about caching, we need to agree on some terminology. Whenever possible, I use words and meanings taken from Internet standards documents. Unfortunately, colloquial usage of web caching terminology is often just different enough to be confusing.

1.1.1 Clients and Servers

The fundamental building blocks of the Web (and indeed most distributed systems) are *clients* and *servers*. A web server manages and provides access to a set of *resources*. The resources might be simple text files and images, or something more complex, such as a relational database. Clients, also known as *user agents*, initiate a transaction by sending a *request* to a server. The server then processes the request and sends a *response* back to the client.

On the Web, most transactions are download operations; the client downloads some information from the server. In these cases, the request itself is quite small (about 200 bytes) and contains the name of the resource, plus a small amount of additional information from the client. The information being downloaded is usually an image or text file with an average size of about 10,000 bytes. This characteristic of the Web makes cable- and satellite-based Internet services viable. The data rates for receiving are much higher than the data rates for sending because web users mostly receive information.

A small percentage of web transactions are more correctly characterized as upload operations. In these cases, requests are relatively large and responses are very small. Examples of uploads include sending an email message and transferring an image file from your computer to a server.

The most common web clients are called *browsers*. These are applications such as Netscape Navigator and Microsoft Internet Explorer. The purpose of a browser is to render the web content for us to view and interact with. Because of the myriad of features present in web browsers, they are really very large and complicated programs. In addition to the GUI-based clients, there are a few simple command-line client programs, such as Lynx and Wget.

A number of different servers are in widespread use on the Web. The Apache HTTP server is a popular choice and freely available. Netscape, Microsoft, and other companies also have server products. Many content providers are concerned with the performance of their servers. The most popular sites on the Net can receive ten million requests per day with peak request rates of 1000 per second. At this scale, both the hardware and software must be very carefully designed to cope with the load. Many sites run multiple servers in parallel to handle their high request rates and for redundancy.

Recently, there has been a lot of excitement surrounding *peer-to-peer* applications, such as Napster. In these systems, clients share files and other resources (e.g., CPU cycles) directly with each other. Napster, which enables people to share MP3 files, does not store the files on its servers. Rather, it acts as a directory and returns pointers to files so that two clients can communicate directly. In the peer-to-peer realm, there are no centralized servers; every client is a server.

The peer-to-peer movement is relatively young but already very popular. It's likely that a significant percentage of Internet traffic today is due to Napster alone. However, I won't discuss peer-to-peer clients in this book. One reason for this is that Napster uses its own transfer protocol, whereas here we'll focus on HTTP.

1.1.2 Proxies

Much of this book is about *proxies*. A proxy is an intermediary in a web transaction. It is an application that sits somewhere between the client and the origin server. Proxies are often used on firewalls to provide security. They allow (and record) requests from the internal network to the outside Internet.

A proxy behaves like both a client and a server. It acts like a server to clients, and like a client to servers. A proxy receives and processes requests from clients, and then it forwards those requests to origin servers. Some people refer to proxies as "application layer gateways." This name reflects the fact that the proxy lives at the application layer of the OSI reference model, just like clients and servers. An important characteristic of an application layer gateway is that it uses two TCP connections: one to the client and one to the server. This has important ramifications for some of the topics we'll discuss later.

Proxies are used for a number of different things, including logging, access controls, filtering, translation, virus checking, and caching. We'll talk more about these and the issues they create in Chapter 3.

1.1.3 Web Objects

I use the term *object* to refer to the entity exchanged between a client and a server. Some people may use *document* or *page*, but these terms are misleading because they imply textual information or a collection of text and images. "Object" is generic and better describes the different types of content returned from servers, such as audio files, ZIP files, and C programs. The standards documents (RFCs) that describe web components and protocols prefer the terms *entity*, *resource*, and *response*. My use of object corresponds to their use of entity, where an object (entity) is a particular response generated from a particular resource. Web objects have a number of important characteristics, including size (number of bytes), type (HTML, image, audio, etc.), time of creation, and time of last modification.

In broad terms, web resources can be considered either *dynamic* or *static*. Responses for dynamic resources are generated on the fly when the request is made. Static responses are pregenerated, independent of client requests. When people think of dynamic responses, often what comes to mind are stock quotes, live camera images, and web page counters. Digitized photographs, magazine articles, and software distributions are all static information. The distinction between dynamic and static content is not necessarily so clearly defined. Many web resources are updated at various intervals (perhaps daily) but not uniquely generated on a per-request basis. The distinction between dynamic and static resources is important because it has serious consequences for cache consistency.

1.1.4 Resource Identifiers

Resource identifiers are a fundamental piece of the architecture of the Web. These are the names and addresses for web objects, analogous to street addresses and telephone numbers. Officially, they are called *Universal Resource Identifiers*, or URIs. They are used by both people and computers alike. Caches use them to identify and index the stored objects. According to the design specification, RFC 2396, URIs must be extensible, printable, and able to encode all current and future naming schemes. Because of these requirements, only certain characters may appear in URIs, and some characters have special meanings.

Uniform Resource Locators (URLs) are the most common form of URI in use today. The URL syntax is described in RFC 1738. Here are some sample URLs:

> *http://www.zoidberg.net*
> *http://www.oasis-open.org/docbook/index.html*
> *ftp://ftp.freebsd.org/pub/FreeBSD/README.TXT*

URLs have a very important characteristic worth mentioning here. Every URL includes a network host address—either a hostname or an IP address. Thus, a URL is bound to a specific server, called the *origin server*. This characteristic has some negative side effects for caching. Occasionally, the same resource exists on two or more servers, as occurs with mirror sites. When a resource has more than one name, it can get cached under different names. This wastes storage space and bandwidth.

Uniform Resource Names (URNs) are similar to URLs, but they refer to resources in a location-independent manner. RFC 2141 describes URNs, which are also sometimes called *persistent names*. Resources named with URNs can be moved from one server (location) to another without causing problems. Here are some sample (hypothetical) URNs:

> *urn:duns:002372413:annual-report-1997*
> *urn:isbn:156592536X*

In 1995, the World Wide Web Project left its birthplace at CERN in Geneva, Switzerland, and became the World Wide Web Consortium. In conjunction with this move, their web site location changed from *info.cern.ch* to *www.w3c.org*. Everyone who used a URL with the old location received a page with a link to the new location and a reminder to "update your links and hotlist."* Had URNs been implemented and in use back then, such a problem could have been avoided.

Another advantage of URNs is that a single name can refer to a resource replicated at many locations. When an application processes such a URN request, it must select one of the locations (presumably the closest or fastest) from which to retrieve the object. RFC 2168 describes methods for resolving URNs.

Unfortunately, URNs have been very slow to catch on. Very few applications are able to handle URNs, while everyone and everything knows about URLs. Through the remainder of this book, I'll use both URI and URL somewhat interchangeably. I won't say much more about URNs, but keep in mind that URI is a generic term that refers to both URLs and URNs.

1.2 Web Transport Protocols

Clients and servers use a number of different transport protocols to exchange information. These protocols, built on top of TCP/IP, comprise the majority of all Internet traffic today. The *Hypertext Transfer Protocol* (HTTP) is the most common because it was designed specifically for the Web. A number of legacy protocols, such as the *File Transfer Protocol* (FTP) and *Gopher*, are still in use today. According to Merit's measurements from the NSFNet, HTTP replaced FTP as the dominant protocol in April of 1995.† Some newer protocols, such as *Secure Sockets Layer* (SSL) and the *Real-time Transport Protocol* (RTP), are increasing in use.

1.2.1 HTTP

Tim Berners-Lee and others originally designed HTTP to be a simple and lightweight transfer protocol. Since its inception, HTTP has undergone three major revisions. The very first version, retroactively named HTTP/0.9, is extremely simple and almost trivial to implement. At the same time, however, it lacks any real features. The second version, HTTP/1.0 [Berners-Lee, Fielding and Frystyk, 1996], defines a small set of features and still maintains the original goals of being simple and lightweight. However, at a time when the Web was experiencing phenomenal growth, many developers found that HTTP/1.0 did not provide all the functionality they required for new services.

The HTTP Working Group of the Internet Engineering Task Force (IETF) has worked long and hard on the protocol specification for HTTP/1.1. New features in this version include persistent connections, range requests, content negotiation,

---

* Many years after this change, accessing *info.cern.ch* still generated a response with a link to *http://www.w3c.org*.

† The source of this data is *ftp://ftp.merit.edu/nsfnet/statistics/*.

and improved cache controls. RFC 2616 is the latest standards track document describing HTTP/1.1. Unlike the earlier versions, HTTP/1.1 is a very complicated protocol.

HTTP transactions use a well-defined message structure. A message, which can be either a request or a response, has two parts: the *headers* and the *body*. Headers are always present, but the body is optional. Headers are represented as ASCII strings terminated by carriage return and linefeed characters. An empty line indicates the end of headers and the start of the body. Message bodies are treated as binary data. The headers are where we find information and directives relevant to caching.

An HTTP header consists of a name followed by a colon and then one or more values separated by commas. Multiword names are separated with dashes. Header names and reserved words are case-insensitive. For example, these are all HTTP headers:

```
Host: www.slashdot.org
Content-type: text/html
Date: Sat, 03 Mar 2001 13:41:06 GMT
Cache-control: no-cache,private,no-store
```

HTTP defines four categories of headers: entity, request, response, and general. Entity headers describe something about the data in the message body. For example, `Content-length` is an entity header. It describes the length of the message body. Request headers should appear only in HTTP requests and are meaningless for responses. `Host` and `If-modified-since` are request headers. Response headers, obviously, apply only to HTTP responses. `Age` is a response header. Finally, general headers are dual-purpose: they can be found in both requests and responses. `Cache-control` is a general header, one that we'll talk about often.

The first line of an HTTP message is special. For requests, it's called the *request line* and contains the *request method*, a URI, and an HTTP version number. For responses, the first line is called the *status-line*, and it includes an HTTP version number and a *status code* that indicates the success or failure of the request. Note that most request messages do not have a body, but most response messages do.

Here's a simple GET request:

```
GET /index.html HTTP/1.1 .
Host: www.web-cache.com
Accept: */*
```

And here's a simple POST request with a message body:

```
POST /cgi-bin/query.pl HTTP/1.1
Host: www.web-cache.com
Accept: */*
```

```
Content-Length: 19

args=foo+bar&max=10
```

Here's a successful response:

```
HTTP/1.1 200 Ok
Date: Wed, 21 Feb 2001 09:57:56 GMT
Last-Modified: Mon, 19 Feb 2001 20:45:26 GMT
Server: Apache/1.2.5
Content-Length: 13
Content-Type: text/plain

Hello, world.
```

And here's an error response:

```
HTTP/1.0 404 Not Found
Date: Fri, 23 Feb 2001 00:46:54 GMT
Server: Apache/1.2.5
content-Type: text/html

<HTML><HEAD>
<TITLE>404 File Not Found</TITLE>
</HEAD><BODY>
<H1>File Not Found</H1>
The requested URL /foo.bar was not found on this server.<P>
</BODY></HTML>
```

RFC 2616 defines the request methods listed in Table 1.1. Other RFCs, such as 2518, define additional methods for HTTP. Applications may even make up their own *extension methods*, although proxies are not required to support them. A proxy that receives a request with an unknown or unsupported method should respond with a 405 (Method Not Allowed) message. The descriptions in Table 1.1 are necessarily brief. Refer to Section 9 of RFC 2616 for full details.

Table 1.1. HTTP Request Methods Defined by RFC 2616

Method	Description
GET	A request for the information identified by the request URI.
HEAD	Identical to GET, except the response does not include a message body.
POST	A request for the server to process the data present in the message body.
PUT	A request to store the enclosed body in the named URI.
TRACE	A "loopback" method that essentially echoes a request back to the client. It is also useful for discovering and testing proxies between the client and the server.
DELETE	A request to remove the named URI from the origin server.

Table 1.1. HTTP Request Methods Defined by RFC 2616 (continued)

Method	Description
OPTIONS	A request for information about a server's capabilities or support for optional features.
CONNECT	Used to tunnel certain protocols, such as SSL, through a proxy.

For our purposes, GET, HEAD, and POST are the only interesting request methods. I won't say much about the others in this book. We'll talk more about HTTP in Chapter 2.

1.2.2 FTP

The File Transfer Protocol (FTP) has been in use since the early years of the Internet (1971). The current standard document, RFC 959, by Postel, is very different from the original specification, RFC 172. FTP consumed more Internet backbone bandwidth than any other protocol until about March of 1995.

An FTP session is a bit more complicated than an HTTP transaction. FTP uses a *control channel* for commands and responses and a separate *data channel* for actual data transfer. Before data transfer can occur, approximately six command and reply exchanges take place on the control channel. FTP clients must "log in" to a server with a username and password. Many servers allow anonymous access to their publicly available files. Because FTP is primarily intended to give access to remote filesystems, the protocol supports commands such as *CWD* (change working directory) and *LST* (directory listing). These differences make FTP somewhat awkward to implement in web clients. Regardless, FTP remains a popular way of making certain types of information available to Internet and web users.

1.2.3 SSL/TLS

Netscape invented the Secure Sockets Layer (SSL) protocol in 1994 to foster electronic commerce applications on the Internet. SSL provides secure, end-to-end encryption between clients and servers. Before SSL, people were justifiably afraid to conduct business online due to the relative ease of sniffing network traffic. The development and standardization of SSL has moved into the IETF, where it is now called *Transport Layer Security* (TLS) and documented in RFC 2246.

The TLS protocol is not restricted to HTTP and the Web. It can be used for other applications, such as email (SMTP) and newsgroups (NNTP). When talking about HTTP and TLS, the correct terminology is "HTTP over TLS," the particulars of which are described in RFC 2818. Some people refer to it as HTTPS because HTTP/TLS URLs use "https" as the protocol identifier:

```
https://secure.shopping.com/basket
```

Proxies interact with HTTP/TLS traffic in one of two ways: either as a connection endpoint or as a device in the middle. If a proxy is an endpoint, it encrypts and decrypts the HTTP traffic. In this case, the proxy may be able to store and reuse responses. If, on the other hand, the proxy is in the middle, it can only tunnel the traffic between the two endpoints. Since the communication is encrypted, the responses cannot be cached and reused.

1.2.4 Gopher

The Gopher protocol is slowly becoming all but extinct on the Web. In principle, Gopher is very similar to HTTP/0.9. The client sends a single request line, to which the server replies with some content. The client knows a priori what type of content to expect because each request includes an encoded, Gopher-specific content-type parameter. The extra features offered by HTTP and HTML made Gopher obsolete.

1.3 Why Cache the Web?

The short answer is that caching saves money. It saves time as well, which is sometimes the same thing if you believe that "time is money." But how does caching save you money?

It does so by providing a more efficient mechanism for distributing information on the Web. Consider an example from our physical world: the distribution of books. Specifically, think about how a book gets from publisher to consumer. Publishers print the books and sell them, in large quantities, to wholesale distributors. The distributors, in turn, sell the books in smaller quantities to bookstores. Consumers visit the stores and purchase individual books. On the Internet, web caches are analogous to the bookstores and wholesale distributors.

The analogy is not perfect, of course. Books cost money; web pages (usually) don't. Books are physical objects, whereas web pages are just electronic and magnetic signals. It's difficult to copy a book, but trivial to copy electronic data.

The point is that both caches and bookstores enable efficient distribution of their respective contents. An Internet without caches is like a world without bookstores. Imagine 100,000 residents of Los Angeles each buying one copy of *Harry Potter and the Sorcerer's Stone* from the publisher in New York. Now imagine 50,000 Internet users in Australia each downloading the Yahoo! home page every time they access it. It's much more efficient to transfer the page once, cache it, and then serve future requests directly from the cache.

In order for caching to be effective, the following conditions must be met:

- Client requests must exhibit locality of reference.

- The cost of caching must be less than the cost of direct retrieval.

We can intuitively conclude that the first requirement is true. Certain web sites are very popular. Classic examples are the starting pages for Netscape and Microsoft browsers. Others include searching and indexing sites such as Yahoo! and Altavista. Event-based sites, such as those for the Olympics, NASA's Mars Pathfinder mission, and World Cup Soccer, become extremely popular for days or weeks at a time. Finally, every individual has a few favorite pages that he or she visits on a regular basis.

It's not always obvious that the second requirement is true. We need to compare the costs of caching to the costs of not caching. Numerous factors enter into the analysis, some of which are easier to measure than others. To calculate the cost of caching, we can add up the costs for hardware, software, and staff time to administer the system. We also need to consider the time users save waiting for pages to load (latency) and the cost of Internet bandwidth.

Let's take a closer look at the three primary benefits of caching web content:

- To make web pages load faster (reduce latency)

- To reduce wide area bandwidth usage

- To reduce the load placed on origin servers

1.3.1 Latency

Latency refers to delays in the transmission of data from one point to another. The transmission of data over electrical or optical circuits is limited by the speed of light. In fact, electrical and optical pulses travel at approximately two-thirds the speed of light in wires and fibers. Theoretically, it takes at least 25 milliseconds to send a packet across the U.S. In practice, it takes a little longer, say about 30 milliseconds. Transoceanic delays are in the 100-millisecond range.

Another source of latency is network congestion. When network links are close to full utilization, packets experience queuing delays inside routers and switches. Queuing, which can occur at any number of points along a path, is occasionally a source of significant delay. When a device's queue is full, it is forced to discard incoming (or outgoing) packets. With reliable protocols, such as TCP, lost packets are eventually retransmitted. TCP's retransmission algorithms are much too complex to describe here. However, a relatively small amount of packet loss can result in a dramatic decrease in throughput.

A web cache located close to its users reduces latency for cache hits. Transmission delays are much lower because the systems are close to each other. Additionally, queuing and retransmission delays are less likely because fewer routers and links are involved. If the service is designed properly, a cache miss should not be delayed much longer than a direct transfer between the client and origin server. Thus, cache hits reduce the average latency of all requests.

To some extent, latency due to congestion can be eliminated by upgrading network links and/or hardware (faster switches, fatter pipes). In reality, you may find this option too costly. Very fast routers and high-speed, wide-area data circuits can be prohibitively expensive. Furthermore, you cannot upgrade equipment you do not control. For example, there is almost nothing a person living in Japan can do to increase the capacity of major exchange points in the United States. Installing a cache, however, avoids congested parts of the network for some web requests.

Content providers and online shopping companies have an incentive to develop cache-friendly web sites. A 1999 study by Zona Research concluded that e-commerce sites may have been losing up to US$362 million per month due to page loading delays and network failures [Zona Research, 1999]. In Chapter 6, we'll talk about ways that content providers can make their servers cache-friendly.

1.3.2 Bandwidth

Another reason to utilize web caches is *bandwidth reduction*. Every request that results in a cache hit saves bandwidth. If your Internet connection is congested, installing a cache is likely to improve performance for other applications (e.g., email, interactive games, streaming audio), because all your network applications compete for bandwidth. A web cache reduces the amount of bandwidth consumed by HTTP traffic, leaving a larger share for the others. It is also correct to say that a web cache increases your effective bandwidth. If your network supports 100 users without a cache, you can probably support 150 users with a cache.

Even if your Internet connection has plenty of spare bandwidth, you may still want to use a cache. In the United States, Internet service is typically billed at flat rates. Many other countries, however, have usage-based billing. That is, you pay only for the bandwidth you use. Australia and New Zealand were among the first countries to meter bandwidth usage. Not surprisingly, these countries were also the first to widely deploy web caches.

1.3.3 Server Load

In the same way that caching reduces bandwidth, it also reduces the load imposed upon origin servers. A server's response time usually increases as the request rate increases. An idle server is faster than a busy one. A very busy server is slow, regardless of the network conditions between the server and its clients. Banga and Druschel show specifically how web server performance degrades when overloaded [Banga and Druschel, 1997].

It seems strange that an ISP should install a caching proxy to reduce the load on content providers. In fact, some content providers don't want caching proxies to reduce their request rates. As we'll see in Chapter 3, they would rather receive all requests.

However, more and more content providers are using *surrogates* (commonly called *server accelerators* or *reverse caches*) to more efficiently distribute their data. Surrogates are used extensively by content distribution network (CDN) providers such as Akamai and Digital Island. A surrogate is much like a caching proxy, except that it works on behalf of an origin server rather than a user agent. This means that surrogates interpret some HTTP headers differently.

CDNs (and surrogates) are a good way for content providers to make their sites faster for end users. However, it's not the only way. By carefully configuring their web servers, content providers can take full advantage of all the caching proxies on the Internet. As we'll see in Chapter 6, it's even possible to get accurate access counts while making most of the content cachable.

1.4 Why Not Cache the Web?

By now, you may have the impression that web caching is a wonderful solution without any negative side effects. In fact, there are a number of important issues and consequences to understand about web caching. I'll mention some of them here, with a deeper discussion to follow in Chapter 3.

Unlike more tightly coupled systems, it can be difficult for a web cache to guarantee consistency. This means that a cache might return out-of-date information to a user. Why should this be the case? One important factor is that web servers provide only weak hints about freshness. Many responses don't have any hints at all. On-demand validation is the only way to guarantee a cached response is up-to-date. Given the relatively high latencies involved (compared to other systems), validation can take a significant amount of time. Furthermore, the cache may not even be able to reach the server due to a network or server failure. If a validation request fails, the cache doesn't really know if its response is up-to-date or not. Some caching products can be configured to intentionally return stale responses.

If you've ever set up and maintained a web server, you understand how good it feels to watch the access log file and see people visiting your site. Many content providers feel the same way. They want to know exactly who their users are, which pages they view, and how often. Caches complicate their analysis. Requests served as cache hits are not logged at the origin server. Proxies also tend to hide the identity of users. For example, all users behind a caching proxy come from the same IP address. Furthermore, some products also have features to remove or modify HTTP request headers that can otherwise identify individual users.

Copyright has been controversial with respect to caching for quite some time. Some people feel that caches violate an author's right to control the distribution of her work. The possibility of being sued for copyright infringement prevents some people from providing caching services. HTTP does allow content providers to specify if, and how, their information should be handled and distributed by different types of caches. However, the protocol does not address copyright directly.

Some people predict that the percentage of web content that is dynamic and personalized is increasing. Dynamic responses usually should not be cached, because they cannot be reused for a future request; Jane should not receive a page that was customized for Bob. If the prediction is true, then caching will become less important over time. However, other people believe that web content is increasingly static, and that it's becoming easier to differentiate static and dynamic data. In this case, caching becomes more efficient. (Note that movies, Java applets, and Macromedia Flash are all static content, even though they can display changing images on your screen.)

These problems all highlight the ongoing struggle for control of web content. Users and their service providers want a high percentage of cache hits, because cache hits save them time and bandwidth. Some content providers, on the other hand, want fewer hits delivered from caching proxies. They don't want their content stored in servers they don't control, and they want to accurately count page accesses and track users throughout their site.

Despite these potential problems, I still feel that web caching is a worthwhile practice. This is not to say that the problems should be ignored. In fact, we'll continue talking about them throughout the rest of this book.

1.5 Types of Web Caches

Web content can be cached at a number of different locations along the path between a client and an origin server. First, many browsers and other user agents have built-in caches. For simplicity, I'll call these *browser caches*. Next, a caching proxy (a.k.a. "proxy cache") aggregates all of the requests from a group of clients. Lastly, a surrogate can be located in front of an origin server to cache popular responses. In this book, we'll spend more time talking about caching proxies than the others.

1.5.1 Browser Caches

Browsers and other user agents benefit from having a built-in cache. When you press the *Back* button on your browser, it reads the previous page from its cache. Nongraphical agents, such as web crawlers, cache objects as temporary files on disk rather than keeping them in memory.

Netscape Navigator lets you control exactly how much memory and disk space to use for caching, and it also allows you to flush the cache. Microsoft Internet Explorer lets you control the size of your local disk cache, but in a less flexible way. Both have controls for how often cached responses should be validated. People generally use 10–100 MB of disk space for their browser cache.

A browser cache is limited to just one user, or at least one user agent. Thus, it gets hits only when the user revisits a page. As we'll see later, browser caches can store "private" responses, but shared caches cannot.

1.5.2 Caching Proxies

Caching proxies, unlike browser caches, service many different users at once. Since many different users visit the same popular web sites, caching proxies usually have higher hit ratios than browser caches. As the number of users increases, so does the hit ratio [Duska, Marwood and Feely, 1997].

Caching proxies are essential services for many organizations, including ISPs, corporations,. and schools. They usually run on dedicated hardware, which may be an appliance or a general-purpose server, such as a Unix or Windows NT system. Many organizations use inexpensive PC hardware that costs less than $1,000. At the other end of the spectrum, some organizations pay hundreds of thousands of dollars, or more, for high-performance solutions from one of the many caching vendors. We'll talk more about equipment in Chapter 10 and performance in Chapter 12.

Caching proxies are normally located near network gateways (i.e., routers) on the organization's side of its Internet connection. In other words, a cache should be located to maximize the number of clients that can use it, but it should not be on the far side of a slow, congested network link.

As I've already mentioned, a proxy sits between clients and servers. Unlike browser caches, a caching proxy alters the path of packets flowing through the network. A proxy splits a web request into two separate TCP connections, one to the client and the other to the server. Since the proxy forwards requests to origin servers, it hides the client's network address. This characteristic raises a number of interesting issues that we'll explore in later chapters.

One of the most difficult aspects of operating a caching proxy is getting clients to use the service. As we'll see in Chapter 4, configuring browsers to use a proxy is a little complicated. Users might not configure their browsers correctly, and they can even disable the caching proxy if they feel like it. Many organizations use interception caching to divert their network's HTTP traffic to a cache. Network administrators like interception caching because it reduces their administrative burdens and increases the number of clients using the cache. However, the technique is controversial because it violates and breaks protocols (such as TCP and HTTP) in subtle ways. I'll cover interception caching extensively in Chapter 5.

1.5.3 Surrogates

Until recently, we didn't have a good name for reverse proxies, server accelerators, and other devices that pretend to be origin servers. RFC 3040 defines a surrogate:

> A gateway co-located with an origin server, or at a different point in the network, delegated the authority to operate on behalf of, and typically working in close co-operation with, one or more origin servers. Responses are typically delivered from an internal cache.

Surrogates are useful in a number of situations. Content distribution networks use them to replicate information at many different locations. Typically, clients are directed to the nearest surrogate that has a given resource. In this manner, it seems like all users are closer to the origin server.

Another common use for surrogates is to "accelerate" slow web servers. Of course, the acceleration is accomplished simply by caching the server's responses. Some web servers are slow because they generate pages dynamically. For example, they may use Java to assemble an HTML page from different components stored in a relational database. If the same page is delivered to all the clients who visit, a surrogate will accelerate the server. If the pages are customized to each client, a surrogate would not speed things up significantly.

Surrogates are also often used to decrypt HTTP/TLS connections. Such decryption requires a fair amount of processing power. Rather than put that burden on the origin server itself, a surrogate encrypts and decrypts the traffic. Although communication between the surrogate and the origin server is unencrypted, there is little risk of eavesdropping because the two devices are usually right next to each other.

Surrogates that cache origin server responses are not much different from caching proxies. It's likely that any product sold as a client-side caching proxy can also function as an origin server surrogate. It may not work automatically, however. You'll probably have to configure it specifically for surrogate operation.

The workload for a surrogate is generally much different from that of a caching proxy. In particular, a surrogate receives requests for a small number of origin servers, while client-side proxies typically forward requests to more than 100,000 different servers. Since the traffic arriving at the surrogate is focused on a small number of servers, the hit ratio is significantly higher. In many cases, surrogates achieve hit ratios of 90% or more.

1.6 Caching Proxy Features

The key feature of a caching proxy is its ability to store responses for later use. This is what saves you time and bandwidth. Caching proxies actually tend to have a wide range of additional features that many organizations find valuable. Most of these are things you can do only with a proxy but which have relatively little to do with caching. For example, if you want to authenticate your users, but don't care about caching, you might use a caching proxy product anyway. I'll introduce some of the features here, with detailed discussions to follow in later chapters of this book.

Authentication

A proxy can require users to authenticate themselves before it serves any requests. This is particularly useful for firewall proxies. When each user has a unique username and password, only authorized individuals can surf the Web from inside your network. Furthermore, it provides a higher quality audit trail in the event of problems.

Request filtering

Caching proxies are often used to filter requests from users. Corporations usually have policies that prohibit employees from viewing pornography at work. To help enforce the policy, the corporate proxy can be configured to deny requests to known pornographic sites. Request filtering is somewhat controversial. Some people equate it with censorship and correctly point out that filtering schemes are not perfect.

Response filtering

In addition to filtering requests, proxies can also filter responses. This usually involves checking the contents of an object as it is being downloaded. A filter that checks for software viruses is a good example. Some organizations use proxies to filter out Java and JavaScript code, even when it is embedded in an HTML file. I've also heard about software that attempts to prevent access to pornography by searching images for a high percentage of flesh-tone pixels.*

---

* For example, see *http://www.heartsoft.com*, *http://www.eye-t.com*, and *http://www.thebair.com*.

Prefetching

> *Prefetching* is the process of retrieving some data before it is actually requested. Disk and memory systems typically use prefetching, also known as "read ahead." For the Web, prefetching usually involves requesting images and hyperlinked pages referenced in an HTML file.
>
> Prefetching represents a tradeoff between latency and bandwidth. A caching proxy selects objects to prefetch, assuming that a client will request them. Correct predictions result in a latency reduction; incorrect predictions, however, result in wasted bandwidth. So the interesting question is, how accurate are prefetching predictions? Unfortunately, good measurements are hard to come by. Companies with caching products that use prefetching are secretive about their algorithms.

Translation and transcoding

> Translation and transcoding both refer to processes that change the content of something without significantly changing its meaning or appearance. For example, you can imagine an application that translates text pages from English to German as they are downloaded.
>
> Transcoding usually refers to low-level changes in digital data rather than high-level human languages. Changing an image file format from GIF to JPEG is a good example. Since the JPEG format results in a smaller file than GIF, they can be transferred faster. Applying general-purpose compression is another way to reduce transfer times. A pair of cooperating proxies can compress all transfers between them and uncompress the data before it reaches the clients.

Traffic shaping

> A significant number of organizations use application layer proxies to control bandwidth utilization. In some sense, this functionality really belongs at the network layer, where it's possible to control the flow of individual packets. However, the application layer provides extra information that network administrators find useful. For example, the level of service for a particular request can be based on the user's identification, the agent making the request, or the type of data being requested (e.g., HTML, Postscript, MP3).

1.7 Meshes, Clusters, and Hierarchies

There are a number of situations where it's beneficial for caching proxies to talk to each other. There are different names for some different configurations. A *cluster* is a tightly coupled collection of caches, usually designed to appear as a single service. That is, even if there are seven systems in a cluster, to the outside world it looks like just one system. The members of a cluster are normally located together, both physically and topologically. As I explain in Chapter 9, many people like cache clusters because they provide scalability and reliability.

A loosely coupled collection of caches is called a *hierarchy* or *mesh*. If the arrangement is tree-like, with a clear distinction between upper- and lower-layer nodes, it is called a hierarchy. If the topology is flat or ill-defined, it is called a mesh. A hierarchy of caches make sense because the Internet itself is hierarchical. However, when a mesh or hierarchy spans multiple organizations, a number of issues arise. We'll talk more about hierarchies in Chapter 7. Then, in Chapter 8, we'll explore the various protocols and techniques that caches use to communicate with each other.

1.8 Products

By now you should have a pretty good view of the web caching landscape. In the rest of this book, we'll explore many of the topics of this chapter in much greater detail, so you can fully comprehend all the issues involved. When you finish this book, you'll be able to design and operate a web cache for your environment. You might even think about writing your own software. But since I'm sure most of you have other responsibilities, you'll probably want to use an existing product. Following is a list of caching products that are currently available, many of which are mentioned throughout this book:

Squid
http://www.squid-cache.org
> Squid is an open source software package that runs on a wide range of Unix platforms. There has also been some recent success in porting Squid to Windows NT. As with most free software, users receive technical support from a public mailing list. Squid was originally derived from the Harvest project in 1996.

Netscape Proxy Server
http://home.netscape.com/proxy/v3.5/index.html
> The Netscape Proxy Server was the first caching proxy product available. The lead developer, Ari Luotonen, also worked extensively on the CERN HTTP server during the Web's formative years in 1993 and 1994. Netscape's Proxy runs on a handful of Unix systems, as well as Windows NT.

Microsoft Internet Security and Acceleration Server
http://www.microsoft.com/isaserver/
> Microsoft currently has two caching proxy products available. The older Proxy Server runs on Windows NT, while the newer ISA product requires Windows 2000.

Volera
http://www.volera.com

> Volera is a recent spin-off of Novell. The product formerly known as Internet Caching System (ICS) is now called Excelerator. Volera does not sell this product directly. Rather, it is bundled on hardware appliances available from a number of OEM partners.

Network Appliance Netcache
http://www.netapp.com/products/netcache/

> Network Appliance was the second company to sell a caching proxy, and the first to sell an appliance. The Netcache products also have roots in the Harvest project.

Inktomi Traffic Server
http://www.inktomi.com/products/network/traffic/

> Inktomi boasts some of the largest customer installations, such as America Online and Exodus. Their Traffic Server product has been available since 1997.

CacheFlow
http://www.cacheflow.com

> Intelligent prefetching and refreshing features distinguish CacheFlow from their competitors.

InfoLibria
http://www.infolibria.com

> InfoLibria's products are designed for high reliability and fault tolerance.

Cisco Cache Engine
http://www.cisco.com/go/cache/

> The Cisco 500 series Cache Engine is a small, low-profile system designed to work with their Web Cache Control Protocol (WCCP). As your demand for capacity increases, you can easily add more units.

Lucent imminet WebCache
http://www.lucent.com/serviceprovider/imminet/

> Lucent's products offer carrier-grade reliability and active refresh features.

iMimic DataReactor
http://www.imimic.com

> iMimic is a relative newcomer to this market. However, their DataReactor product is already licensed to a number of OEM partners. iMimic also sells their product directly.

2

How Web Caching Works

What makes an object cachable or uncachable? How does a cache know when a request is a hit or when to revalidate a cached object? This chapter gives you some background on how web caches work. Many of the topics in this chapter are covered definitively in the HTTP/1.1 draft standard document, RFC 2616. The material here tells you what you need to know; for all the gory details, you'll need to consult the actual RFC document.

To start, we'll see what a typical HTTP request looks like and how it's different when talking to a proxy. Next, we'll see how caches decide if they can store a particular response. After that, we'll talk about cache hits, stale objects, and validation techniques. I'll explain how users can force caches to return an up-to-date response. Finally, we'll see what happens when a cache becomes full and must choose to remove some objects.

2.1 HTTP Requests

Clients always use HTTP when talking to a caching proxy. This is true even when the client requests an FTP or Gopher URL, as we'll see shortly. A client issues a slightly different request when it knows it is talking to a proxy server rather than to an origin server. Occasionally, requests to a cache are referred to as *proxy HTTP* requests.

2.1.1 Origin Server Requests

First, let's examine a request sent to an origin server. In this example, the user is requesting the URL *http://www.nlanr.net/index.html*. When the client is not configured to use a proxy, it connects directly to the origin server (*www.nlanr.net*) and writes this request:

```
GET /index.html HTTP/1.1
Host: www.nlanr.net
Accept: */*
Connection: Keep-alive
```

In reality, the request includes many more headers than are shown here. Note how the URL has been split into two parts. The *request line* (the first line) includes only the pathname component of the URL, while the hostname part appears later in a Host header. The Host header is an HTTP/1.1 feature, primarily intended to support virtual hosting of multiple logical web sites on one physical server (one IP address). If the origin server is not serving virtual domains, the Host header is redundant. Note that we can rebuild a full URL from the request line and the Host header. This is an important feature of HTTP/1.1, especially for interception proxies.

2.1.2 Proxy Requests

When a client talks to a proxy, the request is slightly different. The request line of a proxy request includes the full URI:

```
GET http://www.nlanr.net/index.html HTTP/1.1
Host: www.nlanr.net
Accept: */*
Proxy-connection: Keep-alive
```

The origin server name is in two places: the full URI and the Host header. This may seem redundant, but when HTTP/1.0 and proxying techniques were invented, the Host header did not exist.*

HTTP provides for the fact that requests and responses can pass through a number of proxies between a client and origin server. Some HTTP headers are defined as *end-to-end* and some as *hop-by-hop*. The end-to-end headers convey information for the end systems (client and origin server), and they generally must not be modified by proxies. The Cookie header is end-to-end. Conversely, the hop-by-hop header information is meant for intermediate systems, and it must often be modified or removed before being forwarded. The Proxy-connection and Proxy-authorization headers are hop-by-hop. A client uses the Proxy-connection request header to ask the proxy to make the TCP connection "persistent," so that it can be reused for a future request. The Proxy-authorization header contains credentials for access to the proxy, not the origin server.

---

* Since the hostname exists in two places, it's possible they don't match. When this occurs, the URL hostname takes precedence. To avoid incorrect operation, a caching proxy must ignore the original Host value and replace it with the URL hostname.

2.1.3 Non-HTTP Proxy Requests

Finally, let's look at how proxies handle non-HTTP URIs. Most user-agents have built-in support for other transfer protocols, such as FTP and Gopher. In other words, these clients know how to talk directly to FTP and Gopher servers. Most caching proxies, however, do not emulate FTP and Gopher servers. That is, you can't FTP *to* a caching proxy. This restriction, for better or worse, comes about because it's hard to actually proxy these legacy transport protocols. You might say it's a limitation of their design.

Since HTTP knows about proxies, non-HTTP URIs are proxied as HTTP requests. For example, the user-agent's request looks something like this:

```
GET ftp://ftp.freebsd.org/pub/ HTTP/1.1
Host: ftp.freebsd.org
Accept: */*
```

Because this is an HTTP request, the proxy generates an HTTP response. In other words, it is the role of the proxy to convert from FTP on one side to HTTP on the other. The proxy acts like an FTP client when it talks to an FTP server. The response sent to the user-agent, however, is an HTTP response.

Non-HTTP requests are somewhat difficult for caching proxies in a couple of ways. Both FTP and Gopher services rely heavily on the use of directory listings. Convention dictates that directory listings are displayed with cute little icons and hyperlinks to each of the directory entries. A web client that connects directly to an FTP or Gopher server parses the directory listing and generates a nice HTML page. HTTP servers, however, work differently. For HTTP, the HTML page is generated by the server, not the client. Since FTP and Gopher are proxied via HTTP, it becomes the proxy's responsibility to generate pleasant-looking pages for directory listings. This causes directory pages to look different, depending on whether you proxy FTP and Gopher requests.

Another difficult aspect is that HTTP has certain attributes and features missing from these older protocols. In particular, it can be hard to get values for the Last-modified and Content-length headers. Of course, FTP and Gopher servers don't understand anything about expiration and validation.* Usually, the caching proxy just selects an appropriate freshness lifetime for non-HTTP objects. Because the proxy has little information, it may return more stale responses for FTP files than for HTTP resources.

---

* Some FTP servers do support nonstandard commands for getting a file's modification time (MDTM) and length (SIZE). These might be used to implement validation. The IETF is currently considering a document that would finally standardize these commands.

Determining a response's content type is another hard problem. Proxies and servers often use the filename extension to determine the content type. For example, URLs that end with *.jpg* have the Content-type *image/jpeg*. For FTP files, the proxy must guess the Content-type, and it's relatively common to find mysterious filename extensions, such as *.scr*. The proxy's choice for a content-type affects the way a browser handles the response. For *text* types, the browser displays the data in a window. For others, such as the catchall *application/octet-stream*, the browser brings up a "Save as" dialog window. As new filename extensions and content types are brought into use, caching proxies must be updated.

Because of problems such as these, many organizations don't bother to cache non-HTTP requests. As we'll see in Chapter 4, you can easily configure user agents to send or not send FTP and other types of URLs to a caching proxy.

2.2 Is It Cachable?

The primary purpose of a cache is to store some of the responses it receives from origin servers. A response is said to be *cachable* if it can be used to answer a future request. For typical request streams, about 75% of responses are cachable.

A cache decides if a particular response is cachable by looking at different components of the request and response. In particular, it examines the following:

- The response status code
- The request method
- Response Cache-control directives
- A response validator
- Request authentication

These different factors interact in a somewhat complicated manner. For example, some request methods are uncachable unless allowed by a Cache-control directive. Some status codes are cachable by default, but authentication and Cache-control take precedence.

Even though a response is cachable, a cache may choose not to store it. Many products include heuristics—or allow the administrator to define rules—that avoid caching certain responses. Some objects are more valuable than others. An object that gets requested frequently (and results in cache hits) is more valuable than an object that is requested only once. Many dynamic responses fall into the latter category. If the cache can identify worthless responses, it saves resources and increases performance by not caching them.

2.2.1 *Status Codes*

One of the most important factors in determining cachability is the HTTP server response code, or status code. The three-digit status code indicates whether the request was successful or if some kind of error occurred. The status codes are divided into the following five groups:

1xx

An informational, intermediate status. The transaction is still being processed.

2xx

The request was successfully received and processed.

3xx

The server is redirecting the client to a different location.

4xx

There is an error or problem with the client's request. For example, authentication is required, or the resource does not exist.

5xx

An error occurred on the server for a valid request.

Refer to Appendix F for the complete list, or see Section 10 of RFC 2616.

The most common status code is 200 (OK), which means the request was successfully processed. The 200 code and a number of others shown in Table 2.1 are cachable by default. However, some other aspect of the request or response can make the response uncachable. In other words, the status code alone is not enough to make a response cachable. We'll talk about the other factors shortly.

Table 2.1.   Cachable Response Codes

Code	Description	Explanation
200	OK	Request was processed successfully.
203	Non-Authoritative Information	This is similar to 200, but it can be used when the sender has reason to believe the given entity headers are different from those that the origin server would send.
206	Partial Content	The 206 response is similar to 200, but it is a response to a range request. A 206 response is cachable if the cache fully supports range requests.[a]
300	Multiple Choices	The response includes a list of appropriate choices from which the user should make a selection.

Table 2.1. Cachable Response Codes (continued)

Code	Description	Explanation
301	Moved Permanently	The requested resource has been moved to a new location. The new URL is given in the response headers.
410	Gone	The requested resource has been intentionally and permanently removed from the origin server.

ª HTTP/1.1 defines the range request. It allows clients to request a specific subset of a resource, rather than the entire thing. For example, a user agent can request specific pages from a large PDF document instead of transferring the whole file.

All other response codes are uncachable by default but can be cached if explicitly allowed by other means. For example, if a 302 (Moved Temporarily) response also has an Expires header, it can be cached. In reality, there is relatively little to gain from caching these uncachable-by-default status responses, even when allowed. These status codes occur infrequently to begin with. It's even more unlikely that the response also includes Expires or Cache-control headers to make them cachable. Thus, it is simpler and safer for a cache never to store one of these responses.

2.2.2 Request Methods

Another significant factor in determining cachability is the request method. Here, the rules are somewhat simpler. As shown in Table 2.2, we really have to worry about only three methods: GET, HEAD, and POST.

Table 2.2. Request Methods and Cachability

Request Method	Cachable?
GET	Yes, cachable by default
HEAD	May be used to update previously cached entry
POST	Uncachable by default; cachable if Cache-control headers allow
PUT	Never cachable
DELETE	Never cachable
OPTIONS	Never cachable
TRACE	Never cachable

GET is the most popular request method, and responses to GET requests are by default cachable. Responses to HEAD requests are treated specially. HEAD response messages do not include bodies, so there is really nothing to cache. However, we can use the response headers to update a previously cached response's metadata. For example, a HEAD response can return a new expiration time. Similarly, the response may instead indicate that the resource has changed, which means the cached copy is now invalid. A POST response is cachable only if the response includes an expiration time or one of the Cache-control directives that overrides the default. Cachable POST responses are quite rare in reality.

Responses from all other request methods are always uncachable. In addition, caching proxies must not reuse responses from unknown ("extension") methods. Some RFCs, such as 2518 (WEBDAV) define extensions to HTTP including new request methods. It's possible that such extensions allow responses from new methods to be cached. RFC 2518, however, does not state that any of the WEBDAV methods are cachable.

2.2.3 Expiration and Validation

HTTP/1.1 provides two ways for caches to maintain consistency with origin servers: expiration times and validators. Both ensure that users always receive up-to-date information. Ideally, every cachable response would include one or both; in reality, a small but significant percentage of responses have neither.

Expiration and validation affect cachability in two important ways. First, RFC 2616 says that responses with neither an expiration time nor a cache validator should not be cached. Without these pieces of information, a cache can never tell if a cached copy is still valid. Note, however, that this is only a recommendation, not a requirement. Storing and reusing these types of responses does not violate the protocol. Second, an expiration time turns normally uncachable responses into cachable ones. For example, responses to POST requests and 302 status messages become cachable when the origin server provides an expiration time.

It's very important to understand the subtle difference between expiration and cachability. *Cachable* means that the response can be stored in the proxy. Expired responses may still be cached, but they must be validated before being used again. Even though a response expires, it does not mean that the resource has changed.

In fact, some web sites send *pre-expired* responses. This means that the cache must validate the response the next time someone requests it. Pre-expiration is useful for origin servers that want to closely track accesses to their site but also want their content to be cachable. The proper way to pre-expire a response is to set the Expires header equal to the Date header. For example:

```
Date: Sun, 01 Apr 2001 18:32:48 GMT
Expires: Sun, 01 Apr 2001 18:32:48 GMT
```

An alternative method is to send an invalid date or use the value "0":

```
Expires: 0
```

Unfortunately, the meaning of an expiration time in the past and an invalid expiration value has changed over time. Under HTTP/1.0 (RFC 1945), caches are not supposed to store such responses.* However, HTTP/1.1 allows them to be cached. This causes confusion, as well as problems for people running old HTTP servers, which RFC 2616 recognizes:

> Many HTTP/1.0 cache implementations treat an Expires value that is less than or equal to the response Date value as being equivalent to the Cache-Control response directive "no-cache". If an HTTP/1.1 cache receives such a response, and the response does not include a Cache-Control header field, it SHOULD consider the response to be non-cachable in order to retain compatibility with HTTP/1.0 servers.

We'll talk more about expiration in Section 2.3, "Hits, Misses, and Freshness," and about validation in Section 2.5, "Validation." For now, the important point is this: in order to be cachable, a response should have an expiration time, a validator, or both. Responses with neither should not be cached. However, HTTP/1.1 allows them to be cached anyway without violating the protocol.

2.2.4 Cache-control

The Cache-control header is a new feature of HTTP/1.1 used to tell caches how to handle requests and responses. The value of the header is one or more directive keywords, for example:

```
Cache-control: private
```

```
Cache-control: public,max-age=86400
```

Although Cache-control appears in both requests and responses, our discussion in this section focuses only on directives that appear in a response. We're not interested in request directives yet because, with one exception, they don't affect response cachability.

Note that the Cache-control directives override the defaults for most status codes and request methods when determining cachability. In other words, some Cache-control directives can turn a normally cachable GET response into one that is uncachable, and vice-versa for POST responses.

---

* Since HTTP/1.0 lacks other cache-specific headers, this was the only way to mark a response as uncachable. Some HTTP/1.0 agents won't cache a response that includes Pragma: no-cache, but this is not mentioned in RFC 1945.

Here are the `Cache-control` directives that may appear in an HTTP response and affect its cachability:

no-cache

> The `no-cache` directive is, unfortunately, somewhat confusing. Its meaning has changed in a significant way over time. The January 1997 draft standard RFC for HTTP/1.1, number 2068, says: "no-cache indicates that all or part of the response message MUST NOT be cached anywhere." This statement is quite clear and matches what people intuitively think "no-cache" means.
>
> In RFC 2616 (June 1999), however, the directive's meaning has changed. Now, responses with `no-cache` can be stored but may not be reused without validation ("a cache MUST NOT use the response to satisfy a subsequent request without successful revalidation with the origin server"). Not only is this counterintuitive, but it seems to mean the same thing as `must-revalidate` with `max-age=0`.
>
> Note that, even though a response with `no-cache` can be stored, it is not one of the `Cache-control` directives that turns uncachable responses into cachable ones. In fact, it doesn't affect cachability at all. Rather, it instructs a cache to always validate the response if it has been cached.
>
> The `no-cache` directive also has a secondary use. When the directive specifies one or more header names, those headers must not be sent to a client without validation. This enables origin servers to prevent sharing of certain headers while allowing the response content to be cached and reused. An example of this usage is:
>
> ```
> Cache-control: no-cache=Set-cookie
> ```

private

> The `private` directive gives user agent caches permission to store a response but prevents shared caching proxies from doing so. The directive is useful if the response contains content customized for just one person. An origin server might also use it to track individuals and still allow responses to be cached.
>
> For a shared cache, the `private` directive makes a normally cachable response uncachable. However, for a nonshared cache, a normally uncachable response becomes cachable. For example, a browser may cache a response to a POST request if the response includes the `Cache-control: private` directive.

public

> The `public` directive makes normally uncachable responses cachable by both shared and nonshared caches.
>
> The `public` directive takes even higher precedence than authorization credentials. That is, if a request includes an `Authorization` header, and the response headers contain `Cache-control: public`, the response is cachable.

max-age

> The max-age directive is an alternate way to specify an expiration time. Recall from the previous section that some normally uncachable responses become cachable when an expiration time is given. Also, RFC 2616 recommends that responses with neither a validator nor an expiration time should not be cached. When a response contains the max-age directive, the public directive is implied as well.

s-maxage

> The s-maxage directive is very similar to max-age, except it only applies to shared caches. Like its cousin, the s-maxage directive allows normally uncachable responses to be cached. If both are present in a response, a shared cache uses the s-maxage value and ignores all other expiration values.

> Unlike max-age, s-maxage does not also imply the public directive. It does, however, imply the proxy-revalidate directive.

must-revalidate

> This directive also allows caches to store a response that is normally uncachable. Since the must-revalidate directive deals with validation, we'll talk about it in the following section.

proxy-revalidate

> The proxy-revalidate directive is similar to must-revalidate, except it applies only to shared caches. It also allows caches to store a normally uncachable response.

no-store

> The no-store directive causes any response to become uncachable. It may also be present in a request, in which case the corresponding response is uncachable.

> Section 14.9.2 of RFC 2616 describes no-store with relatively strong language. Requests and responses with this directive must never be written to non-volatile storage (i.e., disk), even temporarily. It is a way for paranoid content providers to decrease the probability that sensitive information is inadvertently discovered or made public.

> Now that no-cache has a different meaning, however, no-store becomes very important. It is the only directive (except private) that prevents a response from getting cached. Thus, we're likely to see no-store used for many types of responses, not just super-sensitive data.

To summarize, public, max-age, s-maxage, must-revalidate, and proxy-revalidate turn normally uncachable responses into a cachable ones. no-store and private turn normally cachable responses into uncachable ones for a (shared) caching proxy. At the same time, `private` turns an uncachable response into a cachable one for a (nonshared) user agent cache.

The HTTP/1.1 standard defines additional cache-control directives for responses that are not presented here. Section 14.9 of RFC 2616 gives the full specification. Cache-control directives appear in HTTP requests as well, but since they generally do not affect cachability, we'll talk about those directives in Section 2.6, "Forcing a Cache to Refresh."

2.2.5   Authentication

Requests that require authentication are not normally cachable. Only the origin server can determine who is allowed to access its resources. Since a caching proxy doesn't know which users are authorized, it cannot give out unvalidated hits.

Origin servers typically use a simple challenge-response scheme to authenticate users. When you first try to access a protected resource, the server returns a message with a 401 (Unauthorized) status code. The response also includes a `WWW-Authenticate` header, which contains the challenge. Upon receipt of this response, your user-agent prompts you for your authorization credentials. Normally this is a username and password. The user-agent then resubmits the request, this time including an `Authorization` header. When a caching proxy finds this header in a request, it knows that the corresponding response is uncachable unless the origin server explicitly allows it.

The rules for caching authenticated responses are somewhat tricky. Section 14.8 of RFC 2616 talks about the conditions under which shared caches can store and reuse such responses. They can be cached only when one of the following `Cache-control` headers is present: `s-maxage`, `must-revalidate`, or `public`. The `public` directive alone allows the response to be cached and reused for any subsequent request, subject to normal expiration. The `s-maxage` directive allows the response to be reused until the expiration time is reached. After that, the caching proxy must revalidate it with the origin server. The `must-revalidate` directive instructs the cache to revalidate the response for every subsequent request.

The HTTP RFC doesn't say how nonshared (user-agent) caches should handle authenticated responses. It's safe to assume that they can be cached and reused, since, by definition, the cache is not shared with other users. However, nonshared caches can actually be shared by multiple users. For example, consider terminals in university labs or Internet cafes.

I wouldn't expect many authenticated responses to include `public` or `s-maxage` cache controls. However, the `must-revalidate` and `proxy-revalidate` directives can be quite useful. They provide a mechanism that allows responses to be cached, while still giving the origin server full control over who can and cannot access the protected information.

There is another issue related to authentication, but not cachability. Origin servers sometimes use address-based authentication rather than passwords. That is, the client's IP address determines whether or not the request is allowed. In these cases, it's possible for a caching proxy to open a back door into a protected server. If the proxy's IP address is in the range of allowed addresses, and the proxy itself allows requests from anywhere, then anyone can access the protected server via the proxy.

People are often surprised to discover that HTTP does not have a request header that specifies the client's IP address. Actually, there was such a header in early versions of HTTP/1.1, but it was taken out. The problem with such a feature is that there is no way to validate the correctness of this information. A proxy or other agent that forwards requests can easily spoof the header. It is a bad idea to use such untrustworthy information for authentication.

2.2.6 Cookies

A *cookie* is a device that allows an origin server to maintain session information for individual users between requests [Kristol and Montulli, 2000]. A response may include a `Set-cookie` header, which contains the cookie as a string of random-looking characters. When user-agents receive a cookie, they are supposed to use it in their future requests to that server. Thus, the cookie serves as a session identifier.

Cookies are typically used to represent or reference private information (e.g. a "shopping basket"), and they should not be shared between users. However, in most cases, the cookie itself is usually the only thing that is private. The object in the body of the reply message may be public and cachable. Rather than making the entire response uncachable, HTTP has a way to make only the cookie information uncachable. This is done with the `Cache-control: no-cache` directive. For example:

```
Cache-control: no-cache="Set-cookie"
```

Origin servers can use the `no-cache` directive to prevent caching of other headers as well.

RFC 2965 actually talks about the `Set-cookie2` and `Cookie2` headers. Apparently these new headers are designed to avoid interoperability problems with the older specifications.

2.2.7 Dynamic Content

I mentioned dynamic responses briefly in Chapter 1. RFC 2616 does not directly address cachability of dynamic content. In terms of the protocol, only the request and reply headers determine cachability. It does not matter how the content is generated. Dynamic responses can be cached, subject to the previously described rules. Origin servers usually mark dynamic content as uncachable, so we have very little to worry about. Even so, it's a good idea to understand dynamic content in case problems arise. Additionally, you may experience a slight performance improvement by not caching some responses that would normally be stored.

Some people worry that a cache will incorrectly handle some dynamic content. For example, consider stock quotes and weather reports. If users happen to receive out-of-date information, they can make misinformed decisions with negative consequences. In these cases, the burden of responsibility is really on the content provider. They need to make sure their server marks dynamic responses as uncachable, using one of the HTTP headers described previously. However, rather than trusting servers (and caches) to do the right thing, some cache administrators feel more comfortable not caching any dynamic content.

Lack of popularity is another reason for not caching dynamic responses. Caches are only beneficial when the request stream includes repeat requests. An object that is requested only once has no value for a cache. Rather, it consumes resources (disk space, memory) that can be more efficiently utilized if allocated to some other object. If we can identify objects that are unlikely to be requested again, it leaves more space for more valuable objects.

How can we identify dynamic content? The HTTP reply headers provide a good indication. Specifically, the `Last-modified` header specifies when the resource was last updated. If the modification time is close to the current time, the content is probably dynamic. Unfortunately, about 35% of responses don't include a last-modification timestamp. Another useful technique is to look for specific strings in URLs. The following usually indicates a dynamic response:

/cgi-bin/ or .cgi
>   The presence of */cgi-bin/* or *.cgi* in a URL path indicates the response was generated from a CGI script.

/servlet/
>   When the URL path includes */servlet/*, the response was most likely generated by the execution of a Java servlet on the origin server.

.asp
>   ASP pages normally have the *.asp* extension, for example, *http://www.microsoft.com/default.asp.*

.shtml

> The *.shtml* extension indicates an HTML page that is parsed for server-side includes. These are special tags that the origin server interprets and then replaces with some dynamically generated content. With Apache, for example, you can include a file's time of last modification with this bit of HTML:

```
<--#flastmod-->
```

> Java servlets may also be used this way inside a *.shtml* file.

Query terms

> Another likely indication of dynamic content is the presence of a "?" (question mark) in a URL. This character delineates the optional query terms, or search-part, of a URL. Usually, the query terms are entered by users into HTML forms and then given as parameters to CGI scripts or database frontends.

2.3 Hits, Misses, and Freshness

When a cache receives a request, it checks to see if the response has already been cached. If not, we say the request is a cache miss, and the request is forwarded on to the origin server. Cache misses occur for objects that have never been requested previously, objects that are not cachable, or objects that have been deleted to make room for new ones. It's common for 50–70% of all requests to be cache misses.

If the object is present, then we might have a cache hit. However, the cache must first decide if the stored response is *fresh* or *stale*. A cached response is fresh if its expiration time has not been reached yet; otherwise, it's stale. Fresh responses are best because they are given to the client immediately. They experience no latency and consume no bandwidth to the origin server. I'll call them *unvalidated hits*. Stale responses, on the other hand, require validation with the origin server.

The purpose of a validation request is to ask the origin server if the cached response is still valid. If the resource has changed, we don't want the client to receive a stale response. HTTP also calls these *conditional requests*. The reply to a conditional request is either a small "Not Modified" message or a whole new response. The Not Modified reply, also known as a *validated hit*, is preferable because it means the client can receive the cached response, which saves on bandwidth. A *validated miss*, where the origin server sends an updated response, is really equivalent to a regular cache miss. We'll talk more about validation in Section 2.5, "Validation."

How does the cache know whether an object is fresh or stale? HTTP/1.1 provides two ways for servers to specify the freshness lifetime of a response: the Expires header and the max-age cache control directive. The Expires header has been in use since HTTP/1.0. Its value is the date and time at which a response becomes stale, for example:

```
Date: Mon, 19 Feb 2001 01:46:17 GMT
```

Application developers find dates such as this awkward for a number of reasons. The format is difficult to parse and prone to slight variations (e.g., "Monday" instead of "Mon"). Additionally, absolute timestamps are susceptible to clock skew problems, when different systems have different notions of the current time. For these reasons, HTTP/1.1 includes a number of headers and directives that use relative instead of absolute times. The max-age cache control directive specifies the number of seconds that the response should be considered fresh, for example:

```
Cache-control: max-age=21600
```

This states that the response is fresh for six hours after it is generated. Section 13.2.3 of RFC 2616 describes how to calculate the age of a response.

Even though HTTP provides these two mechanisms, they are not used very often. Recent measurements suggest that less than 10% of all responses have an expiration time. In these cases, caches are free to apply local rules to estimate object freshness lifetimes (RFC 2616, Section 13.2.2). Most products have configuration options that give the administrator control over these objects. A conservative setting is always to validate responses that don't have an expiration time. Sites with poor connectivity are likely to use liberal settings that return such objects as hits without validation.

Many products also utilize an algorithm known as the *last-modified factor* (LM-factor). It is based upon the somewhat intuitive principle that young objects, because they have recently been created or changed, are likely to be changed soon. Similarly, old objects that have not changed for a long time are less likely to change soon.* An object's LM-factor is calculated as the ratio of the time *since* the object entered the cache to the object's age *when* it entered the cache. The object is presumed to be fresh so long as its LM-factor remains below some threshold, which is typically a configurable parameter. If the threshold is 0.2, for example, an object that is 10 days old when it enters a cache remains fresh for the following 2 days. On the first request after two days have passed, the object is validated with the origin server. If the object is still valid (not modified), the timestamps are updated. In this case, the age when entering becomes 12 days, and the age since entering becomes 0. Now, it remains fresh for the following 2.4 days. Most caching products allow you to set different threshold values for different types of objects.

---

* Unfortunately, just the opposite is true for objects updated at fixed intervals (e.g., hourly or daily). As they get older, they are more likely to be updated.

You might find it strange that a cache sometimes returns a hit without validating it first. Given the option, wouldn't it be better to always make sure the user receives absolutely up-to-date information? Unfortunately, it isn't that simple. The penalty you pay for cache consistency is higher latency. In general, validation requests take a significant amount of time compared to simply returning unvalidated hits. If a cache's fresh versus stale predictions are accurate, the latency reductions are a big win. By tuning the cache configuration, namely the LM-factor thresholds, you should be able to find an appropriate balance in the tradeoff between low latency and cache correctness.

HTTP/1.1 allows caches to intentionally return stale responses in some cases. For example, a cache that tries to validate a response, but cannot connect to the origin server, may return the stale response rather than no response at all. The RFC acknowledges that some caching proxies operate under severe bandwidth constraints, and that these may be configured to return stale responses rather than attempt a validation request.

Clients can also indicate their willingness to accept stale responses with the max-stale cache control directive. This directive can be used with or without a numeric value, for example:

```
Cache-control: max-stale
```

means the client will accept a cached response no matter how stale. On the other hand:

```
Cache-control: max-stale=7200
```

means a response that has been stale for 7200 seconds (two hours) or less can be sent to the client without validation.

HTTP/1.1 does not give caches or clients the final say in stale responses. The must-revalidate and proxy-revalidate cache control directives override the cache and client preferences regarding staleness. A response containing this directive must always be validated when it becomes stale. According to RFC 2616, origin servers should use this feature "if and only if failure to revalidate a request on the entity could result in incorrect operation, such as a silently unexecuted financial transaction." proxy-revalidate applies only to shared (proxy) caches, while must-revalidate applies to all caches.

Whenever a cache returns a stale response for any reason, it must include the following Warning: header:

```
Warning: 110 Response is stale
```

User-agents, in turn, are supposed to alert users when they receive a response with a Warning: header.

2.4 Hit Ratios

How can we measure the effectiveness of our caches? One such measurement is called the *cache hit ratio*. This is the percentage of requests that are satisfied as cache hits. Usually, this includes both validated and unvalidated hits. Validated hits can be tricky because these requests are forwarded to origin servers, incurring slight bandwidth and latency penalties. Note that the cache hit ratio tells you only how many requests are hits—it doesn't tell you how much bandwidth or latency has been saved.

The measurement that does tell you about bandwidth is called the *byte hit ratio*. Instead of counting only requests, this measure is based on the number of bytes transferred. Cache hits for large objects contribute more to the byte hit ratio than do small objects. The byte hit ratio measures how much bandwidth your cache has saved, but there are different ways to calculate it.

One way is to compare the sum of object sizes for cache hits and cache misses. However, this technique has a couple of shortcomings. For example, it doesn't include request traffic. Counting the request traffic probably doesn't matter much because it's relatively small, and most of the data flows in the other direction (into your network, not out of it). This technique might not count the small 304 (Not Modified) responses either. However, the bigger problem is in accounting for requests aborted by the user. Consider a cache miss for a 100 KB object. If the cache downloads the entire response, but the user aborts the transfer at 50 KB, we used more server-side bandwidth than on the client-side. If we instead count bytes transferred on the network, we'll get a more accurate figure for bandwidth savings.

What sort of cache hit ratio values can you expect to achieve? Any reasonably-sized cache should be able to reach 30%. Some of the largest and busiest caches deployed today can make it as high as 70%. Byte hit ratios are normally less than cache hit ratios, often by as much as 10%. That is, a 50% cache hit ratio usually corresponds to a 40% byte hit ratio. We'll see the reason for this in Section A.1, "Reply and Object Sizes." Small objects, such as images and HTML pages, tend to have more cache hits than large objects such as audio and PostScript files.

Three factors affect hit ratios: cache size, number of clients, and freshness heuristics. Obviously, a larger cache holds more objects. The chance that any given request is a cache hit increases as the cache size increases, but the relationship is not linear. In other words, doubling your cache size does not double your hit ratio. Research has shown that the relationship is pseudologarithmic [Duska, Marwood and Feely, 1997]. I show the same in Appendix A with cache simulations. Even if your cache size is infinite, there is an upper limit on the hit ratio you can achieve. Section 10.2, "Disk Space," explains how you can determine an appropriate cache size for your installation.

Empirical evidence and simulation studies have shown that hit ratios also increase as the number of cache clients increases [Breslau, Cao, Fan, Phillips and Shenker, 1999]. My simulations in Appendix A show this behavior as well. The primary reason is related to the popularity characteristics of web requests. In order for a request to be a cache hit, the same object must have been requested previously. As the number of cache users (clients) increases, so does the probability that one of those users has already requested the same object that you request.

As mentioned in Section 2.3, "Hits, Misses, and Freshness," most web caches allow you to tune their LM-factor thresholds. Increasing the threshold value causes your cache to return more unvalidated hits. This means there are fewer validated misses, so your hit ratio improves, but your cache clients receive more out-of-date objects. Strictly speaking, higher thresholds increase your hit ratio, but not without a price.

2.5 Validation

I've already discussed cache validation in the context of cache hits versus misses. Upon receiving a request for a cached object, the cache may want to validate the object with the origin server. If the cached object is still valid, the server replies with a short HTTP 304 (Not Modified) message. Otherwise, the entire new object is sent. HTTP/1.1 provides two validation mechanisms: last-modified timestamps and entity tags.

2.5.1 Last-modified Timestamps

Under HTTP/1.0, timestamps are the only type of validator. Even though HTTP/1.1 provides a new technique, last-modified timestamps remain in widespread use. Most HTTP responses include a `Last-modified` header that specifies the time when the resource was last changed on the origin server. The `Last-modified` timestamp is given in Greenwich Mean Time (GMT) with one-second resolution, for example:

```
HTTP/1.1 200 OK
Date: Sun, 04 Mar 2001 03:57:45 GMT
Last-Modified: Fri, 02 Mar 2001 04:09:20 GMT
```

For objects that correspond to regular files on the origin server, this timestamp is the filesystem modification time.

When a cache validates an object, this same timestamp is sent in the `If-modified-since` header of a conditional GET request.

```
GET http://www.ircache.net/ HTTP/1.1
If-Modified-Since: Wed, 14 Feb 2001 15:35:26 GMT
```

If the server's response is 304 (Not Modified), the cache's object is still valid. In this case, the cache must update the object to reflect any new HTTP response header values, such as Date and Expires. If the server's response is not 304, the cache treats the server's response as new content, replaces the cached object, and delivers it to the client.

The use of timestamps as validators has a number of undesirable consequences:

- A file's timestamp might get updated without any change in the actual content of the file. Consider, for example, moving your entire origin server document tree from one disk partition to another. Depending on the method you use to copy the files, the modification times may not be preserved. Then, any If-modified-since requests to your server result in 200 (OK) replies, instead of 304 (Not Modified), even though the content of the files has not changed.*

- Dealing with timestamps becomes complicated when different systems have different notions of the current time. Unfortunately, it is not safe to assume that all Internet hosts are synchronized to the same time. It's easy to find clocks that are off by days, months, and even years. Thus, we can't really compare an origin server timestamp to the local time. It should be compared only to other origin server timestamps, such as the Date and Expires values. All hosts involved in serving web objects, and especially caches, should synchronize their clocks to known, reliable sources using the Network Time Protocol (NTP). Unix hosts can use the *ntpd* or *xntpd* programs.

- If-modified-since values cannot be used for objects that may be updated more frequently than once per second.

On the other hand, timestamps have some nice characteristics as well:

- Timestamps can be stored internally with a relatively small amount of memory (typically four bytes). The fixed data size simplifies data structures and coding.

- We can derive some meaning from the last-modified timestamp. That is, we can use it for more than just validation. As mentioned in the previous section, last-modified times are often used in heuristics to estimate expiration times.

2.5.2 Entity Tags

HTTP/1.1 provides another kind of validator known as an *entity tag*. An entity tag is an opaque string used to identify a specific instance of an object, for example:

```
HTTP/1.1 200 OK
ETag: "8cac4-276e-35b36b6a"
```

---

* On Unix, *cp -p* and *tar -p* preserve modification times and other file attributes.

A cache uses an entity tag to validate its object with the `If-none-match` request header:

```
GET /index.html HTTP/1.1
If-None-Match: "8cac4-276e-35b36b6a"
```

Upon receiving this request, the origin server examines its metadata for the object. If the entity tag (8cac4-276e-35b36b6a) is still valid, the server returns a 304 (Not Modified) reply. Otherwise, the server ignores the `If-none-match` header and processes the request normally. Most likely, it returns a 200 (OK) response with the new, updated content.

The phrase "If-none-match" is a bit difficult to grasp at first. To understand it, you need to realize that HTTP/1.1 allows an origin server to associate multiple entity tags with a single resource. A cache can store different versions of the same object (same URI), each with a unique entity tag. If the cached responses are stale, the cache learns which are still valid by using the `If-none-match` header, listing all of its entity tags for that resource:

```
GET /index.html HTTP/1.1
If-None-Match: "foo","bar","xyzzy"
```

In essence, a cache says to an origin server, "If none of these entity tags are valid, send me the new content."

If the origin server's reply is a 304 (Not Modified) message, it must tell the cache which tag is valid. The valid entity tag is given in the `Etag:` header of a 304 response:

```
HTTP/1.1 304 Not Modified
ETag: "xyzzy"
```

Unlike the `Last-modified` validator, entity tag validators are opaque to the cache. In other words, the cache cannot derive any meaning from an entity tag. The only operation a cache can perform on an entity tag is a test for equality (string comparison). Timestamps, however, are more useful to caches because they do convey some meaning. A cache can use the `Last-modified` timestamp to calculate the LM-factor and apply the heuristics described previously to identify objects likely to still be fresh. If servers all over the world suddenly stopped sending last-modified timestamps and sent only entity tags, caches would find it much more difficult to predict freshness. Fortunately, RFC 2616 (Section 13.3.4) advocates sending both last-modified timestamps and entity tags whenever possible.

2.5.3 *Weak and Strong Validators*

RFC 2616 defines two types of validators: weak and strong. Strong validators are used for exact, byte-for-byte equivalence of the content. Weak validators, on the other hand, are used for semantic equivalence. Consider, for example, a very simple change to a text document, such as correcting a spelling error. The correction does not alter the meaning of the document, but it does change the bits of the file. In this situation, a conditional request with a strong validator would return the new content, while the same conditional request with a weak validator would return "not modified."

HTTP/1.1 requires strong comparison in some circumstances and allows weak comparison in others. When strong comparison is required, only strong validators may be used. When weak comparison is allowed, either type of validator may be used.

An entity tag is, by default, a strong validator. Thus, even the slightest change to an origin server resource requires the entity tag to change as well. The Apache server uses a checksum over the message body as one component of its entity tags, so this happens automatically. If an origin server wants to create a weak entity tag, it prefixes the validator with "w/":

```
Etag: "w/foo-bar-123"
```

`Last-modified` timestamps, by comparison, are implicitly weak, unless a cache can determine that it is strong according to a complex set of rules. The reason is that the timestamp provides only single-second resolution. It's possible that an object gets modified twice (or more) in a one-second interval. If this actually happens, and the protocol requires strong validation, users could receive the wrong response. A caching proxy that does not support entity tags is better off forwarding conditional requests to origin servers when strong comparison is required.

HTTP/1.1 has many rules regarding weak and strong validators. These details are a bit too overwhelming to cover here, but you can find more information in Section 13.3.3 of RFC 2616.

2.6 *Forcing a Cache to Refresh*

One of the tradeoffs of caching is that you may occasionally receive stale data. What can you do if you believe (or know) that a cache has given you stale data? You need some way to refresh or validate the data received from the cache. HTTP provides a couple of mechanisms for doing just that. Clients can generate requests with `Cache-control` directives, the two most common of which are `no-cache` and `max-age`. We'll discuss `no-cache` first because it has been around the longest.

2.6.1 The no-cache Directive

The no-cache directive notifies a cache that it cannot return a cached copy. Even if a fresh copy of the response—with a specific expiration time—is in the cache, the client's request must be forwarded to the origin server. RFC 2616 calls such a request an "end-to-end validation" (Section 14.9.4). The no-cache directive is sent when you click on the *Reload* button on your browser. In an HTTP request, it looks like this:

```
GET /index.html HTTP/1.1
Cache-control: no-cache
```

Recall that the Cache-control header does not exist in the HTTP/1.0 standard. Instead, HTTP/1.0 clients use a Pragma header for the no-cache directive:

```
Pragma: no-cache
```

no-cache is the only directive defined for the Pragma header in RFC 1945. For backwards compatibility, RFC 2616 also defines the Pragma header. In fact, many of the recent HTTP/1.1 browsers still use Pragma for the no-cache directive instead of the newer Cache-control.

Note that the no-cache directive does not necessarily require the cache to purge its copy of the object. The client may generate a conditional request (with If-modified-since or another validator), in which case the origin server's response may be 304 (Not Modified). If, however, the server responds with 200 (OK), then the cache replaces the old object with the new one.

The interaction between no-cache and If-modified-since is tricky and often the source of some confusion. Consider, for example, the following sequence of events:

1. You are viewing an HTML page in your browser. This page is cached in your browser and was last modified on Friday, February 16, 2001, at 12:00:00.

2. The page author replaces the current HTML page with an older, backup copy of the page, perhaps with this Unix command:

    ```
    mv index.html.old index.html
    ```

    Now there is a "new" version of the HTML page on the server, but it has an older modification timestamp.

3. You try to reload the HTML page by using the *Reload* button. Your browser sends this request:

    ```
    GET http://www.foo.com/index.html
    Pragma: no-cache
    If-Modified-Since: Fri, 16 Feb 2001 09:46:18 GMT
    ```

4. The origin server sends a 304 (Not Modified) response and your browser displays the same page as before.

You could click on *Reload* until your mouse wears out and you would never get the "new" HTML page. What can you do to see the correct page?

If you are using Netscape Navigator, you can hold the Shift key down while clicking on *Reload*. This instructs Netscape to leave out the If-modified-since header. If you use Internet Explorer, hold down the Ctrl key while clicking on *Reload*. Alternatively, you can flush your browser's cache and then press *Reload*, which prevents the browser from sending an If-modified-since header in its request. Note that this is a user-agent problem, not a caching proxy problem.

In addition to the above problem, the *Reload* button, as implemented in most web browsers, leaves much to be desired. For example, it is not possible to reload a single inline image object. Similarly, it is not possible to reload web objects that are displayed externally from the browser, such as sound files and other "application" content types. If you need to refresh an image, PostScript document, or other externally displayed object, you may need to ask the cache administrator to do it for you. Some caches may have a web form that allows you to refresh cache objects. For this you need to know (and type in) the object's full URL.

Another problem with *Reload* is that it is often misused simply to rerequest a page. When the Web seems slow, we often interrupt a request as the page is being retrieved. To request the page again, you might use the *Reload* button. This, of course, sends the no-cache directive. Browsers do not have a button which requests a page again without sending no-cache. You can accomplish this by simply moving the cursor to the URL location box and pressing the Enter key.

As a cache administrator, you might wonder if caches ever can, or should, ignore the no-cache directive. A person who keeps a close watch on bandwidth usage might have the impression that the *Reload* button gets used much more often than necessary. Some products, such as Squid, have features that provide special treatment for no-cache requests. However, I personally do not recommend enabling these features because they violate the HTTP/1.1 protocol and leave users unable to get up-to-date information. One Squid option turns a no-cache request into an If-modified-since request. Another ignores the no-cache directive entirely.

2.6.2 *The max-age Directive*

The max-age directive specifies in seconds the maximum age of a cached response that the client is willing to accept. Whereas no-cache means "I won't accept any cached response," max-age says, "I will accept fresh responses that were last validated within this time period." To specify a limit of one hour, a client sends:

```
Cache-control: max-age=3600
```

Note that max-age has lower precedence than an origin server expiration time. For example, if a cached object became stale five seconds ago, and it is requested with max-age=100000000, the cache must still validate the object with the origin server. In other words, max-age can cause validation to occur but can never prevent it from occurring.

RFC 2616 calls a max-age=0 request an *end-to-end revalidation*, because it forces the cache to revalidate its stored response. The client might still get that stored response, unlike with an end-to-end reload (no-cache), where a cache is not allowed to return a cached response. The use of max-age=0, however, is a request to validate a cached response. If the client includes its own validator, then it's a *specific end-to-end validation.* Otherwise, a caching proxy adds its own validator, if any, and the request is an *unspecified end-to-end validation.*

So far as I know, max-age is not widely supported in web browsers at this time. This is unfortunate, because a max-age=0 request is more likely to generate a short 304 (Not Modified) response, whereas a no-cache request is more likely to generate a full 200 (OK) response. It would be helpful if user agents had an option to set a max-age value in their requests. Users who prefer faster access over freshness would use a higher max-age setting. Similarly, those with lots of bandwidth and good response times could use a lower setting to ensure up-to-date responses.

2.6.3 The min-fresh Directive

In the previous section I talked about the max-stale directive, whereby clients can relax freshness requirements. Conversely, the min-fresh directive allows clients to specify more stringent freshness conditions. The value of the min-fresh directive is added to the object's age when performing staleness calculations. For example, if the client gives a min-fresh value of 3,600 seconds, the cache cannot return a response that would become stale within the next hour.

2.7 Cache Replacement

Cache replacement refers to the process that takes place when the cache becomes full and old objects must be removed to make space for new ones. Usually, a cache assigns some kind of value to each object and removes the least valuable ones. The actual meaning of "valuable" may vary from one cache to another. Typically, an object's value is related to the probability that it will be requested again, thus attempting to maximize the hit ratio. Caching researchers and developers have proposed and evaluated numerous replacement algorithms, some of which are described here.

2.7.1   Least Recently Used (LRU)

LRU is certainly the most popular replacement algorithm used by web caches. The algorithm is quite simple to understand and implement, and it gives very good performance in almost all situations. As the name implies, LRU removes the objects that have not been accessed for the longest time. This algorithm can be implemented with a simple list. Every time an object is accessed, it is moved to the top of the list. The least recently used objects then automatically migrate to the bottom of the list.

A strict interpretation of LRU would consider time-since-reference as the only parameter. In practice, web caches almost always use a variant known as LRU-Threshold, where "threshold" refers to object size. Objects larger than the threshold size are simply not cached. This prevents one very large object from ejecting many smaller ones. This highlights the biggest problem with LRU: it doesn't consider object sizes. Would you rather have one large object in your cache or many smaller ones? Your answer probably depends on what you wish to optimize. If saving bandwidth is important, you want the large object. However, caching numerous small objects results in a higher hit ratio.

2.7.2   First In, First Out (FIFO)

A FIFO replacement algorithm is even simpler to implement than LRU. Objects are purged in the same order they were added. This technique does not account for object popularity and gives lower hit ratios than LRU. FIFO is rarely, if ever, used for caching proxies.

2.7.3   Least Frequently Used (LFU)

LFU is similar to LRU, but instead of selecting based on time since access, the significant parameter is the number of accesses. LFU replaces objects with small access counts and keeps objects with high access counts. If the algorithm does not take time since last access into account, the cache tends to fill up with frequently accessed but old objects. If the least frequently used object in the cache was accessed twice, a new object (which is accessed only once) can never be added. LFU implementations are sometimes used in caching products, but not very often.

2.7.4 Size

A size-based algorithm uses the object size as the primary removal criteria. The largest objects in the cache are removed first. The algorithm really needs an aging mechanism as well. That is, old objects must be removed eventually, otherwise the cache fills up with only very small objects. Simulations show that, compared to LRU, a size-based algorithm provides better cache hit ratios but significantly worse byte hit ratios.

2.7.5 GreedyDual-Size (GDS)

The previously mentioned algorithms tend to optimize one extreme or another. For example, LRU tends to have the highest byte hit ratios, while Size usually has higher document hit ratios. If you're looking for a middle ground, GreedyDual-Size is a good alternative.

GDS assigns value to cached objects based on the cost of a cache miss and the size of the object. GDS does not specify exactly what "cost" means. This offers a lot of flexibility to optimize just what you want. For example, cost might be latency—the time it takes to receive the response. Cost might also be the number of packets transmitted over the network or the number of hops between the origin server and the cache. I'll give a brief explanation of the algorithm here, but for full details on GDS, see [Cao and Irani, 1997].

The GreedyDual-Size algorithm associates a value, H, with each object in the cache. When an object is initially brought into the cache, its H value is set to the cost of retrieving the object, divided by its size. When the cache is full, the object with the smallest H value (H_{min}) is removed. Then, the H values of all remaining objects are decreased by H_{min}. When a cache hit occurs, the object's H value is reset to its initial value, as though it were being added for the first time.

Implementation of the algorithm as described is problematic. It's impractical to perform a subtraction for every cache object each time an object is removed. It works just as well to add an "inflation" value to H for new objects and cache hits. The inflation value is simply set to H_{min} each time an object is removed.

2.7.6 Other Algorithms

Numerous other replacement algorithms have been proposed by web caching researchers. Many of these are combinations of the algorithms already mentioned. For example, LRU-size uses size as the primary criteria and LRU as the secondary criteria. The LRU-MIN algorithm attempts to remove an old object of approximately the same size as the new object. This prevents a new, small object from replacing a large object. Further details are not given here because these algo-rithms are not known to be used in caching products available today. Refer to [Williams, Abrams, Standridge, Abdulla and Fox, 1996] for more information.

One reason for the relative popularity of the LRU algorithm is its simplicity. Some of the other algorithms proposed over the years are difficult to implement effi-ciently. Some require computing a metric for every cached object each time the replacement procedure runs. This is not practical for really large caches. Other algorithms require keeping extra metadata for each object. Since memory is usu-ally a scarce resource, programmers are more likely to implement simpler algo-rithms.

3

Politics of Web Caching

In this chapter, we will explore some important and difficult-to-solve issues that surround web caching. The issues pertain to many aspects of caching but are primarily targeted at those of us who operate a caching proxy. For example, as an administrator, you have access to information that, if made available to others, can seriously violate the privacy of your users. If your users cannot trust you to protect their privacy, they will not want to use your cache. Hopefully, both you and your users will perceive the cache as something that protects, rather than violates, their privacy.

A particularly thorny issue with web caching involves the rights of content providers to control the copying and distribution of their works. Some people argue that existing copyright laws cannot be applied to the Internet, but most people look for ways to coerce the two together. By some interpretations, web caches are in gross violation of copyright laws. Various rulings by U.S. courts* seem to support this view, although none of them specifically address web caching. Similar issues surround so-called offensive material and the liability of system operators whose facilities are used for its transmission.

Other issues explored here include dynamic pages, content integrity, and cache busting. When properly generated by origin servers, dynamic pages do not present any problems for web caches. Unfortunately, the problem of ensuring content integrity is not as easy to dismiss. Without a general-purpose digital signature framework, web users are forced to trust that they receive the correct content from both proxy and origin servers.

---

* I'll talk only about U.S. laws here, but other countries' laws are equally vague on the subject of caching.

Something that makes caching politically interesting is the fact that many different organizations are involved in even the simplest web transactions. At one end is the user, and at the other is a content provider. In between are various types of Internet service providers. Not surprisingly, different organizations have different goals, which may conflict with one another. Some users prefer to be anonymous, but some content providers want to collect a lot of personal information about their customers or visitors. Some ISPs want to sell more bandwidth, and others want to minimize their bandwidth costs.

In a sense, these differences can lead to an "arms race." Content providers decide their pages should not be cached, so they add some headers to prevent it. Users and administrators get upset and configure their caches to store the pages anyway. Next, the content providers discover their pages are being cached anyway, so they take further, more extreme steps to prevent caching, and so on. A similar battle exists regarding the information sent in user requests. Some HTTP headers can reveal personal information or allow individuals to be tracked as they navigate within and between sites. If users filter these headers out or alter their values, some sites refuse the requests. Each side, it seems, wants to exercise some control over the information in web requests and responses. Who will win? My fear is that the commerce-driven content providers are already winning.

3.1 *Privacy*

"Privacy is the power to control what others can come to know about you" [Lessig, 1999, p.143]. In the U.S., most people feel they have a right to privacy. Even though the word does not occur in our Constitution, the fourth amendment comes close when talking about "the right of the people to be secure in their persons, houses, papers, and effects, against unreasonable searches and seizures..." In at least one famous case, the Supreme Court ruled that this amendment does provide for an individual's privacy.* Also of relevance is Article 12 of the United Nations Universal Declaration of Human Rights, which states:

> No one shall be subjected to arbitrary interference with his privacy, family, home
> or correspondence, nor to attacks upon his honor and reputation. Everyone has
> the right to the protection of the law against such interference or attacks.

Privacy is a very important issue on the Internet as a whole and the Web in particular. Almost everywhere we go in cyberspace, we leave behind a little record of our visit. Today's computer and networking technology makes it almost trivial for information providers to amass huge amounts of data about their audience. As users, you and I might have different feelings about the importance of privacy. As

---

* Katz v. U.S., 389 U.S. 347 (1967).

cache operators, however, we have a responsibility always to protect the privacy of our cache users.

Privacy concerns are found in almost every aspect of our daily lives, not just while surfing the Net. My telephone company certainly knows which phone numbers I have dialed. The video store where I rent movies knows what kind of movies I like. My bank and credit card company know where I spend my money. Surveillance cameras are commonplace in stores, offices, and even some outdoor, public places.

In the United States, a consumer's privacy is protected by federal laws on a case-by-case basis. Video stores are not allowed to disclose an individual's rental and sales records without that individual's consent or a court order.* However, the law does allow video stores to use detailed personal information for marketing purposes if the consumer is given an opportunity to opt out. Similarly, telephone companies must protect their customer's private information, including call records.† There are no federal laws, however, that address consumer privacy in the banking industry. In fact, under the Banking Secrecy Act, banks must report suspicious transactions, such as large deposits, to federal agencies.‡ The latter is intended to aid in the tracking of money laundering, drug trafficking, and other criminal activities. Banks may be subject to state privacy laws, but for the most part, they are self-regulating in this regard.

As with banking, there are no U.S. laws that protect an individual's privacy on the Internet. This is unfortunate, because web transactions can reveal a significant amount of information about an individual user. Internet companies that specialize in marketing and advertising can determine a person's age, sex, place of residence, and other information by examining only a handful of requests. In the normal course of administering your cache, you are going to encounter personal details about your users. You are in a unique position to either strengthen or weaken your users' privacy. I strongly encourage you to develop and publish a policy that protects the privacy of your users to the fullest extent possible.

3.1.1 Access Logs

One way in which users' privacy can be compromised is by cache access logs. Most web caches in operation make a log entry for each and every request received. A typical log entry includes the time of access, URL requested, the requesting client's network address, and, in some cases, a username. As a cache operator, you have access to a large amount of potentially revealing information

---

* 18 U.S.C. 2710(b). Visit *http://www.law.cornell.edu* to read the actual text for this and other citations.

† 47 U.S.C. 222(c).

‡ 31 C.F.R. 103.21.

about your users, who trust you not to abuse it. If you violate that trust relationship, your users will not want to use your cache.

Note that proxies are not the only applications that can log user requests. A network packet sniffer can produce the same result. Proxy log files are easier to understand and generate, but a sniffer also logs requests that don't go through a proxy cache.

As a cache administrator, you are probably free to choose if, and how much, proxy information is logged. Some operators choose to disable logging, but some may be required to log because of regional laws, company policies, settlements, or other reasons. At the same time, it is the policy of some organizations to log all requests for security reasons.

If the choice is yours to make, a number of factors should affect your decision. First of all, log files provide some amount of accountability. Under normal operation, it is unlikely you will need to examine specific requests. But if you suspect criminal activity, the log files might prove useful. Also, many organizations like to analyze their log files to extract certain statistics and trends. Analysis tools can calculate hit ratios, network utilization (bandwidth), and request service times. Long-term analysis can inform you about growth trends and when your organization may require additional bandwidth. Debugging reported problems is generally made easier by having log files around. As many of us know, users often fail to report details important for finding and fixing problems. Your log files might fill in the missing pieces.

If you decide to keep access logs, it might be sufficient to log partial information, so that users retain some amount of privacy. For example, instead of logging full client IP addresses, the cache could log only the first three octets (or any subnetting/netmask scheme). Instead of logging full URLs, the cache might log only the server hostnames. You should be particularly sensitive to logging the query part of a URL. These appear following a "?", and might contain sensitive information such as names and account numbers. Here are some slightly edited examples from my cache logs (with long lines wrapped):

```
http://komunitas.detik.com/eshare/server/srvgate.dll?action=2&user=XXXP
    &id=68nFdR&rand=975645899050
    &request=248+bye%2Ball%2Bgua%2Bpamit%2Bsebentar
http://edit.yahoo.com/config/ncclogin?.src=bl
    &login=dream_demon_of_night&passwd=XXXXXXXXXXXXX&n=1
http://liveuniverse.com/world?type=world&page=ok
    &dig.password=XXXXXXXX&dig.handle=darkforce
http://mercury.beseen.com/chat/rooms/e/17671/Chat.html?handle=lanunk
    &passkey=XXXXXXXXXXXXX
http://msg.edit.yahoo.com/config/ncclogin?.src=bl&login=XXXXXXXXX
    &passwd=XXXXX&n=1
http://www.creditcardsearchengine.com/?AID=115075&6PID=823653
```

```
http://64.23.37.140/cgi-bin/muslimemail/me.cgi?read=Refresh&login=XXXX
    &myuid=XXXXXXXX&folder=INBOX&startx=1&endx=15
http://64.40.36.143/cdjoin2.asp?sitename=wetdreams
http://ekilat.com/email_login.php?who=XXXXX@ekilat.com
http://join.nbci.com/authlogin_remote_redir.php?u=be_nink
    &hash=XXX...XXX&targetURL=http%3A%2F%2Fwww%2Eemail%2Ecom%2F%3F...
```

Due to their sensitive nature, you should carefully consider who else is able to read your proxy access logs. Limiting the number of people who can read the log files reduces the risk of privacy invasion and other abuses. If your cache runs on a multiuser system such as Unix, pay close attention to file ownership, group, and related permissions. Some caching appliances make log files available for download via FTP. In this case, avoid using a widely-known administrator password, and also find out if other (e.g., address-based) access controls are available.

If you keep access logs, you should also develop a policy for how long the logs are saved. Keeping access logs for long periods of time might be useful for the reasons just described. However, situations might also arise where, in order to protect the privacy of your customers or employees, it would be better to not have the logs at all. In the U.S., the Freedom of Information Act (FOIA)* requires federal agencies to share certain documents and records with the public upon request. Many state governments have similar laws governing their own agencies. Some people feel that the access logs of systems owned and/or operated by the government are subject to these laws.

In order to do long-term analysis, you probably don't need the full log file information. Instead, you can store shorter data files that summarize the information in such a way that it remains useful but no longer compromises the privacy of your users.

3.1.2 Making Requests Anonymous

Caching proxies also serve to strengthen, not just weaken, user privacy. Many organizations run web caches on their firewalls to hide the details of their internal network. External servers see connections coming from only the firewall host. This makes it harder for outsiders to find out the name, address, or type of user machines. Simply hiding internal names and addresses is not really sufficient. A good firewall has additional defense mechanisms in place, but every little bit helps.

Proxies may also protect privacy by filtering outgoing requests. As I alluded to earlier, HTTP requests often include personal or user-specific information. A request can include the browser software, operating system, IP address, and the page being viewed when the new request is made. Older browser software was known

---

* 5 U.S.C. 552.

to send the user's email address as well, but recent versions should not. Some of this information can be quickly indexed to other online databases to acquire, for example, the user's telephone number and street address.

Content providers are quite happy to collect as much personal information as they can. Usually, much of this information can be filtered out without any negative consequences for the user. Some caching proxies, such as Squid, are able to remove certain HTTP headers before forwarding a request. If you have privacy concerns, you might want to filter some of the following headers:

From

> This header, if present, contains the user's email address. In the past, browsers always sent a `From` header if the user had configured that information. These days, the header is rarely seen, probably because of backlash from privacy advocates. RFC 2616 suggests that user agents should not send the header without the user's consent.

> In my experience, it is always safe to remove the `From` header in outgoing requests. I have not encountered or heard of an origin server that requires it to be present.

Referer

> The (historically misspelled) `Referer` header contains the URI from which the requested URI was obtained. For example, consider a page *A* that includes a link to page *B*. When you click on the link for *B*, the request looks something like this:

> ```
> GET B HTTP/1.1
> Referer: A
> ```

> Content providers love the `Referer` header because it tells them how people find out about their site. When you use a search engine such as Altavista and follow one of the links, the `Referer` header is set to the Altavista query URL plus your query terms. Thus, the content provider knows what you are searching for when you find their site through a search engine. The Apache server makes it easy to log `Referer` headers from requests received. Here are some examples from my own web site:

> ```
> http://google.yahoo.com/bin/query?p=%22web+cache%22&hc=0&hs=1 -> /
> http://www.google.com/search?q=wpad+rfc&hl=en -> /writings.html
> http://www.altavista.com/cgi-bin/query?pg=q&q=linux+cache -> /
> http://search.msn.com/spbasic.htm?MT=akamai%20personalization
>       -> /services.html
> http://www.google.com/search?q=web+cache+proxy&hl=en -> /
> http://www.12g.com/topic/Web_Caching -> /writings.html
> http://www.google.com/search?q=what+is+a+web+cache&hl=en -> /
> http://www.altavista.com/cgi-bin/query?q=RFC+WPAD -> /writings.html
> ```

In the previous examples, the `Referer` header is on the left, and the requested URI is to the right of the -> symbol.

The `Referer` header is useful for fixing broken links. A broken link is a hypertext link to a page or object that doesn't exist anymore. They are, unfortunately, all too common on the Web. With the `Referer` header, a content provider can discover the pages that point to nonexistent documents. Presumably, the content provider can contact the author of the other document and ask her to update the page or remove the link. However, that's much easier said than done. Getting the broken links fixed is often quite difficult.

`Referer` violates our privacy by providing origin servers with a history of our browsing activities. It gives content providers probably more information than they really need to satisfy a request. In my experience, it is always safe to filter out `Referer` headers.

User-agent

The `User-agent` header contains a string that identifies your web browser, including operating system and version numbers. Here are some sample `User-agent` values:

```
Mozilla/2.0 (compatible; MSIE 3.01; AK; Windows 95)
Mozilla/4.0 (compatible; BorderManager 3.0)
Mozilla/4.51 [en] (X11; I; Linux 2.2.5-15 i686)
NetAnts/1.00
Mozilla/4.0 (compatible; MSIE 5.0; Windows 95; DigExt)
Mozilla/4.0 (compatible; MSIE 4.01; Windows 98)
Wget/1.5.3
```

`User-agent` is useful to content providers because it tells them what their users are using to view their site. For example, knowing that 90% of requests come from browser *X*, which supports feature *Z*, makes it easier to design a site that takes advantage of that feature. `User-agent` is also sometimes used to return browser-specific content. Netscape may support some nonstandard HTML tags that Internet Explorer does not, and vice versa.

As you can see in the previous examples, the `User-agent` field tells the content provider quite a lot about your computer system. They know if you run Windows 95 or Windows NT. In the Linux example, we can see that the system's CPU is an Intel 686 (Pentium II) or newer.

Unfortunately, it is not always safe to filter out the `User-agent` header. Some sites rely on the header to figure out if certain features are supported. With the header removed, I have seen sites that return a page saying, "Sorry, looks like your browser doesn't support Java, so you can't use our site." I have also seen sites (e.g., *www.imdb.com*) that refuse requests from specific user-agents, usually to prevent intense robot crawling.

`Cookie`

Cookies are used to maintain session state information between HTTP requests. A so-called shopping basket is a common application of a cookie. However, they may also be used simply to track a person's browsing activities. The prospect is truly frightening when you consider the way that advertising companies such as *doubleclick.net* operate. DoubleClick places ads on thousands of servers. The `Cookie` and `Referer` headers together allow them to track an individual's browsing across all of the servers where they place ads.

Unfortunately, filtering `Cookie` headers for all requests is not always practical. Doing so may interfere with sites that you really want to use. As an alternative, users should be able to configure their browsers to require approval before accepting a new cookie. There are also client-side programs for filtering and removing cookies. For more information, visit *http://www.cookiecentral.com.*

Unfortunately, even some presumably harmless headers can be used to track individuals. Martin Pool uncovered a trick whereby content providers use the `Last-modified` and `If-modified-since` headers to accomplish exactly that [Pool, 2000]. In this scheme, the cache validator serves the same purpose as a cookie. It's a small chunk of information that the user-agent receives, probably stores, and then sends back to the server in a future request. If each user receives a unique validator, the content provider knows when that user revisits a particular page.

3.2 Request Blocking

Request blocking refers to the act of denying certain requests based on some part of the request itself (usually the URL). Like it or not, a fair amount of the content available on the Web is generally considered to be offensive, the most obvious example being pornography. Some organizations that connect to the Internet feel it necessary to prevent their users from accessing these sites. A web cache is a logical place to implement per-request blocking.

The issues surrounding request blocking fall mostly into the political realm. Furthermore, these issues are not new or unique to the Web. Just as many companies say employees should not make phone-sex calls while at work, they also say workers should not view pornographic web sites. Similarly, a parent might say that children should not have easy access to sexually explicit material, whether in the form of a magazine, video, or web site. It is a policy decision, for employers and parents, whether and to what extent request blocking should be enabled. Classifying material into offensive or inoffensive categories is a political and ideological issue and far beyond the scope of this book. Even if the classification is not controversial, it is unlikely that a particular technique or implementation is perfect.

Some legitimate sites may be incorrectly blocked. Similarly, sites that should be blocked may still be allowed through.

Several request-blocking products and services are available. Some of these are "plug-ins" for web cache products; others are full proxy implementations that can be used alone or in serial with an existing web cache. The companies offering these products also provide a list of sites (or URLs) to be blocked. Usually these products require a subscription fee to receive list updates. However, some allow new sites to be added manually. A typical blocking list probably includes 100,000 or more entries.

The World Wide Web Consortium (*http://www.w3c.org*) has developed a content labeling scheme known as the Platform for Internet Content Selection. PICS is simply a standard way to label web pages rather than rate them. In other words, PICS specifies the structure of a label, not what to put inside it. However, PICS is often associated with content filtering, because that was one of the primary reasons for its development. A PICS-aware web cache can filter out requests based on one or more rating schemes.

Request blocking has the potential to adversely affect latency. Depending on the type of list and the searching algorithm, a large list could add noticeable delay to every request. In general, web cache systems are I/O-bound and do not require top-of-the-line processors. However, checking every requested URL against a blocking list increases the demand for CPU resources and can change the web cache into a CPU-bound application. The three most popular methods for blocking requests are exact string matches, substring matches, and regular expressions. Exact string matching is straightforward and can be implemented easily in an efficient algorithm. However, exact string matching is essentially useless for blocking URLs. Both substring matching and regular expressions are much more flexible, but at the same time, they are difficult to implement efficiently. The simple (but inefficient) algorithm for searching a list of regular expressions involves sequentially checking every entry in the list. If your cache needs to check requests against a large blocking list, you might want to consider a machine with a fast processor.

If you do employ request blocking on your caching proxy, it's best to be up-front about it. Tell your users that access to certain web sites is being blocked and why this is the case. Provide them with a copy of your organization's policy on appropriate use of your facilities. Periodically (e.g., once per year) remind your users about the policy and its enforcement. Be sure to tell them what to do in case the software incorrectly blocks legitimate content. Finally, be sure that you and your colleagues know how to make exceptions in the filtering rules.

3.3 Copyright

Copyright laws give authors or creators certain rights regarding the copying and distribution of their original works. These laws are intended to encourage people to share their creative works without fear that they will not receive due credit or remuneration. Copyrights are recognized internationally through various treaties (e.g., the Berne Convention and the Universal Copyright Convention). This helps our discussion somewhat, because the Internet tends to ignore political boundaries.

Digital computers and the Internet challenge our traditional thinking about copyrights. Before computers, we only had to worry about making copies of physical objects such as books, paintings, and records. The U.S. copyright statute defines a copy thusly:

> *Copies* are material objects...in which a work is fixed by any method now known or later developed, and from which the work can be perceived, reproduced, or otherwise communicated, either directly or with the aid of a machine or device.[*]

When you memorize a poem, thereby making a copy in your brain, you have not violated a copyright law. Tests for physicality are difficult to apply to computer systems where information exists only as electrostatic or magnetic charges representing ones and zeroes.

Copying is a fundamental characteristic of the Internet. An Internet without copying is like a pizza without cheese—what would be the point? People like the Internet because it lets them share information with each other. Email, newsgroups, web pages, chat rooms: all require copying information from one place to another. The Internet also challenges traditional copyrights in another interesting way. Revenue is often the primary reason we establish and enforce copyrights. I don't want you to copy this book and give it to someone else because I get a bigger royalty check if your friend buys his own copy. On the Internet, however, paying for information is the exception rather than the rule. Some sites require subscriptions, but most do not, and a lot of web content is available for free.

3.3.1 Does Caching Infringe?

The question for us is this: does web caching infringe upon an author's copyright? If so, cache operators are potentially liable and may be subject to litigation. If not, copyright owners have arguably lost the right to exercise control over the distribution of their works. We can make good arguments for both sides of this debate.

---

* 17 U.S.C. 101.

First, let's examine some arguments that suggest that caching does infringe. The Berne Convention text (Article 9) states the following:

> Authors of literary and artistic works protected by this Convention shall have the exclusive right of authorizing the reproduction of these works, in any manner or form.

Web caching most certainly qualifies as "reproduction" in this context, and thus the Berne Convention applies. In fact, judges have already ruled that even relatively transitory and short-term copies of works in computer memory (RAM) are subject to copyright laws. One grey area is whether we can say that a cache has the authorization to make a copy. Some people say "no" because such authorization is almost never explicitly granted, especially at the level of the transfer protocol (HTTP). The author of a web page may write something like "caching of this page is allowed," say, in an HTML comment, but the proxy wouldn't know that.

A more credible pro-caching defense states that web publishers implicitly grant a license to create copies, simply by placing material on a web server. After all, browsers must necessarily copy a page from the server to display it to the user. Content providers are generally aware that such copying between nodes is a fundamental aspect of the Internet's operation, and therefore they may accept that their pages are copied and duplicated at various locations. Furthermore, the laws certainly do not discriminate between caching at a browser versus caching at a proxy. If one infringes, we must conclude the other does as well.

In the U.S., this issue remained unresolved for a number of years. Although the threat of copyright infringement claims always existed, that didn't stop most organizations from deploying caching proxies in their networks. The situation changed dramatically in October of 1998, however, when Congress passed the Digital Millennium Copyright Act (DMCA). But before getting to that, let's look at some previous case law.

3.3.2 Cases and Precedents

It appears that copyright law relating to caching has not yet been tested in any court. Rumors of such lawsuits do exist, but, if the rumors are true, the cases were likely dropped or settled before trial. However, U.S. courts have heard a number of cases alleging copyright infringement by system operators. Eric Schlachter's article in Boardwatch magazine provides a good summary of some of these cases [Schlachter, 1997]. It is enlightening to examine a few details from them.

In 1993, Playboy magazine sued a system operator, George Frena, for, among other things, distribution of copyrighted images. The operator was found guilty of violating Playboy's right of distribution, even though he did not copy the files himself. The court noted that intent is not required to be found liable.

The following year, Sega sued the operators of a bulletin board for providing unauthorized copies of game software. The court initially found the operators both directly and contributorily liable. A second hearing of the case in 1996 found the operators were not directly liable because they did not make the copies. However, they remained contributorily liable because their system encouraged users to upload the pirated software.

More recently, the Religious Technology Center, a group affiliated with the Church of Scientology, instigated a lawsuit against system operators (Netcom and Tom Klemesrud) and a user (Dennis Erlich) over some messages posted to a Usenet newsgroup. One of the claims was copyright infringement of material owned by the Religious Technology Center. In the end, neither Netcom nor Klemesrud were found liable. However, this case contains an interesting twist. Both Netcom and Klemesrud were notified that their systems had distributed copyrighted information. The operators did not attempt to cancel the messages because they felt the copyright claims could not reasonably be verified. The court agreed. Although not stated explicitly, this ruling implies operators could be liable if given adequate notice that an infringement has occurred.

The case against Napster is perhaps one of the highest profile copyright lawsuits in recent years. Napster is a service (and software package) that puts its users in touch with each other so they can share music files. Napster doesn't store the files on its servers, but the comapny maintains a central database detailing the files that each user is willing to share. A number of recording industry companies sued Napster in late 1999 for contributory copyright infringement. One of Napster's defenses is that people can use their system in ways that do not infringe on copyrights. For example, users may share their own music or music that is free from copying restrictions. Sony successfully used this line of reasoning in a 1984 Supreme Court case that established that videocassette recording of television shows qualifies as fair use. After many hearings, the court forced Napster to prevent its customers from swapping copyrighted music unless they pay a royalty to the music producers.

3.3.3 The DMCA

The Digital Millennium Copyright Act was signed into law in October of 1998. Its goal is to bring U.S. law in line with the World Intellectual Property Organization Copyright Treaty and the Performances and Phonograms Treaty. To many people, the DMCA is a travesty. The Electronic Freedom Foundation (*http://www.eff.org*) has a number of anti-DMCA articles on its web site. However, these are all focused on section 1201 of U.S.C. title 17, which makes it illegal to circumvent copyright protection systems.

For this discussion, we focus on a different part of the DMCA. Title II is called the Online Copyright Infringement Liability Limitation Act. It exempts service providers from liability for copyright infringement if certain conditions are met. Surprisingly, this legislation specifically addresses caching! This part of the Act became law as section 512 of U.S.C. title 17. The text of the first two subsections are included in Appendix G.

Subsection (a) doesn't talk about caching, but it's relevant anyway. It exempts service providers for simply providing "transitory digital network communications," for example, routing, transmitting packets, and providing connections through their networks. This language probably applies to proxying (without caching) as well. To avoid liability, certain conditions must be met.

One condition is that the service provider must not modify the content as it passes through its network. Thus, a caching proxy that alters web pages, images, etc., may be liable for copyright infringement. Filtering out "naughty" words from text and changing the resolution or quality of an image both violate this condition. It's not clear to me whether blocking a request for an embedded image (e.g., an advertisement banner) qualifies as content modification.

Subsection (b) deals entirely with caching. It says that "intermediate and temporary storage of material" does not make service providers liable for copyright infringement, but only if the following conditions are met:

- The material is made available by somebody other than the ISP.

- The material is sent to someone other than the content provider.

- The reason for storing the material is to use it in response to future requests from users, subject to a number of additional conditions.

The additional conditions of subsection (b) are quite long and relate to issues such as modification of content, serving stale responses, and access to protected information.

Paragraph (2)(A) says that the service provider can't modify cached responses. Since subsection (a) says the provider can't modify the original response, this implies that all cache hits must be the same as the original.

Paragraph (2)(B) is interesting because it mandates compliance with "rules concerning the refreshing, reloading, or other updating of the material . . . "—in other words, the HTTP headers. This means that if the caching product is configured or operates in a way that violates HTTP, the service provider may be guilty of copyright infringement. What's even more interesting is that this paragraph applies "only if those rules are not used by the [content owner] to prevent or unreasonably impair" caching. To me it seems that if the origin server is cache busting (see Section 3.7, "Cache Busting and Server Busting"), disobeying HTTP headers does not make the service provider liable for infringement. This is somewhat surprising, because HTTP gives content owners ultimate control over how caches handle their content. However, the language in this paragraph is so vague and confusing that it probably makes this condition altogether worthless.

The next condition, paragraph (2)(C), is tricky as well. It says that service providers cannot interfere with the content owner's ability to receive access statistics from caches. Again, this condition does not apply if the collection of such statistics places an undue burden on the service provider. The condition also does not apply if the content provider somehow uses the cache to collect additional information that it wouldn't normally have if users were connecting directly.

The condition in paragraph (2)(D) is relatively straightforward. It says that caches must respect the content provider's ability to limit access to information. For example, if users must authenticate themselves in order to receive a certain web page, the cache must not give that page to unauthenticated users. Doing so makes the service provider liable for copyright infringement. I think there is a small problem with this requirement, however. In some cases, a caching proxy won't know that the content provider is limiting access. For example, this happens if access is granted based only on the client's IP address. The law should require origin servers to explicitly mark protected responses. Otherwise, service providers may be inadvertently violating the owner's copyright.

The final condition, in paragraph (2)(E), is a requirement to remove material (or deny access to it) when someone makes a claim of copyright infringement. For example, a content provider might place a copyrighted image on its server without the copyright owner's permission. The copyright owner can demand that the content provider remove the image from its site. He can also demand that the image be removed from an ISP's caches. Since such a demand must be made to individual service providers, it's difficult to imagine that the copyright owner will get the content removed from all caches in operation.

The first time I read this legislation, I thought that prefetching could make service providers liable for copyright infringement. On closer examination, however, it seems that prefetching is exempt as well. Subsection (a)—which is about routing, not caching—eliminates liability for material requested by "a person other than the service provider." Arguably, when a cache prefetches some objects, those requests are initiated by the service provider, not the user. However, when talking about caching in subsection (b), the exemption covers material requested by a person other than the content provider. Since the ISP is not the content provider, the exemption applies.

One interesting thing to note about this law is that it only exempts ISPs from *liability* for copyright infringement. The service provider may still be guilty of infringement, but the copyright owner is not entitled to compensation for copies made by caches. Before the Online Copyright Infringement Liability Limitation Act became law, some service providers were afraid that caching would invite lawsuits. With these new additions, however, ISPs in the U.S. have nothing to fear as long as they "play nice" and don't violate the rules of HTTP.

3.3.4 HTTP's Role

Even those who feel strongly that caching is a blatant infringement of copyrights generally agree that caching is necessary for efficient and continued operation of the Web. Because caching is here to stay, we need good technical solutions to deal appropriately with information that authors want to control tightly. HTTP/1.1 provides a number of different directives and mechanisms that content authors can use to control the distribution of their works.

One way is to insert one or more of the `Cache-control` directives in the response headers. The `no-store` directive prevents any cache from storing and reusing the response. The `no-cache` and `must-revalidate` directives allow a response to be cached but require validation with the origin server before each subsequent use. The `private` directive allows the response to be cached and reused by a user agent cache but not by a caching proxy. We'll talk further about these in Section 6.1.4, "Cache-control."

Authentication is another way to control the distribution of copyrighted material. To access the information, users must enter a username and password. By default, caching proxies cannot store and reuse authenticated responses. Passwords may be a pain to administer, however. Not many organizations can afford the resources to maintain a database with millions of users.

Encryption is an even more extreme way to control distribution. Recall that end-to-end encryption protocols such as SSL/TLS are opaque to proxies in the middle. In other words, caching proxies cannot interpret encrypted traffic, which makes it impossible to cache. User-agents can cache responses received via an encrypted channel. In this sense, encryption is similar to the `private` cache control.

One of the difficulties with `Cache-control` is that the header must be generated by the server itself; it is not a part of the content. Modifying the server's behavior probably requires assistance from the server administrator; the author may not be able to do it alone. Even if the author wants to use `Cache-control` or other HTTP headers to control caching, she may not be able to, unless the administrator is willing and able to help out. Apache actually makes it possible for authors to insert and remove headers after some initial configuration by the administrator. We'll see how do to this in Chapter 6.

Using the `no-store` header is not a decision to be made lightly. Though preventing caching gives the provider greater control over the distribution of the content, it also increases the time that cache users wait to view it. Anyone who thinks users and cache operators don't notice the difference is wrong. Even if the provider site has enough capacity to handle the load, the user may be sitting behind a congested and/or high-latency network connection. Because people have short attention spans, if the latency is too high, they simply abort the request and move on to another site. Issues relating to servers that don't allow caching are further discussed in Section 3.7, "Cache Busting and Server Busting."

3.4 Offensive Content

As I mentioned earlier, pornography and other potentially offensive material comprise a noticeable proportion of web content.* Most national (and some local) governments have laws that address the selling or transportation of pornography. Could, you, as a cache operator, be liable because your cache stores or distributes such material? Only one thing is certain: there are no simple answers.

In 1996, the U.S. government passed the Communications Decency Act (CDA), which attempted to criminalize the sending of pornography and other obscene material over "telecommunications facilities." Furthermore, it sought to make liable anyone who:

> knowingly permits any telecommunications facility under [his] control to be used for any activity prohibited [above] with the intent that it be used for such activity...†

This might not be as bad as it initially sounds, especially given the use of the words "knowingly" and "intent." Even better, the law also seems to provide an exemption for some providers:

> No person shall be held [liable] solely for providing access or connection to or from a facility, system, or network not under that person's control, including transmission, downloading, intermediate storage, access software, or other related capabilities that are incidental to providing such access or connection that does not include the creation of the content of the communication.‡

This is good news for those of us who operate caches. The presence of the phrase "intermediate storage" is particularly comforting.

However, most of the provisions of the CDA were struck down as unconstitutional by the U.S. Supreme Court in 1997. The CDA was strongly opposed by groups such as the Electronic Freedom Foundation and the American Civil Liberties Union

---

* Certainly not everyone finds pornography offensive. Use of the term here is only for convenience and is not meant to suggest that there is an obvious distinction between offensive and inoffensive material.

† 47 U.S.C. 223(d)(2).

‡ 47 U.S.C. 223(e)(1).

because it violates some fundamental rights (such as freedom of speech) granted by the Bill of Rights.

Admittedly, the discussion here has been very U.S.-centric. Laws of other countries are not discussed here, except to note that the Internet is generally not subject to geopolitical boundaries. The application of local and national laws to a network that connects millions of computers throughout the world is likely to be problematic.

3.5 Dynamic Web Pages

Many people worry that caches do not properly deal with what they call "dynamic pages." Such pages are considered dynamic because the content might be different for every request. Time-sensitive information, such as stock prices and weather reports, logically fall into the category of dynamic pages. Pages that have been customized for the user, to include his name or targeted advertisements, are dynamic as well.

Historically, dynamic pages have been problematic because some web caching software had relatively aggressive caching and refresh policies. Dynamic pages were cached and returned as cache hits when perhaps they should not have been. Part of the blame lies with the early descriptions and implementations of HTTP. The HTTP/1.0 RFC [Berners-Lee, Fielding and Frystyk, 1996] was not published until May of 1996, while active development on web caching had been ongoing since early 1994. Without a stable protocol description, implementors are certainly prone to make some mistakes. Even when HTTP/1.0 became official, it still lacked a good description of what can and cannot be cached. Section 1.3 of RFC 1945 states:

> Some HTTP/1.0 applications use heuristics to describe what is or is not a "cachable" response, but these rules are not standardized.

Some of the blame lies with the origin servers, however. Even though HTTP/1.1 has more caching features than HTTP/1.0, the older protocol does have enough functionality to prevent a compliant proxy from returning hits on dynamic pages. Unfortunately, confusion arises when an origin server's response leaves out some headers. For example, consider a reply such as this:

```
HTTP/1.0 200 OK
Server: MasterBlaster/1.6.9
Date: Mon, 15 Jan 2001 23:01:43 GMT
Content-Type: text/html
```

How should a cache interpret this? There is no Last-modified date, so the cache has no idea how old the resource is. Assuming the server's clock is correct, we know how old the response is, but not the resource. There is no Expires header either, so perhaps the cache can apply local heuristics. Should a cache be allowed to store this reply? Can it return this as a cache hit? In the absence of rigid standards, some applications might consider this cachable.

These days, you are unlikely to encounter a caching product that incorrectly handles dynamic pages. HTTP/1.1 allows servers to be very specific regarding how a response is to be treated by a cache (see Section 6.3, "Being Cache-Unfriendly"). Over the years, people who implement HTTP caching have had a lot of time to "get it right." An application in compliance with HTTP (1.0 or 1.1) should never cache a response if the origin server does not want it to.

3.5.1 Java Applets

The Java programming language is widely used on the Web for generating dynamic content. Some people wonder if web caches are designed to properly handle Java applets. The answer is a resounding "yes" because of the way in which applets work. Rather than executing on the origin server, as CGI programs and Java servlets do, applets run on the client (usually a browser). Thus, a Java applet file is really static, much like an HTML file, when downloaded from an origin server. The user sees something dynamic only when the applet code executes on the client. Java applets are very much like other static objects, such as text files and JPEG images.

3.6 Content Integrity

Can you trust the information you receive from a cache? How do you know it has not been modified? How do you know it is what the origin server intends for you to see?

This is an extremely difficult problem, with no known solutions at this time. TCP does not currently provide any form of end-to-end security, which means this problem is not specific to HTTP or the Web. The Transport Layer Security protocol (TLS, formerly Secure Sockets Layer) does provide end-to-end security on top of the network transport protocols. TLS protocols [Dierks and Allen, 1999] are designed to prevent eavesdropping, tampering, and message forgery. However, the security provided by TLS is in effect only for the duration of the data transfer. It does not guarantee—especially for cache hits—that the object you receive has not been modified since the origin server generated it. Unfortunately, we do not have a general purpose digital signature scheme for web objects. Even if such a thing did exist, to be of any real value it would require out-of-band communication for the key exchange. In other words, it would be pointless to retrieve signing keys from the cache.

Recent security features being added to DNS [Eastlake, 1999] might be able to support a scheme for authenticating web objects. For example, lets say you request the URL *http://www.monkeybrains.net/index.html.* The response is an HTML page that includes, in comments, a digital signature. To validate the signature, you need the public key of the author or owner. Such keys can be entered into a DNS zone. Continuing with our example, we query the DNS for a *http.www.monkeybrains.net* KEY record. The returned key (if any) and the signature are enough to prove that the HTML page is authentic.

To date, I am not aware of any caches that have been broken into and had cache content modified. However, on numerous occasions, origin server security has been compromised, and the perpetrators have replaced the normal home page content with something else. Usually these pranks are short-lived and not a real problem. If the bogus pages make it into web caches, though, some users could receive the wrong content even after the origin server has been restored.

Another way to get bogus content to web users is to attack the DNS. Most networked applications in use today, including proxy caches, inherently trust the answers to their DNS queries. If my cache asks for the IP address of *www.microsoft.com* and gets a wrong answer, it happily connects to that address and retrieves the wrong content. The best way to prevent this from happening is to remain up-to-date with new releases (and patches) of name resolver software (e.g., BIND).

Assuming incorrect objects have been loaded into a cache, what can be done to get rid of them? In most cases, it is sufficient to issue a request with a `Pragma:` no-cache header. This operation, most easily accomplished by clicking the *Reload* button in a browser, replaces the old object with a new one. Occasionally, this may not work, or you may want to remove an object entirely instead of replacing it. Caching products should provide this functionality via their management interface. With Squid, you can use the *client* program to issue a purge request:

```
client -m PURGE http://ircache.nlanr.net/badobject
```

3.7 Cache Busting and Server Busting

Cache busting is a technique that content providers use to prevent their pages from being served as hits from caches. Often this means making every response uncachable. This issue is difficult to assess for a number of reasons. First and foremost, owners and publishers have legal rights to control the distribution of their information. Whether or not we agree with their decision to defeat caching, the choice is theirs to make. Usually, their reasons are unknown to us, but the reasons might include the copyright issues discussed previously or the desire to increase the number and accuracy of their hit counts. Second, some content providers, by the very nature of their business, might serve only uncachable content. We should not be surprised to find that sites that exist only to count advertisement impressions do not allow their responses to be cached. Issues relating to advertising are explored further in the next section.

How would someone be able to claim that an origin server is cache busting? Cache users and administrators sometimes expect certain types of objects to be cachable by default. When users visit a page for the first time and then access it again a short while later, they expect the page to load very quickly because it should be in the cache. When the page loads slowly, they wonder why. If a user is curious and savvy enough, she might find a way to examine the reply headers firsthand. With access to the cache log files, administrators can easily analyze them and generate reports including hit ratios for individual origin servers. Those servers that give a lower than average amount of hits, or no hits at all, might be suspects for cache busting.

On the other side of this issue are the Internet service providers who pay high, or perhaps metered, tariffs for their bandwidth. They turn to caching as a way to save money. In a sense, cache-busting web servers represent additional costs for the ISP. When Internet charges are usage-based, rather than flat-rate, people often feel they have purchased information when they download it, and they should not have to pay to download it again.

Some caching software allows administrators to override the server's instructions for cache behavior. A cache configured in this manner blatantly violates the HTTP standard. *Server busting* might be an appropriate term for such behavior. This is a dangerous path to start down, as it essentially leads to an "arms race" between caches and origin servers. If caches ignore an origin server's requirements, content providers will find new ways to defeat caching. Instead of working against each other, we should be having a dialogue and finding ways to cooperate.

The development of a hit-metering mechanism for HTTP [Mogul and Leach, 1997] is a step in the right direction. Hit metering works in two ways: by reporting unvalidated cache hits back to origin servers and by limiting the number of hits before requiring validation. These mechanisms offer content providers some control over the distribution of their pages, as well as better statistics regarding cache hits. Caches are not required to support both reporting and limiting. For example, a cache can say that it will limit cache hits but not provide hit count statistics. Unfortunately, there has been little demand for hit metering from content providers. Without such demand, we may never see hit metering implemented or widely deployed.

3.8 Advertising

We all know that electronic commerce has been a driving force behind the evolution of the Web. Advertising, in particular, is important because it generates revenue for a large number of web sites. Advertising fees are often based on the number of views or impressions. That is, the advertiser pays the web site some amount for every person who sees their ad. But how do the site owners and the advertisers know how many people have seen a particular ad?

The simplest approach is to count the number of accesses logged by the site's HTTP server. As I'm sure you can guess, with caching in place, some of the requests for an advertisement never reach the origin server. Thus, the web site counts too few accesses and perhaps undercharges the advertiser. The advertiser might not mind being undercharged, but it is probably in everyone's best interest to have accurate access counts. Later, in Section 6.4.2, "What About Advertisements?," I suggest some techniques that content providers can use to increase ad counting accuracy while remaining cache-friendly.

Some people take issue with the notion of counting ad impressions and other page accesses. The fact that *something* requests a page or image does not mean a human being actually views it. Search engines and other web robots can generate a large number of requests. The User-agent request header normally identifies the entity that issued the request. Thus, user requests can be differentiated from robot requests. Another tricky aspect of request counting is related to the *Back* button found on web browsers. When you follow a sequence of hypertext links and then work your way back up the chain, your browser might decide to request some pages or images again. Most people argue that the second request should not be recounted as an ad impression.

Opponents of brute-force access counting suggest using statistical sampling techniques, much like those used to rate television programs. Certainly, the traditional broadcast media (television, radio) and to some extent print publications (newspapers, magazines) have similar needs to gauge readership. Indeed, a few companies now offer high-quality site measurement services. Among them are Media Metrix (*http://www.mediametrix.com*), Nielson NetRatings (*http://www.nielson-netratings.com*), and PC Data Online (*http://www.pcdataonline.com*).

Apart from paying for measurement services, what can a web site with advertisements do to get more accurate access statistics? One way is to make every object uncachable, but this cache-busting is a bad idea for the reasons described in the previous section. A more sensible approach is to include a tiny, uncachable inline image in the pages to be counted. This allows the page itself and large inline images to be cached, yet still delivers a request to the origin server every time someone views the page.

Another clever counting technique uses JavaScript embedded in a web page. When the page is loaded into a browser, the browser executes the JavaScript, which can send a message back to the origin server to indicate that the page has been loaded. Furthermore, the JavaScript can select which advertisement to show to the user. For example, the script can output HTML for an inline image. The nice characteristic of this solution is that both the web page and the images can be cached, yet the origin server still knows every time the page is viewed and exactly which ad images appear on the page.

Unfortunately, there is a fine line between counting visitors and tracking individuals. The Privacy Foundation (*http://www.privacyfoundation.org*) calls these hidden images "Web bugs." Though I think simply counting page requests is not so bad, the same technique allows content providers to closely track your browsing activities. This raises all of the privacy issues discussed earlier in this chapter. The Privacy Foundation suggests that Web bugs should be made visible, so users know when they are being tracked. My advice is to always assume that content providers collect as much information about you as they can.

3.9 *Trust*

When viewed in a broader sense, many of the issues surrounding web caching can be reduced to matters of trust. Cache users must trust administrators not to reveal private information contained in cache log files. This relationship is analogous to those we have with banks, telephone service providers, and movie rental companies.

A very informal trust relationship often exists between cache operators and content providers. In a sense, cache operators trust they will not face litigation, and content providers trust caches to have reasonable expiration and refresh parameters. Of course, some trust more or less than others, and when this tenuous relationship breaks down, both parties seek to regain control. Content providers may turn to cache-busting techniques, and cache administrators to server-busting.

Perhaps the thing we most take for granted is that our caches deliver correct content to users. While it is perhaps unfortunate that we must place so much trust in this aspect of web caching, it is not necessarily unique. As users, we also generally trust that our email messages are authentic and unmodified. At least with email we have some good solutions to this problem (e.g., PGP). The Web will catch up eventually.

3.10 Effects of Proxies

In Chapter 1, I talked briefly about how a proxy sits in between clients and servers. Without a proxy, clients normally connect directly to origin servers. With a proxy, however, clients connect only to the proxy. If needed, the proxy connects to origin servers for cache misses. This characteristic of proxies has two important implications for cache managers: security (of both web servers and caches) and bandwidth.

Because the server only knows about its TCP connection from the proxy, the client remains hidden. This can cause problems for origin servers that use address-based access controls. When a client's request goes through a proxy, the server gets the proxy's address, not the client's. If the server is configured to allow connections from the client's address and deny all others, requests forwarded through the proxy are denied.

As a caching proxy administrator, you must pay close attention to access controls on your web servers and on your proxy. Web servers that authorize connections from your proxy are effectively authorizing connections from anyone who can connect to your proxy. A proxy that accepts requests from any client is open to all sorts of mischief. An open-access proxy creates a back door that enables tricks similar to IP source routing and email relaying. An outsider may be able to route traffic through your proxy. Such abuse can be as harmless as consuming some of your bandwidth or as serious as credit card fraud or threatening the President.

Pay especially close attention to how your caching proxy handles the CONNECT method. This method exists so user agents can tunnel SSL/TLS and other traffic through a firewall. The client specifies a hostname and port number that the proxy should connect to. Once the tunnel is established, it's as though the client has a direct connection to the origin server. The proxy is usually configured to allow connections only to specific ports (*https* and *snews*). If the proxy allows connections to the *smtp* ports of remote servers, for example, then mischievous users can use your proxy as a mail relay, spamming others and leaving you to blame.

Proxies have the power to significantly affect a company's bandwidth. Consider the diagram in Figure 3.1. Two companies, *A* and *B*, receive Internet service from the same ISP. This ISP has two routers, *R1* and *R2*. *R1* exists primarily to collect flow statistics and generate monthly bills, based on a customer's usage.

Company *B* has a proxy cache on its network, and the administrator failed to configure the access controls correctly. Hosts inside company *A*'s network are allowed to use the proxy. For the cache traffic passing through *R1*, the destination IP

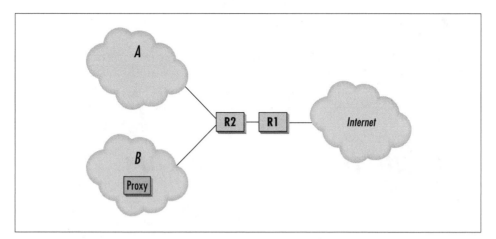

Figure 3.1. How to get some free bandwidth

address is *B*'s proxy cache. Thus, the traffic gets charged to *B*. Router *R1* has no idea the traffic is eventually sent to hosts in company *A*. Since the administrators in company *B* are obviously careless, it's likely they'll never notice the additional traffic flowing through their network.

4

Configuring Cache Clients

After setting up a caching proxy on your network, you'll need to figure out how to make your clients (browsers) use it. For many organizations, this is a particularly daunting task. There are a number of techniques you can use. Your choice is likely to depend on how many users you have, the client software they use, and whether you can configure that software. For example, a corporate information systems department usually supports one or two browsers and has full administrative control over all employee workstations. An ISP's customers, on the other hand, maintain their own computers and run whatever software they like.

The oldest technique is what we call *manual configuration*. The clients are given one or more proxy addresses to use, and, with few exceptions, they forward all requests to the proxy. Manual configuration is relatively straightforward, but it's not something most users can figure out on their own. If naive users are to manually configure their browsers, they require detailed instructions, such as those in the following section. Given the choice, some users won't bother to configure their browser since it's somewhat of a hassle. Another drawback is that many user-agents don't handle failures well when manually configured.

The second-generation configuration technique, pioneered by Netscape, is known as *proxy auto-configuration*. Instead of a static configuration, the browser executes a JavaScript function shortly before making each request. This script gives the browser a list of proxy addresses to which the request is forwarded. The auto-configuration technique also offers improved failure detection and failover compared to manual configuration. For example, if the browser believes the first proxy in the list is down, then it fails over to the next one, and so on.

Although proxy auto-configuration is more flexible, it also requires the user to enter a URL for the JavaScript file. To eliminate this step, some companies are proposing a web proxy auto-discovery protocol. When the browser starts up, it uses DHCP and the DNS to locate a proxy auto-configuration script. If found, the browser automatically loads the script and begins using the caching proxy.

A recent development, known as *interception proxying*, delivers client requests to caching proxies with absolutely no configuration of the client. Instead, you configure your network equipment (e.g., routers, switches) to divert HTTP traffic to the proxies. In this case, the client doesn't even know it's talking to a proxy—it thinks it's talking to the origin server. Interception proxying (a.k.a. transparent proxying) is an interesting and controversial technique; we'll save it for the next chapter.

Finally, this chapter finishes with a few suggestions for configuring browser caches when the browser also utilizes a shared cache.

4.1   Proxy Addresses

As with all other Internet services, such as mail and FTP, a proxy server has an address comprised of a hostname (or IP address) and a port number. However, unlike most other services, proxies do not have a standard default port number. While it is generally sufficient to say, "connect to the FTP server at *ftp.isp.net*," it is not sufficient to say, "use the proxy at *proxy.isp.net*." Thus, proxy addresses always appear with explicit port numbers. Typically, they are written together, separated by a colon, for example:

```
172.16.4.1:8080
squid.ircache.net:3128
proxy1.bigisp.net:80
```

Although there is no default port number, most proxies use one of the following ports: 3128, 8080, 80, or 1080. Most of these are some variation of "80" because that is the default for HTTP. Port number 3128 was arbitrarily selected as the default for the Harvest software, from which Squid evolved. Although port 80 is normally associated with origin servers, it is also popular for proxy servers, probably because the CERN server was able to function simultaneously as both an origin server and as a proxy server. Today's web caches have the ability to listen for requests on multiple ports at the same time. I don't recommend using port 80 for proxy servers unless absolutely necessary. Usually, we identify network applications by port numbers, and the shared approach makes it difficult to separate origin server traffic from proxy traffic.

4.2   Manual Proxy Configuration

A manual configuration is generally characterized by a set of proxy addresses, one for each transfer protocol, and a list of domain names for which the proxies should not be used. The set of proxyable transfer protocols includes HTTP, FTP, Gopher, SSL, and WAIS. Usually, a single proxy supports all of these, so the same proxy address is used for all protocols. Some clients allow you to set a single proxy address rather than requiring you to enter the same address repeatedly.

Depending on your reasons for using proxies, you may not need or want to configure all protocols. If your users are behind a firewall, it is probably necessary to proxy all requests. If not, you might want to proxy only HTTP and FTP. A proxy cannot cache SSL responses because the content is encrypted. Forwarding SSL requests when the client can make a direct connection serves only to increase the load upon the proxy. Gopher and WAIS requests might be cachable, but they typically comprise such a small fraction of total traffic that the cache provides relatively little benefit.

The manual configuration approach has a number of disadvantages. Primarily, it requires a significant amount of individual effort to enter all the settings. Knowledgeable users may not be bothered, but a typical user requires very clear and specific instructions. Additionally, you may need to provide different instructions for different browsers and different versions of the same browser. Another annoyance is that the manual configuration results in poor failover characteristics. When a proxy fails, the browser does not attempt a direct connection or try an alternate proxy. Arguably, browsers should support this feature, but at the time of this writing, they do not. Finally, a manual configuration is not flexible enough to accommodate systems with multiple proxy machines. For example, you might want to forward one class of requests to one proxy and the remaining traffic to another.

4.2.1 Configuring Microsoft Internet Explorer

To configure Microsoft Internet Explorer Version 5, select *View → Internet Options* from the menu. This brings up a new window with six "tabs" along the top. Select the *Connection* tab and you will see the window shown in Figure 4.1. The proxy settings are buried under *LAN Settings...*, so click on that button and you should see the window shown in Figure 4.2.

The *LAN Settings* window has a subwindow titled *Proxy server.* Here you can enter an IP address or hostname and the proxy port number. This configures Internet Explorer to use the proxy for all transfer protocols.

If you want to use different proxies or no proxy for some protocols (such as FTP or SSL), click on the *Advanced...* button. Now you should see the window shown in Figure 4.3. You can enter hostnames or IP addresses for each transfer protocol separately. Note that "Secure" refers to SSL. You can enter a list of domain names in the *Exceptions* subwindow. URLs that match these domains are not sent to your proxies. With Internet Explorer, you must separate domains with semicolons instead of commas. When you finish configuring the proxies, be sure to return to the browser and try a new request.

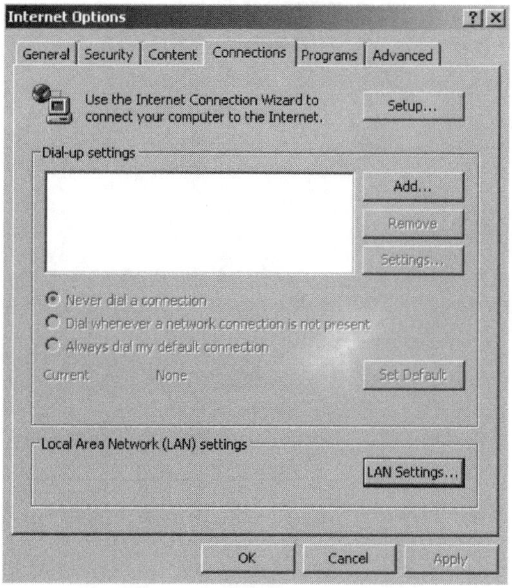

Figure 4.1. Microsoft Internet Explorer Internet Options window

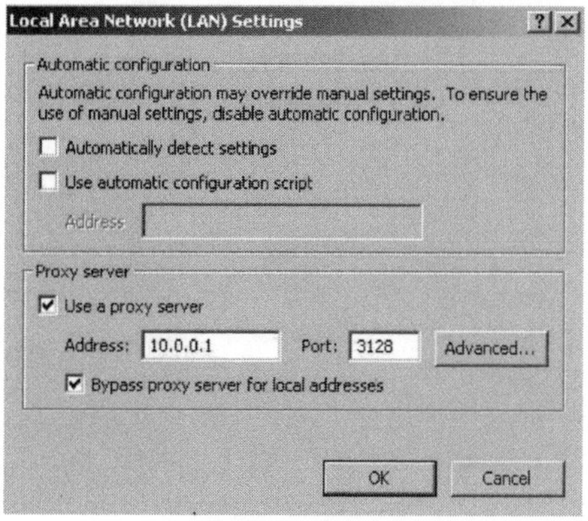

Figure 4.2. Microsoft Internet Explorer LAN Settings window

4.2.2 Configuring Netscape Navigator

Netscape's browser products allow you to set proxy addresses in pop-up windows. To bring up the configuration window in Netscape Navigator Version 4, select *Edit → Preferences...* from the main menu bar. In the Preferences window, click on the small triangle next to *Advanced.* This adds two more entries to the

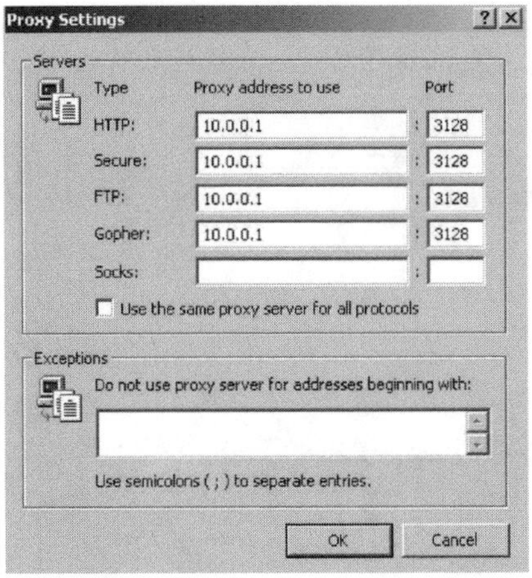

Figure 4.3. Microsoft Internet Explorer Proxy Settings window

menu, one of which is *Proxies.* Next, select *Manual proxy configuration* and click on the *View...* button. You should now see the window shown in Figure 4.4.

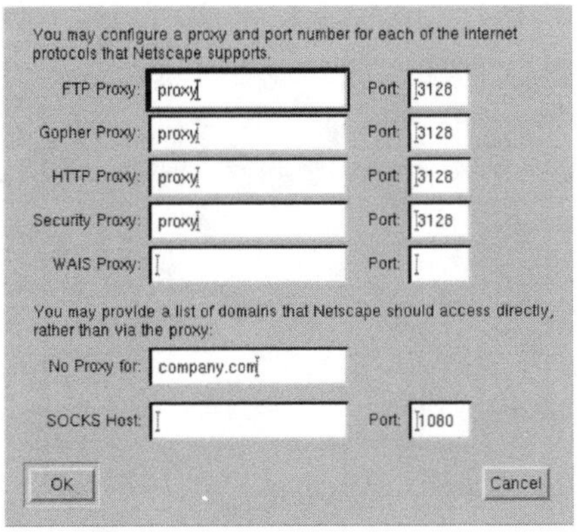

Figure 4.4. Netscape Navigator manual proxy configuration

Once you have the manual proxy configuration window, you can enter proxy addresses. Usually, you enter the same proxy address for every protocol (HTTP, FTP, Gopher, Wais). *Security Proxy* refers to SSL (a.k.a. HTTPS) requests. SSL requests are never cached by proxies, so the only reason to configure an SSL proxy is to tunnel through a firewall. Do not set the SSL proxy if you are not behind a firewall. In the *No Proxy for* field, you can enter a comma-separated list

of domains that should not be requested through the proxy. When you are finished, return to the main browser window by clicking the *OK* button, and then try
to load a new URL.

Note that Netscape hasn't changed the proxy configuration in the newer versions
of Navigator. The windows may look a little bit different, but the pull-down menus
and text boxes are the same for Version 6.

4.2.3 NCSA Mosaic, Lynx, and Wget

Unix-based clients such as NCSA Mosaic for X, Lynx, and Wget look for proxy
addresses in environment variables. Note that the variable names are lowercase.
For historical reasons, these environment variables look just like URLs:*

```
http_proxy="http://squid.nlanr.net:3128/"
ftp_proxy="http://squid.nlanr.net:3128/"
```

These clients also look for environment variables named *gopher_proxy*,
https_proxy, and *wais_proxy*.

The *no_proxy* variable holds URL domain names that should not be forwarded to
the proxy. In most cases, this includes your local domain (or domains). To specify
multiple domains, simply separate them with commas. For example:

```
no_proxy="nlanr.net,sdsc.edu"
```

Netscape Navigator for Unix actually reads these environment variables as well,
but only if the user's preferences file does not exist.

4.3 Proxy Auto-Configuration Script

The proxy auto-configuration (PAC) technique is designed to fix many of the manual configuration problems described previously. Instead of using static proxy
addresses, the browser executes a function for every request. This function returns
a list of proxy addresses that the browser tries until the request is successfully forwarded.

The PAC function is written in JavaScript. In theory, any browser that supports
JavaScript can also support PAC. Netscape invented the PAC feature, and it was
first available in Version 2 of their browser. Microsoft added PAC support to MSIE
Version 3.

Both the Netscape and Microsoft browsers retrieve the PAC script as a URL. This is
perhaps the biggest drawback to proxy auto-configuration. Setting the PAC URL

---

* This is because very early proxies simply prepended these proxy URLs to the original URL and then
  processed the request normally.

requires someone to enter the URL in a pop-up window, or the browser must be preconfigured with the URL.

The best thing about proxy auto-configuration is that it allows administrators to reconfigure the browsers without further intervention from the users. If the proxy address changes, the administrator simply edits the PAC script to reflect the change. The browsers fetch the PAC URL every time they are started, but apparently not while the browser is running, unless the user forces a reload.

Another very nice feature is failure detection, coupled with the ability to specify multiple proxy addresses. If the first proxy in the list is not available, the browser tries the next entry, and so on until the end of the list. Failure is detected when the browser receives a `Connection Refused` error or a timeout during connection establishment.

The PAC script provides greater flexibility than a manual configuration. Instead of forwarding all HTTP requests to a single proxy address, the auto-configuration script can select a proxy based on the URI. As mentioned in Section 2.2.7, "Dynamic Content," objects with "cgi" in the URI are usually not cachable. A proxy auto-configuration script can detect these requests and forward them directly to origin servers. Unfortunately, the auto-configuration script is not given the request method, so we cannot have similar checks for POST and PUT requests, which are also rarely cachable.

The PAC script can also be used creatively to implement load sharing. Without a PAC script, one way to do load sharing is by entering multiple address records for the cache's hostname in the DNS. This results in a somewhat random scheme. There is no guarantee that the same URI always goes to the same proxy cache. If possible, we would rather have requests for the same URIs always going to the same caches, to maximize our hit ratios. We can accomplish this by writing a function that always returns the same proxy list for a given URI. An example of this is shown later in Example 4.1.

4.3.1 Writing a Proxy Auto-Configuration Function

The proxy auto-configuration function is named `FindProxyForURL()` and has two arguments: *url* and *host*.* The return value is a string specifying how to forward the request. The return string is one or more of the following, separated by semicolons:

```
PROXY host:port
SOCKS host:port
DIRECT
```

---

* Of course, the *url* includes *host*, but it has been extracted for your convenience.

For example:

```
"PROXY proxy.web-cache.net:3128; DIRECT;
 SOCKS socks.web-cache.net:1080;"
```

When writing FindProxyForURL(), you may want to use some of the built-in
functions for analyzing the URL. The most useful ones are described here. For the
full details, see Netscape's PAC documentation at *http://home.netscape.com/eng/
mozilla/2.0/relnotes/demo/proxy-live.html.*

- The isPlainHostName(*host*) function returns true if *host* is a single-component hostname rather than a fully qualified domain name. If *host* contains
  any periods, this function returns false.

  Many PAC scripts are written so that requests with plain hostnames are sent
  directly to the origin server. It's likely that such a request refers to an internal
  server, which probably doesn't benefit from caching anyway. Also, the caching
  proxy may not be able to resolve unqualified hostnames, depending on how
  the proxy is configured.

- The dnsDomainIs(*host, domain*) function returns true if *host* is a member of *domain*. For example, *foo.bar.com* is a member of *bar.com*, whereas
  www.foobar.com is not.

- The isResolvable(*host*) function returns true if a DNS lookup for *host*
  results in an IP address. This function allows the browser, instead of the
  proxy, to generate error pages for invalid hostnames. When the browser generates an error message rather than the proxy, users are less likely to complain
  that the proxy cache is broken. Fewer complaints, of course, means less
  headaches for your support staff.

- The shExpMatch(*string, pattern*) function performs Unix shell-style pattern matching on *string*. For example, to match URLs that end with *.cgi*,
  you can write:

  ```
  shExpMatch(url, "*.cgi")
  ```

  To match the request protocol at the beginning of the URL, use:

  ```
  shExpMatch(url, "ftp:*")
  ```

Some sample FindProxyForURL() functions are given in the next section.

The PAC script must be placed on a web server, and the server must be configured
to return a specific MIME Content-type header in the response. If Content-type is
not set to application/x-ns-proxy-autoconfig, browsers do not recognize it as a
proxy auto-configuration script. Generally, administrators name the PAC script with

a *.pac* extension and then instruct the HTTP server to return the desired Content-
type for all URIs with that extension. With Apache, you can add this line to
srm.conf:

```
AddType application/x-ns-proxy-autoconfig .pac
```

4.3.2 Sample PAC Scripts

First, let's look at a very simple proxy auto-configuration script that returns a single
proxy address for all HTTP and FTP requests. For all other requests, it instructs the
browser to forward the request directly to the origin server:

```
function FindProxyForURL(url, host)
{
  if (shExpMatch(url, "http:*"))
    return "PROXY proxy.isp.net:8080";
  if (shExpMatch(url, "ftp:*"))
    return "PROXY proxy.isp.net:8080";
  return "DIRECT";
}
```

Now, let's look at a more complicated example for a company with a firewall. We
want to forward all internal requests directly and all external requests via the firewall proxy. First, we look for internal hosts. These are single-component hostnames or fully qualified hostnames inside our domain (*company.com*). We use the
isResolvable() trick so error messages for invalid hostnames come directly from
the browser instead of the proxy. This trick works only if the internal hosts can
look up addresses for external hosts:

```
function FindProxyForURL(url, host)
{
  if (isPlainHostName(host))
    return "DIRECT";
  if (dnsDomainIs(host, "company.com"))
    return "DIRECT";
  if (!isResolvable(host))
    return "DIRECT";
  return "PROXY proxy.company.com:8080";
}
```

Next, let's see how you can use a proxy auto-configuration script for load sharing
and redundancy. Three methods are commonly used for sharing the load between
a set of *N* caches. One simple approach is to assign *N* IP addresses to a single
hostname. While this spreads the load, it has the undesirable effect of randomizing
mappings from requests to caches. It is better to have the same request always
sent to the same cache. A *hash function* accomplishes this effect. A hash function
takes a string (e.g., a URL) as input and returns an integer value. Given the same
input, a hash function always returns the same value. We apply the modulo operator to the hash result to select from the *N* caches. This scheme works well, but the

mappings change entirely when additional caches are added. The final technique is to use some aspect of the URL, such as the domain name or perhaps the file-name extension. For example, *.com* requests can be sent to one cache and all other domains to another cache. Depending upon the incoming requests, this approach might result in significantly unbalanced load sharing, however.

Example 4.1 uses the hash function technique. We have four caches, and the hash function is simply the length of the URL, modulo four. Furthermore, for redundancy, we return multiple proxy addresses. If the first is unavailable, the browser tries the second. This failover breaks the partitioning scheme, but the users are more likely to get service.

Example 4.1: Sample PAC Script with Hashing

```
var N = 4;

function FindProxyForURL(url, host)
{
    var i = url.length % N;
    if (i == 0)
        return "PROXY a.proxy.company.com:8080; "
             + "PROXY b.proxy.company.com:8080; "
             + "DIRECT";
    else if (i == 1)
        return "PROXY b.proxy.company.com:8080; "
             + "PROXY c.proxy.company.com:8080; "
             + "DIRECT";
    else if (i == 2)
        return "PROXY c.proxy.company.com:8080; "
             + "PROXY d.proxy.company.com:8080; "
             + "DIRECT";
    else if (i == 3)
        return "PROXY d.proxy.company.com:8080; "
             + "PROXY a.proxy.company.com:8080; "
             + "DIRECT";
}
```

4.3.3 Setting the Proxy Auto-Configuration Script

Once a PAC script has been written and placed on a server, configuring a browser to use it is relatively simple. All you need to do is enter the PAC script URL in the appropriate configuration window for your browser.

For Netscape's browser, set the proxy auto-configuration URL in one of the same windows used for manual proxy configuration. Start by selecting *Edit → Prefer-ences...* from the main menu bar. In the Preferences window, click on the small tri-angle next to *Advanced* and select *Proxies*. Select the "Automatic proxy configuration" option and enter the URL as shown in Figure 4.5.

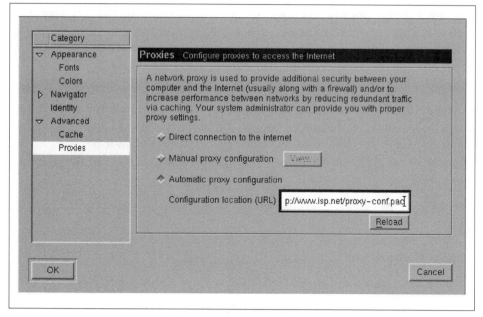

Figure 4.5. Netscape Navigator proxy configuration window

If you're using Microsoft Internet Explorer, select *View → Internet Options* from the main menu bar. Select the *Connection* tab; the window shown in Figure 4.1 appears. Again, click on *LAN Settings...* and you'll see the window in Figure 4.2. At the top is a subwindow titled *Automatic configuration*. If you select "Automatically detect settings," Explorer will try to use WPAD, which we'll talk about next. To use a PAC script, select "Use automatic configuration script" and enter its URL in the *Address* box.

Normally, browsers read the PAC URL only at startup. Thus, if you change the PAC script, users do not get the changes until they exit and restart their browser. Users can force a reload of the PAC script at any time by going to the proxy auto-configuration window and clicking on the *Reload* or *Refresh* button. Unfortunately, the Netscape browser does not obey the Expires header for PAC replies. That is, you cannot make Netscape Navigator reload the PAC script by providing an expiration time in the response.

Organizations with hundreds or even thousands of desktop systems may want to preconfigure browsers with a PAC URL. One way to accomplish this is to use a special kit from the manufacturer that allows you to distribute and install specially configured browsers. Microsoft calls theirs the Internet Explorer Administration Kit.

Netscape's is the Client Customization Kit, but it works only on the Microsoft Windows and Macintosh versions of Netscape Navigator. Both kits are available for download at no charge.*

4.4 *Web Proxy Auto-Discovery*

As I mentioned earlier, proxy auto-configuration usually requires the user to manually enter a URL in the proxy configuration window. Recent efforts by browser developers seek to eliminate that step. This new feature is called web proxy auto-discovery, or WPAD. WPAD is designed to let browsers automatically learn the auto-configuration URL with no assistance from the user.

WPAD uses a number of protocols and services to find the auto-configuration URL. The preferred protocol is DHCP (Dynamic Host Configuration Protocol). If DHCP fails, the user-agent may try the Service Location Protocol (SLP, RFC 2068) next. If SLP fails as well, it queries the DNS for A, SRV, and TXT records. A client that implements WPAD must support at least the DHCP and DNS A record queries. Support for SLP is optional.

Using the DNS is likely to be the simplest and most popular approach for network administrators. The first step is to select an HTTP server and place a proxy auto-configuration script there under the name */wpad.dat*. Then the administrator needs only to add a DNS entry for a host named *wpad*. For example, if *wpad.company.com* is an alias for *company.com*'s web server, and the *wpad.dat* file is installed there, all of the company's web browsers can automatically configure themselves.

WPAD was submitted to the IETF as an Internet Draft in December of 1999. Unfortunately, it has not yet been updated or moved beyond that stage, and the draft is now expired. Even so, Microsoft's Internet Explorer (Version 5) already supports WPAD. The protocol authors seem uninterested in advancing the protocol within the IETF. Their lack of enthusiasm may be due to some negative reactions to WPAD on various mailing lists and in IETF working-group meetings. One of the issues is that WPAD refers to (i.e., requires) JavaScript, which is not a standardized language. The situation is unfortunate because many of us believe WPAD is a much better way to get clients talking to a caching proxy.

---

* You can download the Internet Explorer Administration Kit from *http://www.microsoft.com/windows/ ieak/en/download/default.asp*, and Netscape's Client Customization Kit is available for download at *http://home.netscape.com/download/cck.html.*

4.5 Other Configuration Options

Most browsers have two other settings that you may want to consider changing: the browser cache and the refresh settings. In some cases, a shared proxy cache may make the browser cache redundant, especially if the browser has good network connectivity to the proxy.

With Netscape Navigator, I recommend setting the disk cache size to 0 and using a memory cache only. 1–3 MB of memory cache should be sufficient. In addition to freeing disk space for other uses, this configuration has another advantage. The memory cache is not persistent between browser sessions. If you think you are getting stale responses from the browser cache, you can just quit and restart. When Netscape Navigator starts again, the browser cache is empty and the suspicious request is sent to the proxy cache. In Version 4 of Netscape Navigator, the browser cache settings are found under *Edit* → *Preferences* → *Advanced* → *Cache*.

Internet Explorer (Versions 4 and 5) allow you to control the amount of disk space—but not memory—used for caching. The setting is found under *Tools* → *Internet Options* → *Temporary Internet Files* → *Settings....* Apparently, you can't disable disk caching. Explorer enforces a minimum cache size.* However, there is an option to remove all temporary files each time Explorer exits.

Both Netscape Navigator and Internet Explorer also have settings that control validation of objects in the browser cache. The three options are to validate the cached object every request, once per session, or never. Validating every request ensures pages are up-to-date but may incur additional delays. Choosing never to validate makes cached pages load very quickly, but at the risk of loading stale pages. However, in my experience, these settings often do not work as I expect them to. Even when validation is set to never, some requests are still validated. Sometimes, when it's set to always, cached objects are not validated. Most likely, the browser's validation algorithm is more complicated than these settings imply. I recommend using the *always* setting if you have a good Internet connection and the *never* setting if your connection is slow or highly congested.

4.6 The Bottom Line

If you are thinking about deploying a web caching service for your organization, do not discount the difficulties of configuring the clients. Small organizations, or those where using the proxy is optional, might be able to use manual configuration. Large organizations probably want to use proxy auto-configuration scripts,

---

* See Microsoft Knowledgebase article Q145766, *http://support.microsoft.com/support/kb/articles/Q145/7/66.asp.*

however. If you do not want your employees or customers to configure their own browsers, you need to preconfigure them or use some other technique to change the settings without the user's intervention. Both Netscape and Microsoft have freely available toolkits that allow organizations to distribute browsers with customized settings.

The web proxy auto-discovery protocol looks like a very promising method to eliminate that final, time-consuming configuration hassle. Even so, many organizations are not entirely comfortable with proxy auto-configuration, and they have instead turned to interception caching because it requires no browser configuration whatsoever. Furthermore, it works with all web clients, not just the most popular browsers. Interception caching is becoming increasingly prevalent because it makes administrator's lives easier, but not everyone embraces it so openly. The issues and technologies around interception caching are discussed in Chapter 5.

5

Interception Proxying and Caching

As we discussed in Chapter 4, one of the most difficult problems you might face in deploying a web caching service is getting users to use your cache. In some cases, the problem is mostly political; users might resist caching because of privacy concerns or fears they will receive stale information. But even if users are convinced to use the cache—or have no choice—administrative hurdles may still be a problem. Changing the configuration of thousands of installed clients is a daunting task. For ISPs, the issue is slightly different—they have little or no control over their customers' browser configurations. An ISP can provide preconfigured browsers to their customers, but that doesn't necessarily ensure that customers will continue to use the caching proxy.

Because of problems such as these, *interception caching* has become very popular recently. The fundamental idea behind interception caching (or proxying) is to bring traffic to your cache without configuring clients. This is different from a technique such as WPAD (see Section 4.4, "Web Proxy Auto-Discovery"), whereby clients automatically locate a nearby proxy cache. Rather, your clients initiate TCP connections directly to origin servers, and a router or switch on your network recognizes HTTP traffic and redirects it to your cache. Web caches require only minor modifications to process requests received in this manner.

As wonderful as this may sound, a number of issues surround interception caching. Interception caching breaks the rules of the Internet Protocol. Routers and switches are supposed to deliver IP packets to their intended destination. Diverting web traffic to a cache is similar to a postal service that opens your mail

and reads it before deciding where to send it or whether it needs to be sent at all.*
The phrase *connection hijacking* is often used to describe interception caching, as
a reminder that it violates the Internet Protocol standards. Interception also leads
to problems with HTTP. Clients may not send certain headers, such as Cache-control, when they are unaware of the caching proxy.

Interception proxies are also known as *transparent proxies*. Even though the word
"transparent" is very common, it is a poor choice for several reasons. First of all,
"transparent" doesn't really describe the function. We hope that users remain
unaware of interception caches, and all web caches for that matter. However,
interception proxies are certainly not transparent to origin servers. Furthermore,
interception proxies are known to break both HTTP and IP interoperability.
Another reason is that RFC 2616 defines a transparent proxy to mean something
different. In particular, it states, "A 'transparent proxy' is a proxy that does not
modify the request or response beyond what is required for proxy authentication
and identification." Thus, to remain consistent with documents produced by the
IETF Web Replication and Caching working group, I use the term interception
caching.

In this chapter, we'll explore how interception caching works and the issues surrounding it. The technical discussion is broken into three sections, corresponding
to different networking layers. We start near the bottom, with the IP layer. As
packets traverse the network, a router or switch diverts HTTP packets to a nearby
proxy cache. At the TCP layer, we'll see how the diverted packets are accepted,
possibly modified, and then sent to the application. Finally, at the application
layer, the cache uses some simple tricks to turn the original request into a proxy-
HTTP request.

5.1 Overview

Figure 5.1 shows a logical diagram of a typical interception proxy setup. A client
opens a TCP connection to the origin server. As the packet travels from the client
towards the server, it passes through a router or a switch. Normally, the TCP/IP
packets for the connection are sent to the origin server, as shown by the dashed
line. With interception proxying, however, the router/switch diverts the TCP/IP
packets to the cache.

Two techniques are used to deliver the packet to the cache. If the router/switch
and cache are on the same subnet, the packet is simply sent to the cache's layer
two (i.e., Ethernet) address. If the devices are on different subnets, then the original IP packet gets encapsulated inside another packet that is then routed to the

---

* Imagine how much work the postal service could avoid by not delivering losing sweepstakes entries.
  Imagine how upset Publisher's Clearinghouse would be if they did!

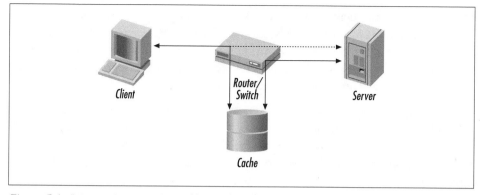

Figure 5.1. Interception proxying schematic diagram

cache. Both of these techniques preserve the destination IP address in the original IP packet, which is necessary because the cache pretends to be the origin server.

The interception cache's TCP stack is configured to accept "foreign" packets. In other words, the cache pretends to be the origin server. When the cache sends packets back to the client, the source IP address is that of the origin server. This tricks the client into thinking it's connected to the origin server.

At this point, an interception cache operates much like a standard proxy cache, with one important difference. The client believes it is connected to the origin server rather than a proxy cache, so its HTTP request is a little different. Unfortunately, this difference is enough to cause some interoperability problems. We'll talk more about this in Section 5.6, "Issues."

You might wonder how the router or switch decides which packets to divert. How does it know that a particular TCP/IP packet is for an HTTP request? Strictly speaking, nothing in a TCP/IP header identifies a packet as HTTP (or as any other application-layer protocol, for that matter). However, convention dictates that HTTP servers usually run on port 80. This is the best indicator of an HTTP request, so when the device encounters a TCP packet with a source or destination port equal to 80, it *assumes* that the packet is part of an HTTP session. Indeed, probably 99.99% of all traffic on port 80 is HTTP, but there is no guarantee. Some non-HTTP applications are known to use port 80 because they assume firewalls would allow those packets through. Also, a small number of HTTP servers run on other ports (see Table A.9). Some devices may allow you to divert packets for these ports as well.

Note that interception caching works anywhere that HTTP traffic is found: close to clients, close to servers, and anywhere in between. Before interception, clients had to be configured to use caching proxies. This meant that most caches were located close to clients. Now, however, we can put a cache anywhere and divert traffic to it. Clients don't need to be told about the proxy. Interception makes it possible to put a cache, or surrogate, close to origin servers. Interception caches can also be located on backbone networks, although I and others feel this is a bad idea, for reasons I'll explain later in this chapter. Fortunately, it's not very common.

5.2 The IP Layer: Routing

Interception caching begins at the IP (network) layer, where all sorts of IP packets are routed between nodes. Here, a router or switch recognizes HTTP packets and diverts them to a cache instead of forwarding them to their original destination. There are a number of ways to accomplish the interception:

Inline

> An inline cache is a device that combines both web caching and routing (or bridging) into a single piece of equipment. Inline caches usually have two or more network interfaces. Products from Cacheflow and Network Appliance can operate in this fashion, as can Unix boxes running Squid.

Layer four switch

> Switching is normally a layer two (datalink layer) activity. A layer four switch, however, can make forwarding decisions based on upper layer characteristics, such as IP addresses and TCP port numbers. In addition to HTTP redirection, layer four switches are also often used for server load balancing.

Web Cache Coordination Protocol

> WCCP is an encapsulation protocol developed by Cisco Systems that requires implementation in both a router (or maybe even a switch) and the web cache. Cisco has implemented two versions of WCCP in their router products; both are openly documented as Internet Drafts. Even so, use of the protocol in a product may require licensing from Cisco.

Cisco policy routing

> Policy routing refers to a router's ability to make forwarding decisions based on more than the destination address. We can use this to divert packets based on destination port numbers.

5.2.1 Inline Caches

An inline cache is a single device that performs both routing (or bridging) and web caching. Such a device is placed directly in the network path so it captures HTTP traffic passing through it. HTTP packets are processed by the caching application, while other packets are simply routed between interfaces.

Not many caching products are designed to operate in this manner. An inline cache is a rather obvious single point of failure. Let's face it, web caches are relatively complicated systems and therefore more likely to fail than a simpler device, such as an Ethernet switch. Most caching vendors recommend using a third-party product, such as a layer four switch, when customers need high reliability.

You can build an inexpensive inline cache with a PC, FreeBSD or Linux, and Squid. Any Unix system can route IP packets between two or more network interfaces. Add to that a web cache plus a little packet redirection (as described in Section 5.3, "The TCP Layer: Ports and Delivery"), and you've got an inline interception cache. Note that such a system does not have very good failure-mode characteristics. If the system goes down, it affects all network traffic, not just caching. If Squid goes down, all web traffic is affected. It should be possible, however, to develop some clever scripts that monitor Squid's status and alter the packet redirection rules if necessary.

InfoLibria has a product that fits best in the inline category. They actually use two tightly coupled devices to accomplish inline interception caching. The DynaLink is a relatively simple device that you insert into a 100BaseT Ethernet segment. Two of the DynaLink's ports are for the segment you are splitting. The other two deliver packets to and from an attached DynaCache. The DynaLink is a layer one (physical) device. It does not care about Ethernet (layer two) packets or addresses. When the DynaLink is on, electromechanical switches connect the first pair of ports to the second. The DynaCache then skims the HTTP packets off to the cache while bridging all other traffic through to the other side. If the DynaLinks loses power or detects a failure of the cache, the electromechanical switches revert to the passthrough position.

If you want to use an inline caching configuration, carefully consider your reliability requirements and the failure characteristics of individual products. If you choose an inexpensive computer system and route all your traffic through it, be prepared for the fact that a failed disk drive, network card, or power supply can totally cut off your Internet traffic.

5.2.2 Layer Four Switches

Recently, a new class of products known as layer four switches* have become widely available. The phrase "layer four" refers to the transport layer of the OSI reference model; it indicates the switch's ability to forward packets based on more than just IP addresses. Switches generally operate at layer two (datalink) and don't know or care about IP addresses, let alone transport layer port numbers. Layer four switches, on the other hand, peek into TCP/IP headers and make forwarding decisions based on TCP port numbers, IP addresses, etc. These switches also have

---

* You might also hear about "layer seven" or "content routing" switches. These products have additional features for looking even deeper into network traffic. Unfortunately, there is no widely accepted term to describe all the smart switching products.

other intelligent features, such as load balancing and failure detection. When used for interception caching, a layer four switch diverts HTTP packets to a connected web cache. All of the other (non-HTTP) traffic is passed through.

Layer four switches also have very nice failure detection features (a.k.a. health checks). If the web cache fails, the switch simply disables redirection and passes the traffic through normally. Similarly, when the cache comes back to life, the switch once again diverts HTTP packets to it. Layer four switches can monitor a device's health in a number of ways, including the following:

ARP

The switch makes Address Resolution Protocol (ARP) requests for the cache's IP address. If the cache doesn't respond, then it is probably powered off, disconnected, or experiencing some other kind of serious failure.

Of course, this only works for devices that are "layer two attached" to the switch. The cache might be on a different subnet, in which case ARP is not used.

ICMP echo

ICMP echo requests, a.k.a. "pings," also test the cache's low-level network configuration. As with ARP, ICMP tells the switch if the cache is on the network. However, ICMP can be used when the switch is on a different subnet.

ICMP round-trip time measurements can sometimes provide additional health information. If the cache is overloaded, or the network is congested, the time between ICMP echo and reply may increase. When the switch notices such an increase, it may send less traffic to the cache.

TCP

ARP and ICMP simply tell the switch that the cache is on the network. They don't, for example, indicate that the application is actually running and servicing requests. To check this, the switch sends connection probes to the cache. If the cache accepts the connection, that's a good indication that the application is running. If, however, the cache's TCP stack generates a reset message, the application cannot handle real traffic.

HTTP

In some cases, even establishing a TCP connection is not sufficient evidence that the cache is healthy. A number of layer four/seven products can send the cache a real HTTP request and analyze the response. For example, unless the HTTP status code is 200 (OK), the switch marks the cache as "down."

SNMP

Layer four switches can query the cache with SNMP. This can provide a variety of information, such as recent load, number of current sessions, service times, and error counts. Furthermore, the switch may be able to receive SNMP traps from the cache when certain events occur.

Load balancing is another useful feature of layer four switches. When the load placed on your web caches becomes too large, you can add additional caches and the switch will distribute the load between them. Switches often support numerous load balancing techniques, not all of which are necessarily good for web caches:

Round-robin
> A counter is kept for each cache and incremented for every connection sent to it. The next request is sent to the cache with the lowest counter.

Least connections
> The switch monitors the number of active connections per cache. The next request is sent to the cache with the fewest active connections.

Response time
> The switch measures the response time of each cache, perhaps based on the time it takes to respond to a connection request. The next request is sent to the cache with the smallest response time.

Packet load
> The switch monitors the number of packets traversing each cache's network port. The next request is sent to the cache with the lowest packet load.

Address hashing
> The switch computes a hash function over the client and/or server IP addresses. The hash function returns an integer value, which is then divided by the number of caches. Thus, if I have three caches, each cache receives requests for one-third of the IP address space.

URL hashing
> Address hashing doesn't always result in a well-balanced distribution of load. Some addresses may be significantly more popular than others, causing one cache to receive more traffic than the others. URL hashing is more likely to spread the load evenly. However, it also requires more memory and CPU capacity.
>
> With address hashing, the forwarding decision can be made upon receipt of the first TCP packet. With URL hashing, the decision cannot be made until the entire URL has been received. Usually, URLs are quite small, less than 100 bytes, but they can be much larger. If the switch doesn't receive the full URL in the first data packet, it must store the incomplete URL and wait for the remaining piece.

If you have a cluster of caches, URL hashing or destination address hashing are the best choices. Both ensure that the same request always goes to the same cache. This partitioning maximizes your hit ratio and your disk utilization because a given object is stored in only one cache. The other techniques are likely to spread requests around randomly so that, over time, all of the caches come to hold the same objects. We'll talk more about cache clusters in Chapter 9.

Table 5.1 lists switch products and vendors that support layer four redirection. The Linux Virtual Server is an open source solution for turning a Linux box into a redirector and/or load balancer.

Table 5.1. Switches and Products That Support Web Redirection

Vendor	Product Line	Home Page
Alteon, bought by Nortel	AceSwitch	*http://www.alteonwebsystems.com*
Arrowpoint, bought by Cisco	Content Smart Switch	*http://www.arrowpoint.com*
Cisco	Local Director	*http://www.cisco.com*
F5 Labs	Big/IP	*http://www.f5.com*
Foundry	ServerIron	*http://www.foundrynet.com*
Linux Virtual Server	LVS	*http://www.linuxvirtualserver.org*
Radware	Cache Server Director	*http://www.radware.com*
Riverstone Networks	Web Switch	*http://www.riverstonenet.com*

These smart switching products have many more features than I've mentioned here. For additional information, please visit the products' home pages or *http://www.lbdigest.com.*

5.2.3 WCCP

Cisco invented WCCP to support interception caching with their router products. At the time of this writing, Cisco has developed two versions of WCCP. Version 1 has been documented within the IETF as an Internet Draft. The most recent version is dated July 2000. It's difficult to predict whether the IETF will grant any kind of RFC status to Cisco's previously proprietary protocols. Regardless, most of the caching vendors have already licensed and implemented WCCPv1. Some vendors are licensing Version 2, which was also recently documented as an Internet Draft. The remainder of this section refers only to WCCPv1, unless stated otherwise.

WCCP consists of two independent components: the control protocol and traffic redirection. The control protocol is relatively simple, with just three message types: HERE_I_AM, I_SEE_YOU, and ASSIGN_BUCKETS. A proxy cache advertises itself to its home router with the HERE_I_AM message. The router responds with an I_SEE_YOU message. The two devices continue exchanging these messages periodically to monitor the health of the connection between them. Once the router knows the cache is running, it can begin diverting traffic.

As with layer four switches, WCCP does not require that the proxy cache be connected directly to the home router. Since there may be additional routers between
the proxy and the home router, diverted packets are encapsulated with GRE
(Generic Routing Encapsulation, RFC 2784). WCCP is hardcoded to divert only
TCP packets with destination port 80. The encapsulated packet is sent to the proxy
cache. Upon receipt of the GRE packet, the cache strips off the encapsulation
headers and pretends the TCP packet arrived there normally. Packets flowing in
the reverse direction, from the cache to the client, are not GRE-encapsulated and
don't necessarily flow through the home router.

WCCP supports cache clusters and load balancing. A WCCP-enabled router can
divert traffic to many different caches.* In its I_SEE_YOU messages, the router tells
each cache about all the other caches. The one with the lowest numbered IP
address nominates itself as the *designated cache*. The designated cache is responsible for coming up with a partitioning scheme and sending it to the router with
an ASSIGN_BUCKETS message. The buckets—really a lookup table with 256
entries—map hash values to particular caches. In other words, the value for each
bucket specifies the cache that receives requests for the corresponding hash value.
The router calculates a hash function over the destination IP address, looks up the
cache index in the bucket table, and sends an encapsulated packet to that cache.
The WCCP documentation is vague on a number of points. It does not specify the
hash function, nor how the designated cache should divide up the load. WCCPv1
can support up to 32 caches associated with one router.

WCCP also supports failure detection. The cache sends HERE_I_AM messages
every 10 seconds. If the router does not receive at least one HERE_I_AM message
in a 30-second period, the cache is marked as unusable. Requests are not diverted
to unusable caches. Instead, they are sent along the normal routing path towards
the origin server. The designated cache can choose to reassign the unusable
cache's buckets in a future ASSIGN_BUCKETS message.

WCCPv1 is supported in Cisco's IOS versions 11.1(19)CA, 11.1(19)CC, 11.2(14)P,
and later. WCCPv2 is supported in all 12.0 and later versions. Most IOS 12.x versions also support WCCPv1, but 12.0(4)T and earlier do not. Be sure to check
whether your Cisco hardware supports any of these IOS versions.

When configuring WCCP in your router, you should refer to your Cisco documentation. Here are the basic commands for IOS 11.x:

```
ip wccp enable
!
interface fastethernet0/0
ip wccp web-cache redirect
```

---

* Each cache can have only one home router, however.

Use the following commands for IOS 12.x:

```
ip wccp version 1
ip wccp web-cache
!
interface fastethernet0/0
ip wccp web-cache redirect out
```

Notice that with IOS 12.x you need to specify which WCCP version to use. This command is only available in IOS releases that support both WCCP versions, however. The fastethernet0/0 interface may not be correct for your installation; use the name of the router interface that connects to the outside Internet. Note that packets are redirected on their way *out* of an interface. IOS does not yet support redirecting packets on their way *in* to the router. If needed, you can use access lists to prevent redirecting requests for some origin server or client addresses. Consult the WCCP documentation for full details.

5.2.4 Cisco Policy Routing

Interception caching can also be accomplished with Cisco policy routing. The next-hop for an IP packet is normally determined by looking up the destination address in the IP routing table. Policy routing allows you to set a different next-hop for packets that match a certain pattern, specified as an IP access list. For interception caching, we want to match packets destined for port 80, but we do not want to change the next-hop for packets originating from the cache. Thus, we have to be a little bit careful when writing the access list. The following example does what we want:

```
access-list 110 deny   tcp host 10.1.2.3 any eq www
access-list 110 permit tcp any any eq www
```

10.1.2.3 is the address of the cache. The first line excludes packets with a source address 10.1.2.3 and a destination port of 80 (www). The second line matches all other packets destined for port 80. Once the access list has been defined, you can use it in a route-map statement as follows:

```
route-map proxy-redirect permit 10
match ip address 110
set ip next-hop 10.1.2.3
```

Again, 10.1.2.3 is the cache's address. This is where we want the packets to be diverted. The final step is to apply the policy route to specific interfaces:

```
interface Ethernet0
ip policy route-map proxy-redirect
```

This instructs the router to check the policy route we specified for packets received on interface Ethernet0.

On some Cisco routers, policy routing may degrade overall performance of the router. In some versions of the Cisco IOS, policy routing requires main CPU processing and does not take advantage of the "fast path" architecture. If your router is moderately busy in its normal mode, policy routing may impact the router so much that it becomes a bottleneck in your network.

Some amount of load balancing can be achieved with policy routing. For example, you can apply a different next-hop policy to each of your interfaces. It might even be possible to write a set of complicated access lists that make creative use of IP address netmasks.

Note that policy routing does not support failure detection. If the cache goes down or stops accepting connections for some reason, the router blindly continues to divert packets to it. Policy routing is only a mediocre replacement for sophisticated layer four switching products. If your production environment requires high availability, policy routing is probably not for you.

5.3 The TCP Layer: Ports and Delivery

Now that we have fiddled with the routing, the diverted HTTP packets are arriving at the cache's network interface. Usually, an Internet host rejects received packets if the destination address does not match the host's own IP address. For interception caching to work, the cache must accept the diverted packet and give it to the TCP layer for processing.

In this section, we'll discuss how to configure a Unix host for interception caching. If you use a caching appliance, where the vendor supplies both hardware and software, this section may not be of interest to you.

The features necessary to support interception caching on Unix rely heavily on software originally developed for Internet firewalls. In particular, interception caching makes use of the software for packet filtering and, in some cases, network address translation. This software does two important things. First, it tells the kernel to accept a diverted packet and give it to the TCP layer. Second, it gives us the option to change the destination port number. The diverted packets are destined for port 80, but our cache might be listening on a different port. If so, the filtering software changes the port number to that of the cache before giving the packet to the TCP layer.

I'm going to show you three ways to configure interception caching: first with Linux, then with FreeBSD, and finally with the IP Filter package, which runs on numerous Unix flavors. In all the examples, 10.1.2.3 is the IP address of the cache (and the machine that we are configuring). The examples also assume that the cache is running on port 3128, and that an HTTP server, on port 80, is also running on the system.

5.3.1 *Linux*

Linux has a number of different ways to make interception caching work. Mostly, it depends on your kernel version number. For Linux-2.2 kernels, you'll probably want to use *ipchains*; for 2.4 kernels, you'll want to use *iptables* (a.k.a. Netfilter).

Most likely, the first thing you'll need to do is compile a kernel with certain options enabled. If you don't already know how to build a new kernel, you'll need to go figure that out, and then come back here. A good book to help you with this is *Linux in a Nutshell* [Siever, Spainhour, Hekman and Figgins, 2000]. Also check out the "Linux Kernel HOWTO" from the Linux Documentation Project at *http://www.linuxdoc.org*.

5.3.1.1 *ipchains*

To begin, make sure that your kernel has the necessary options enabled. On most systems, go to the kernel source directory (*/usr/src/linux*) and type:

```
# make menuconfig
```

Under *Networking options*, make sure the following are set:

```
[*] Network firewalls
[*] Unix domain sockets
[*] TCP/IP networking
[*] IP: firewalling
[*] IP: always defragment (required for masquerading)
[*] IP: transparent proxy support
```

Once the kernel has been configured, you need to actually build it, install it, and then reboot your system.

After you have a running kernel with the required options set, you need to familiarize yourself with the *ipchains* program. *ipchains* is used to configure IP firewall rules in Linux. Firewall rules can be complicated and unintuitive to many people. If you are not already familiar with *ipchains*, you should probably locate another reference that describes in detail how to use it.

The Linux IP firewall has four rule sets: input, output, forwarding, and accounting. For interception caching, you need to configure only the input rules. Rules are evaluated in order, so you need to list any special cases first. This example assumes we have an HTTP server on the Linux host, and we don't want to redirect packets destined for that server:

```
/sbin/ipchains -A input -p tcp -s 0/0 -d 10.1.2.3/32 80 -j ACCEPT
/sbin/ipchains -A input -p tcp -s 0/0 -d 0/0 80 -j REDIRECT 3128
```

The -A input option means we are appending to the set of input rules. The -p tcp option means the rule matches only TCP packets. The -s and -d options specify source and destination IP addresses with optional port numbers. Using 0/0 matches any IP address. The first rule accepts all packets destined for the local HTTP server. The second rule matches all other packets destined for port 80 and redirects them to port 3128 on this system, which is where the cache accepts connections.

Finally, you need to enable routing on your system. The easiest way to do this is with the following command:

```
echo 1 > /proc/sys/net/ipv4/ip_forward
```

After you get the *ipchains* rules figured out, be sure to save them to a script that gets executed every time your machine boots up.

5.3.1.2 iptables

In the Linux-2.4 kernel, *iptables* has replaced *ipchains*. Unfortunately, I don't have operational experience with this new software. Setting up *iptables* is similar to *ipchains*. You'll probably need to build a new kernel and make sure the *iptables* features are enabled. According to Daniel Kiracofe's "Transparent Proxy with Squid mini-HOWTO," the only command you need to intercept connections is:

```
/sbin/iptables -t nat -D PREROUTING -i eth0 -p tcp --dport 80 \
-j REDIRECT --to-port 3128
```

You'll also need to enable routing, as described previously.

Since *iptables* is relatively new, the information here may be incomplete. Search for Daniel's mini-HOWTO or see the Squid FAQ (*http://www.squid-cache.org/Doc/ FAQ/*) for further information.

5.3.2 FreeBSD

Configuring FreeBSD for interception caching is very similar to configuring Linux. The examples here are known to work for FreeBSD Versions 3.x and 4.x. These versions have all the necessary software in the kernel source code, although you need to specifically enable it. If you are stuck using an older version (like 2.2.x), you should consider upgrading, or have a look at the IP Filter software described in the following section.

First, you probably need to generate a new kernel with the IP firewall code enabled. If you are unfamiliar with building kernels, read the *config(8)* manual page. The kernel configuration files can usually be found in */usr/src/sys/i386/conf.* Edit your configuration file and make sure these options are enabled:

```
options        IPFIREWALL
options        IPFIREWALL_FORWARD
```

Next, configure and compile your new kernel as described in the *config(8)* manual page. After your new kernel is built, install it and reboot your system.

You need to use the *ipfw* command to configure the IP firewall rules. The following rules should get you started:

```
/sbin/ipfw add allow tcp from any to 10.1.2.3 80 in
/sbin/ipfw add fwd 127.0.0.1,3128 tcp from any to any 80 in
/sbin/ipfw add allow any from any to any
```

The first rule allows incoming packets destined for the HTTP server on this machine. The second line causes all remaining incoming packets destined for port 80 to be redirected (forwarded, in the *ipfw* terminology) to our web cache on port 3128. The final rule allows all remaining packets that didn't match one of the first two. The final rule is shown here because FreeBSD denies remaining packets by default.

A better approach is to write additional `allow` rules just for the services running on your system. Once all the rules and services are working, you can have FreeBSD deny all remaining packets. If you do that, you'll need some special rules so the interception proxy works:

```
/sbin/ipfw add allow tcp from any 80 to any out
/sbin/ipfw add allow tcp from 10.1.2.3 to any 80 out
/sbin/ipfw add allow tcp from any 80 to 10.1.2.3 in established
/sbin/ipfw add deny any from any to any
```

The first rule here matches TCP packets for intercepted connections sent from the proxy back to the clients. The second rule matches packets for connections that the proxy opens to origin servers. The third rule matches packets from the origin servers coming back to the proxy. The final rule denies all other packets. Note that this configuration is incomplete. It's likely that you'll need to add additional rules for services such as DNS, NTP, and SSH.

Once you have the firewall rules configured to your liking, be sure to save the commands to a script that is executed when your system boots up.

5.3.3 *Other Operating Systems*

If you don't use Linux or FreeBSD, you might still be able to use interception caching. The IP Filter package runs on a wide range of Unix systems. According to their home page (*http://cheops.anu.edu.au/~avalon/ip-filter.html*), IP Filter works with FreeBSD, NetBSD, OpenBSD, BSD/OS, Linux, Irix, SunOS, Solaris, and Solaris-x86.

As with the previous Linux and FreeBSD instructions, IP Filter also requires kernel modifications. Some operating systems support loadable modules, so you might not actually need to build a new kernel. Configuring the kernels of all the different platforms is too complicated to cover here; see the IP Filter documentation regarding your particular system.

Once you have made the necessary kernel modifications, you can write an IP Filter configuration file. This file contains the redirection rules for interception caching:

```
rdr ed0 10.1.2.3/32 port 80 -> 127.0.0.1 port 80 tcp
rdr ed0 0.0.0.0/0 port 80 -> 127.0.0.1 port 3128 tcp
```

Note that the second field is a network interface name; the name ed0 may not be appropriate for your system.

To install the rules, you must use the *ipnat* program. Assuming that you saved the rules in a file named */etc/ipnat.rules*, you can use this command:

```
/sbin/ipnat -f /etc/ipnat.rules
```

The IP Filter package works a little differently than the Linux and FreeBSD firewalls. In particular, the caching application needs to access */dev/nat* to determine the proper destination IP address. Thus, your startup script should also make sure the caching application has read permission on the device:

```
chgrp nobody /dev/ipnat
chmod 644 /dev/ipnat
```

If you are using Squid, you need to tell it to compile in IP Filter support with the --enable-ipf-transparent configure option.

5.4 *The Application Layer: HTTP*

Recall that standard HTTP requests and proxy-HTTP requests are slightly different (see Section 2.1, "HTTP Requests"). The first line of a standard request normally includes only an absolute pathname. Proxy-HTTP requests, on the other hand, use the full URL. Because interception proxying does not require browser configuration, and the browser thinks it is connected directly to an origin server, it sends only the URL-path in the HTTP request line. The URL-path does not include the origin server hostname, so the cache must determine the origin server hostname by some other means.

The most reliable way to determine the origin server is from the HTTP/1.1 Host header. Fortunately, all of the recent browser products do send the Host header, even if they use "HTTP/1.0" in the request line. Thus, it is a relatively simple matter for the cache to transform this standard request:

```
GET /index.html HTTP/1.0
Host: www.ircache.net
```

into a proxy-HTTP request, such as:

```
GET http://www.ircache.net/index.html HTTP/1.0
```

In the absence of the `Host` header, the cache might be able to use the socket interface to get the IP address for which the packet was originally destined. The Unix sockets interface allows an application to retrieve the local address of a connected socket with the `getsockname()` function. In this case, the local address is the origin server that the proxy pretends to be. Whether this actually works depends on how the operating system implements the packet redirection. The native Linux and FreeBSD firewall software preserves the destination IP address, so `getsockname()` does work. The IP Filter package does not preserve destination addresses, so applications need to access */dev/nat* to get the origin server's IP address.

If the cache uses `getsockname()` or */dev/nat*, the resulting request looks something like this:

```
GET http://192.52.106.29/index.html HTTP/1.0
```

While either a hostname or an IP address can be used to build a complete URL, hostnames are highly preferable. The primary reason for this is that URLs typically use hostnames instead of IP addresses. In most cases, a cache cannot recognize that both forms of a URL are equivalent. If you first request a URL with a hostname, and then again with its IP address, the second request is a cache miss, and the cache now stores two copies of the same object. This problem is made worse because some hostnames have many different IP addresses.

5.5 *Debugging Interception*

Many people seem to have trouble configuring interception caching on their networks. This is not too surprising, because configuration requires a certain level of familiarity with switches and routers. The rules and access lists these devices use to match certain packets are particularly difficult. If you set up interception caching and it doesn't seem to be working, these hints may help you isolate the problem.

First of all, does the caching proxy receive redirected connections? The best way to determine this is with *tcpdump*. For example, you can use:

```
tcpdump -n port 80
```

You should see a fair amount of output if the switch or router is actually diverting connections to the proxy. Note that if you have an HTTP server running on the same machine, it is difficult to visually differentiate the proxy traffic from the server traffic. You can use additional *tcpdump* parameters to filter out the HTTP server traffic:

```
tcpdump -n port 80 and not dst 10.1.2.3
```

If you don't see any output from *tcpdump*, then it's likely your router/switch is incorrectly configured.

If your browser requests just hang, then it's likely that the switch is redirecting traffic, but the cache cannot forward misses. Running *tcpdump* in this case shows a lot of TCP SYN packets sent out but no packets coming back in. You can also check for this condition by running *netstat -n*. If you see a lot of connections in the SYN_SENT state, it is likely that the firewall/*nat* rules deny incoming packets from origin servers. Turn on firewall/*nat* debugging if you can.

You may also find that your browser works fine, but the caching proxy doesn't log any of the requests. In this case, the proxy machine is probably simply routing the packets. This could happen if you forget, or mistype, the redirect/forward rule in the *ipchains*/*ipfw* configuration.

5.6 Issues

Interception caching is still somewhat controversial. Even though it sounds like a great idea initially, you should carefully consider the following issues before deploying it on your network.

5.6.1 It's Difficult for Users to Bypass

If for some reason, one of your users encounters a problem with interception caching, he or she is going to have a difficult time getting around the cache. Possible problems include stale pages, servers that are incompatible with your cache (but work without it), and IP-based access controls. The only way to get around an interception cache is to configure a different proxy cache manually. Then the TCP packets are not sent to port 80 and thus are not diverted to the cache. Most likely, the user is not savvy enough to configure a proxy manually, let alone realize what the problem is. And even if he does know what to do, he most likely does not have access to another proxy on the Internet.

In my role as a Squid developer, I've received a number of email messages asking for help bypassing ISP settings. The following message is real; only the names have been changed to protect the guilty:

Duane,

I am Zach Ariah, a subscriber of XXX Internet - an ISP who has
recently installed... Squid/1.NOVM.21. All of my HTTP requests are

now being forced through the proxy(proxy-03-real.xxxxx.net). I really
don't like this, and am wondering if there is anyway around this. Can
I do some hack on my client machine, or put something special into the
browser, which will make me bypass the proxy??? I know the proxy looks
at the headers. This is why old browsers don't work.

Anyway... Please let me know what's going on with this.
Thank you and Best regards,

Zach Ariah

This is a more serious issue for ISPs than it is for corporations. Users in a corporate environment are more likely to find someone who can help them. Also, corporate users probably expect their web traffic to be filtered and cached. ISP customers have more to be angry about, since they pay for the service themselves.

All layer four switching and routing products have the ability to bypass the cache for special cases. For example, you can tell the switch to forward packets normally if the origin server is *www.hotmail.com* or if the request is from the user at 172.16.4.3. However, only the administrator can change the configuration. Users who experience problems need to ask the administrator for assistance. Getting help may take hours, or even days. In some cases, users may not understand the situation well enough to ask for help. It's also likely that such a request will be misinterpreted or perhaps even ignored. ISPs and other organizations that deploy interception caching must be extremely sensitive to problem reports from users trying to surf the Web.

5.6.2 *Packet Transport Service*

What exactly is the service that one gets from an Internet service provider? Certainly, we can list many services that a typical ISP offers, among them email accounts, domain name service, web hosting, and access to Usenet newsgroups. The primary service, however, is the transportation of TCP/IP packets to and from our systems. This is, after all, the fundamental function that enables all the other services.

As someone who understands a little about the Internet, I have certain expectations about the way in which my ISP handles my packets. When my computer sends a TCP/IP packet to my ISP, I expect my ISP to forward that packet towards its destination address. If my ISP does something different, such as divert my packets to a proxy cache, I might feel as though I'm not getting the service that I pay for.

But what difference does it make? If I still get the information I requested, what's wrong with that? One problem is related to the issues raised in Chapter 3. Users might assume that their web requests cannot be logged because they have not configured a proxy.

Another, more subtle point to be made is that some users of the network expect the network to behave *predictably*. The standards that define TCP connections and IP routing do not allow for connections to be diverted and accepted under false pretense. When I send a TCP/IP packet, I expect the Internet infrastructure to handle that packet as described in the standards documents. Predictability also means that a TCP/IP packet destined for port 80 should be treated just like a packet for ports 77, 145, and 8333.

5.6.3 *Routing Changes*

Recall that most interception caching systems expose the cache's IP address when forwarding requests to origin servers. This might alter the network path (routing) for the HTTP packets coming from the origin server to your client. In some cases, the change can be very minor; in others, it might be significant. It's more likely to affect ISPs than corporations and other organizations.

Some origin servers expect all requests from a client to come from the same IP address. This can really be a problem if the server uses HTTP/TLS and unencrypted HTTP. The unencrypted (port 80) traffic may be intercepted and sent through a caching proxy; the encrypted traffic is not intercepted. Thus, the two types of requests come from two different IP addresses. Imagine that the server creates some session information and associates the session with the IP address for unencrypted traffic. If the server instructs the client to make an HTTP/TLS request using the same session, it may refuse the request because the IP address doesn't match what it expects. Given the high proliferation of caching proxies today, it is unrealistic for an origin server to make this requirement. The session key alone should be sufficient, and the server shouldn't really care about the client's IP address.

When an interception cache is located on a different subnet from the clients using the cache, a particularly confusing situation may arise. The cache may be unable to reach an origin server for whatever reason, perhaps because of a routing glitch. However, the client is able to *ping* the server directly or perhaps even *telnet* to it and see that it is alive and well. This can happen, of course, because the *ping* (ICMP) and *telnet* packets take a different route than HTTP packets. Most likely, the redirection device is unaware that the cache cannot reach the origin server, so it continues to divert packets for that server to the cache.

5.6.4 *It Affects More Than Browsers and Users*

Web caches are deployed primarily for the benefit of humans sitting at their computers, surfing the Internet. However, a significant amount of HTTP traffic does not originate from browsers. The client might instead be a so-called web robot, or a program that mirrors entire web sites, or any number of other things. Should these clients also use proxy caches? Perhaps, but the important thing is that with interception proxying, they have no choice.

This problem manifested itself in a sudden and very significant way in June of 1998, when Digex decided to deploy interception caching on their backbone network. The story also involves Cybercash, a company that handles credit card payments on the Internet. The Cybercash service is built behind an HTTP server, thus it uses port 80. Furthermore, Cybercash uses IP-based authentication for its services. That is, Cybercash requires transaction requests to come from the known IP addresses of its customers. Perhaps you can see where this is leading.

A number of other companies that sell merchandise on the Internet are connected through Digex's network. When a purchase is made at one of these sites, the merchant's server connects to Cybercash for the credit card transaction. However, with interception caching in place on the Digex network, Cybercash received these transaction connections from a cache IP address instead of the merchant's IP address. As a result, many purchases were denied until people finally realized what was happening.

The incident generated a significant amount of discussion on the North American Network Operators Group (NANOG) mailing list. Not everyone was against interception caching; many applauded Digex for being forward-thinking. However, this message from Jon Lewis (*jlewis@fdt.net*) illustrates the feelings of people who are negatively impacted by interception caching:

> My main gripe with Digex is that they did this (forced our traffic into a transparent proxy) without authorization or notification. I wasted an afternoon, and a customer wasted several days worth of time over a 2–3 week period trying to figure out why their cybercash suddenly stopped working. This customer then had to scan their web server logs, figure out which sales had been "lost" due to proxy breakage, and see to it that products got shipped out. This introduced unusual delays in their distribution, and had their site shut down for several days between their realization of a problem and resolution yesterday when we got Digex to exempt certain IP's from the proxy.

Others took an even stronger stance against interception caching. For example, Karl Denninger (*karl@denninger.net*) wrote:

> Well, I'd love to know where they think they get the authority to do this from in the first place.... that is, absent active consent. I'd be looking over contracts and talking to counsel if someone tried this with transit connections that I was involved in. Hijacking a connection without knowledge and consent might even run afoul of some kind of tampering or wiretapping statute (read: big trouble).....

5.6.5 No-Intercept Lists

Given that interception caching does not work with some servers, how can we fix it? Currently, the only thing we can do is configure the switch or router not to divert certain connections to the cache. This must be a part of the switch/router configuration because, if the packets are diverted to the cache, there is absolutely nothing the cache can do to "undivert" them. Every interception technique allows you to specify special addresses that should not be diverted.

The maintenance of a no-intercept list is a significant administrative headache. Proxy cache operators cannot really be expected to know of every origin server that breaks with interception caching. At the same time, discovering the list of servers the hard way makes the lives of users and technical support staff unnecessarily difficult. A centrally maintained list has certain appeal, but it would require a standard format to work with products from different vendors.

One downside to a no-divert list is that it may also prevent useful caching of some objects. Routers and switches check only the destination IP address when deciding whether to divert a connection. Any given server might have a large amount of cachable content but only a small subset of URLs that do not work through caches. It is unfortunate that the entire site must not be diverted in this case.

5.6.6 Are Port 80 Packets Always HTTP?

I've already made the point that packets destined for port 80 may not necessarily be HTTP. The implied association between protocols and port numbers is very strong for low-numbered ports. Everyone knows that port 23 is telnet, port 21 is FTP, and port 80 is HTTP. However, these associations are merely conventions that have been established to maximize interoperation.

Nothing really stops me from running a telnet server on port 80 on my own system. The *telnet* program has the option to connect to any port, so I just need to type *telnet myhostname 80*. However, this won't work if there is an interception proxy between my telnet client and the server. The router or switch assumes the port 80 connection is for an HTTP request and diverts it to the cache.

This issue is likely to be of little concern to most people, especially in corporate networks. Only a very small percentage of port 80 traffic is not really HTTP. In fact, some administrators see it as a positive effect, because it can prevent non-HTTP traffic from entering their network.

5.6.7 HTTP Interoperation Problems

Interception caching is known to impair HTTP interoperability. Perhaps the worst instance is with Microsoft Internet Explorer. When you click on *Reload*, and Explorer thinks it's connecting to the origin server, it omits the Cache-control: no-cache directive. The interception cache doesn't know the user clicked on *Reload*, so it serves a cache hit instead of forwarding the request to the origin server.*

Interception proxies also pose problems for maintaining backwards compatibility. HTTP allows clients and servers to utilize new, custom request methods and headers. Ideally, proxy caches should be able to pass unknown methods and headers between the two sides. However, in practice, many caching products cannot process new request methods. A smart client can bypass the proxy cache for the unknown methods, unless interception caching is used.

5.6.8 IP Interoperation Problems

There are a number of ways that interception proxies impact IP interoperability. For example, consider path MTU† discovery. Internet hosts use the IP *don't fragment* option and ICMP feedback messages to discover the smallest MTU of all links between them. This technique is almost worthless when connection hijacking creates two network paths for a single pair of IP addresses.

Another problem arises when attempting to measure network proximity. One way to estimate how close you are to another server is to time how long it takes to open a TCP connection. Using this technique with an interception proxy in the way produces misleading results. Connections to port 80 are established quickly and almost uniformly. Connections to other ports, however, take significantly longer and vary greatly. A similar measurement tactic times how long it takes to complete a simple HTTP request. Imagine that you've developed a service that rates content providers based on how quickly their origin servers respond to your requests. Everything is working fine, until one day your ISP installs an interception cache. Now you're measuring the proxy cache rather than the origin servers.

I imagine that as IP security (RFC 2401) becomes more widely deployed, many people will discover problems caused by interception proxies. The IP security protocols and architecture are designed to ensure that packets are delivered end-to-end without modification. Indeed, connection hijacking is precisely one of the reasons to use IP security.

---

* See Microsoft Knowledgebase article Q266121, *http://support.microsoft.com/support/kb/articles/Q266/1/21.ASP*.

† The Maximum Transmission Unit is the largest packet size that can be sent in a single datalink-layer frame or cell.

5.7 To Intercept or Not To Intercept

Interception caching, a.k.a. connection hijacking, is extremely attractive to proxy and network administrators because it eliminates client configuration headaches. Users no longer need to know how to configure proxies in their browser. Furthermore, it works with all web clients; administrators don't need specific instructions for Lynx, Internet Explorer, Netscape Navigator, and their different versions. With interception caching, administrators have greater control over the traffic sent to each cache. It becomes very easy to add or remove caches from a cluster or to disable caching altogether.

A related benefit is the sheer number of users using the cache. When users are given a choice to use proxies, most choose not to. With interception caching, however, they have no choice. The larger user base drives up hit ratios and saves more wide-area Internet bandwidth.

The most significant drawback to interception caching is that users lose some control over their web traffic. When problems occur, they can't fix the problem themselves, assuming they even know how. Another important consequence of connection hijacking is that it affects more than just end users and web browsers. This is clearly evident in the case of Digex and Cybercash.

Certainly, interception caching was in use long before Digex decided to use it on their network. Why, then, did the issue with Cybercash never come up until then? Mostly because Digex was the first to deploy interception caching in a *backbone* network. Previously, interception caching had been installed close to web clients, not web servers. There seems to be growing consensus in the Internet community that interception caching is acceptable at the edges of the network, where its effects are highly localized. When used in the network core (i.e., backbones), its effects are widely distributed and difficult to isolate, and thus unacceptable.

Many people feel that WPAD (or something similar) is a better way to "force" clients to use a caching proxy. With WPAD, clients at least understand that they are talking to a proxy rather than the origin server. Of course, there's no reason you can't use both. If you use interception proxying, you can still use WPAD to configure those clients that support it.

6

Configuring Servers to Work with Caches

This chapter is intended as a guide for web server administrators. I offer some techniques and advice on how to make your server friendly to web caches.

HTTP—Version 1.1 in particular—provides a number of headers for the exchange of information between origin servers and caches. For one reason or another, servers often fail to include these headers in their responses. This is rather unfortunate, because it can lead to undesirable or even incorrect behavior. The absence of these headers gives caches a lot of freedom to determine whether and for how long a given response may be cached. In particular, we are interested in the Date, Last-modified, Expires, Cache-control, and Content-length headers. You have already been introduced to these HTTP headers in Chapter 2, but we will explore them in greater detail here.

As a server administrator, you may be forced to choose between control on one hand and performance on the other. Uncachable objects give you more control and accurate access counts. Cachable responses take away some of your control but give better performance to your viewers. I will argue that your servers should be as cache-friendly as possible. This means carefully identifying which pages can be cached and which cannot. Cachable pages should include expiration times in keeping with their update frequency.

You will also find information here on how to configure your server to be cache-unfriendly. Essentially, this means telling the server to generate uncachable responses. As a proponent of web caching, I personally don't like to find cache-unfriendly servers. Of course, the decision is yours, not mine. I hope that, in reading this chapter, you come to believe that your viewers and customers will be better served by a cache-friendly server.

Much of this chapter deals with the HTTP reply headers that affect cachability. Although it is important to understand these aspects of the protocol, you also need to know how to make your server send the headers. If you are lucky enough to be using the Apache server, I have some specific examples you can follow. For other HTTP servers, consult your user's manual.

6.1 Important HTTP Headers

To understand what makes web objects cachable (or uncachable), you need to know how HTTP presents certain information to caches. In this chapter, we will discuss five HTTP headers that are particularly important and useful for web caches: Date, Last-modified, Expires, Cache-control, and Content-length. Although some of these headers may appear in requests, for this chapter, we are interested only in response headers.

6.1.1 Date

When an origin server generates an HTTP response, it places the current time in the Date header. The time is represented in a common format and always as Greenwich Mean Time (GMT), so clients and servers around the globe do not need to worry about time zone conversions.

The Date header allows a cache or other agent to derive some useful information about a response. Obviously, you can determine the age of the response (but not the resource!) from this header. If the given date is equal to the current time, you probably have a response that just came from the origin server. On the other hand, if the date is in the past, you probably have a response that came from a cache.

You can never be absolutely sure about the Date header because you don't know if the origin server's clock is correct. We call this the clock skew problem. There is no guarantee that the origin server's clock is synchronized to your own. Either clock may be incorrectly set. If you find a Date header with a future time, then you know that either your clock or the server's clock is wrong. If the time is in the past, either a clock is out of sync, or it is a cached response. A number of new features in HTTP/1.1 are designed to eliminate ambiguities and reliance on absolute dates. For example, the Age header represents the age (in seconds) of the response. Previously, caches had to determine the age by calculating the difference between the Date header and the current time. Even though HTTP/1.1 has these new headers, you should always use NTP to keep your system clocks synchronized.

The Date header is also important to caches because it provides a basis for comparing the other timestamp headers in a response. For example, to calculate the resource's age when the response was generated, caches subtract the Date value from the `Last-modified` value. Caches may also need to compare the `Expires` value to the response date. If they are equal, or if the expires time is earlier, the response is preexpired and must be revalidated upon its next request.

RFC 2616 requires origin servers to generate a `Date` header for every response. In reality, a `Date` header is present in about 91% of responses (see Section A.3.2, "Client Reply Headers"). The RFC also says that proxies should insert their own `Date` header if none exists.

6.1.2 Last-modified

The `Last-modified` header specifies the time when the resource was most recently modified. This timestamp is important to web caches because it is used as a cache validator. A cache says to an origin server, "I have this object with this last-modified timestamp; is it still current?" The server compares the validator timestamp with the resource's modification time. If they are the same, the resource has not been modified, and the server returns a 304 (Not Modified) response. Recall from Section 2.2, "Is It Cachable?," that RFC 2616 recommends a response should not be cached unless it includes either a cache validator or an explicit expiration time. The last-modified timestamp is not the only type of cache validator, however. With HTTP/1.1, entity tags (see Section 2.5.2, "Entity Tags") may be used as well.

Last-modified times are also useful in another way. As I mentioned earlier, by subtracting the date from the last-modified time, we know how old the resource was when the server generated the response. We call this the *last-modified age*, or LM-age. Caches may use the LM-age to estimate the stability of the resource. A young resource is considered unstable and more likely to change; an old resource, however, is more stable and less likely to change. This heuristic is often used for revalidation when a resource does not have a specific expiration time. The LM-age can also be used in a cache replacement algorithm. When choosing objects for deletion, it may be better to select the youngest ones because they have probably changed and need to be transferred again upon the next request anyway.

Unfortunately, we see `Last-modified` headers in responses less frequently than `Date` headers. The statistics in Section A.3.2, "Client Reply Headers," show that only about 52 percent of responses have a last-modified timestamp. RFC 2616 says that an origin server "should send a Last-Modified value if it is feasible to send one . . . ". For objects stored as plain disk files, it is trivial to retrieve the modification time from the filesystem. However, responses generated from CGI scripts, Active Server Pages, and HTML with server-side includes often do not have a last-modified timestamp.

6.1.3 Expires

The Expires header is great for caches because it tells the cache exactly how long the response may be considered fresh. A response that includes an Expires header may be reused without validation (i.e., a cache hit) until the expiration time is reached. This removes a lot of guesswork from the cache and places responsibility with the origin server. Without an Expires header, a cache may be to blame for returning an out-of-date (stale) response. By providing an expiration time, the content provider takes responsibility for ensuring users receive fresh responses.

The presence of an Expires header can also turn an otherwise uncachable response into a cachable one. For example, responses to POST requests are uncachable by default, but they can be cached if there is an Expires line in the reply headers.

Expires headers appear relatively infrequently in practice. Today, we see expiration values in about 12% of all responses (see Section A.3.2, "Client Reply Headers"). Fortunately, the trend is increasing over time. When I started analyzing cache logs in 1995, only about 5% of responses had expiration times. But why was this number so low? The most likely reason is that, by default, web servers never send Expires headers. Another is that it can be very difficult to predict when a resource will actually change. When will you change your home page next? When will a product's price go up or down? What if you guess wrong? It is not too difficult to imagine a situation where an information provider wants or needs to retract a document before its expiration time is reached. It could be as harmless as a spelling mistake or as serious as slanderous accusations against an innocent person. Note, however, that this problem is not unique to the Web. Newspaper, television, and radio also often publish or broadcast information that later requires a correction.

Another difficult aspect of expiration times is the interface (or lack thereof) between humans and the HTTP server. Who should set expiration times? The document author or the server administrator? The answer depends on the actual HTTP server being used. Some, like Apache, provide ways for authors to insert or modify certain HTTP headers, as we'll see later. Others require configuration that only the server administrator may perform.

6.1.4 Cache-control

The Cache-control header has a number of directives, all of which are important to caching in one way or another. In this chapter, we are only concerned with the reply directives. We already talked about most of these in Section 2.2.4, "Cache-control," but we'll go over them again here:

max-age *and* s-maxage

> max-age is an alternate form of the Expires header. Both specify the amount of time until a response becomes stale. max-age uses relative values, while Expires uses absolute times. The max-age directive is preferred for some of the reasons already described. Another good thing about max-age is that it can change a response from uncachable to cachable. The s-maxage directive is the same, but it only applies to shared caches.

public

> The public directive designates a response as cachable. Many responses are cachable by default, so public is not always needed. However, responses that are uncachable by default become cachable when this Cache-control directive is present. If you want a particular response to be cached, it is a good idea to add the public directive just to be safe.

private

> When an origin server wants to allow the response to be cached by a browser but not by a proxy, it includes the private cache-control directive. Such a response must not be cached by a shared (proxy) cache, but the user's browser may cache the response and reuse it if all other standard conditions are met.

no-cache

> This directive is somewhat tricky. It is similar to the must-revalidate directive. Responses that include the no-cache directive can be stored, but they must be revalidated before reuse. The no-cache directive can also specify a list of header names, in which case those headers must be removed before storing the response.

no-store

> The no-store directive is the best way to make a response uncachable. It is intended to prevent even temporary storage of information that the owner considers highly sensitive. RFC 2616 says that "the cache MUST NOT intentionally store the information in non-volatile storage, and MUST make a best-effort attempt to remove the information from volatile storage as promptly as possible after forwarding it." Some caching products might prefer to buffer incoming data on disk, which is especially useful if the client is slower than the server. This should not happen, however, if the no-store directive is present.

no-transform

> By and large, caching proxies are allowed to change, or transform, the objects they serve to clients. For example, a proxy might recode images from one format to another that uses less space and less transmission time. Similarly, a cache might apply compression to text objects before giving them to clients and storing them on disk. According to RFC 2616, these sorts of

transformations have been known to cause problems in some cases—for instance, when clients and servers communicate using SOAP or XML-RPC over HTTP.

To prevent such modifications, the server includes a no-transform directive. With this directive, a proxy cache cannot change the type, length, or encoding of the object content.

must-revalidate

RFC 2616 permits caches to intentionally return stale responses in some circumstances, such as extremely poor network connectivity. The must-revalidate directive is a way for the server to prevent stale responses in those cases. In other words, this directive takes higher precedence than the user-agent and/or cache configuration. Section 14.9.4 of the RFC advises servers to send must-revalidate "if and only if failure to revalidate a request on the entity could result in incorrect operation."

must-revalidate and no-cache are quite similar. The difference is that no-cache supersedes expiration times, but must-revalidate does not. In other words, must-revalidate responses are validated only after becoming stale, whereas no-cache responses are always validated. Both should be used with extreme caution.

proxy-revalidate

proxy-revalidate is just like must-revalidate, except that it applies only to shared (proxy) caches, not to single-user (browser) caches. A response with proxy-revalidate may be reused by a browser cache without revalidation. A proxy cache, on the other hand, is required to revalidate the response before giving it to a client.

6.1.5 Content-length

The Content-length header specifies the size of the HTTP message body in a response. Knowing the body size allows a cache to determine whether it received a complete response. If a cache or client doesn't know what the body size should be, it might store a partial response and believe it received the whole thing. A future request for the object may then result in the partial response being sent as a cache hit.

There are two ways to find the end of an HTTP message body when the response doesn't have a Content-length value. The simplest approach is just to close the connection. However, since HTTP/1.1 wants connections to be persistent, it provides something called *chunked transfer encoding.*

Under HTTP/1.0, connections are always closed at the end of a transfer; HTTP/1.1 agents can do the same when the headers don't include a content length.

Unfortunately, this makes it hard for a client to tell whether it got the whole message successfully or received just part of the message due to an error. The client doesn't know how big the message body is supposed to be. Consider the case when a proxy is reading such a response from an origin server and relaying it to the client. Remember that there are two TCP connections—one to the client and one to the server. The proxy gets a read error, such as "connection reset by peer," during the middle of the transfer. The proxy knows the response is most likely incomplete. But how does it notify the client? HTTP does not provide any way to indicate an error condition while sending the message body. If we just close the client's connection, the client is likely to believe the response is complete. The proxy should instead perform an *abortive close* so the client also receives a TCP reset packet.*

HTTP/1.1 has persistent connections designed to reduce retrieval latencies by eliminating the TCP connection handshake for every request. Though closing a persistent connection to indicate end-of-message is allowed, it is not desirable. To support unknown message sizes and persistent connections together, HTTP/1.1 uses a chunked transfer encoding. The chunked transfer encoding divides the message body into a sequence of chunks, each of which includes the chunk size. This allows the server to tell the client, "Here are N more bytes of data, but it's not the end yet." The server indicates the end-of-message with a chunk of size of 0. If a client doesn't receive the 0-sized chunk, it should assume the response is incomplete.

The `Content-length` header is useful to caches in a number of other ways as well. It can be used to preallocate cache storage space or calculate the amount of data left to be transferred. When a user aborts an HTTP transfer before it has finished, a cache may want to finish the download anyway. If resources have been used to transfer 95% of an object, the cache may just as well get the remaining 5%, especially if there is a chance it could result in a cache hit. The content length is an important factor in deciding whether to finish an aborted transfer.

6.2 Being Cache-Friendly

This section is directed to content providers: I want to convince you to engineer a cache-friendly web site. If you stick with me through the motivation section, I'll give you some practical advice and even show you how to implement many of the tips on the Apache server.

---

* To make an abortive close with Berkeley sockets, use the `SO_LINGER` option with a linger time of 0, and then close the socket.

6.2.1 Why?

Why should you, as a content provider, care about web caching? For at least the following three reasons:

- When people access your web site, pages will load faster.

- Caches isolate clients from network failures.

- Caches reduce the load placed on your servers and network connections.

Let's examine each of these reasons in more detail.

6.2.1.1 Latency

It should be pretty obvious that caching objects close to web clients can greatly reduce the amount of time it takes to access those objects. This is the reason why web browsers have their own built-in cache. Retrieving an object from the browser cache is almost always faster than retrieving it over the network. When considering how your web site interacts with caches, don't forget browser caches!

What if the requested objects are not in the browser cache but might be stored in a proxy cache? Now the benefits of caching are strongly correlated to relative proximity of the client, cache, and origin server. Here, *proximity* refers to network topology rather than geography. Both latency and throughput characterize network proximity. As an example, let's consider two different users accessing the *www.cnn.com* home page. The first user is connected to a U.S. ISP with a 56K modem, using the ISP's proxy cache. The second is in a classroom on the campus of a university in Perth, Australia, using the university's proxy cache. The dial-up user is actually "far away" from the ISP cache because the dial-up connection is a major bottleneck. Throughput between the user's home computer and the proxy cache is limited to about 4 KB per second. The ISP cache probably does not speed up transfers for the dial-up user because both cache hits and misses are limited to the modem speed. However, the Australian student is very close to her cache, probably connected via a local area network. In her case, the major bottleneck is the transoceanic link between Australia and the United States. The cache provides a significant speedup because cache hits are transferred much faster than cache misses.

When discussing how caches reduce latency, it is very important to include the differences between validated and unvalidated cache hits (see Section 2.3, "Hits, Misses, and Freshness"). While validation requests can contribute significantly to reducing network bandwidth, they still incur high latency penalties. In some situations, a validated cache hit takes just about as long as a cache miss. For users who enjoy high-speed network connections, round-trip delays, rather than transmission delays, are the primary source of latency. Thus, validated cache hits do not appear to be significantly faster on high-speed networks. For dial-up users, however, transmission time is the primary source of delay, and a validated hit from the browser cache should be faster than a cache miss.

6.2.1.2 Hiding network failures

Most likely, you have experienced a network outage or failure when using the Internet. An outage may be due to failed hardware (such as routers and switches) or a telecommunication breakdown (fiber cut). Whatever the cause, network failures are frustrating because they prevent users from reaching certain web sites.

People who use web caches, however, may still be able to receive your site's pages, even during a network outage. As long as the user has network connectivity to the cache, pages already in the cache can be sent to the user. If a cached object is considered fresh, there is no need to contact the origin server anyway. For an unvalidated cache hit, both the user and the cache would never even know about the network outage.

For a stale cached object, the cache forwards a validation request to the origin server. If the validation request fails because of the network outage, the cache may be able to send the cached copy to the user anyway. HTTP/1.1 generally allows caches to do this, but the cache must insert a Warning header, which looks like this:

```
Warning: 111 (cache.foo.com:3128) Revalidation Failed
```

Note that caches are not required to send stale responses for failed validation requests. This is up to the caching proxy implementation or is perhaps an option for the cache administrator. Also recall that if the cached response includes the must-revalidate cache-control directive, the cache cannot send a stale response to the client.

6.2.1.3 Server load reduction

As a content provider, you probably want your users to receive your information as quickly as possible. Many people spend a lot of time thinking about and working on ways to optimize their HTTP servers. The load placed upon an origin server affects its overall performance. In other words, as the load increases, the average response time increases as well.

Server load is usually measured in terms of requests per second. Numerous factors affect a server's performance, including network speed, CPU power, disk access times, and TCP implementations. At the time of this writing, state-of-the-art web servers can handle about 10,000 requests per second. That's much more than most of us require.

It should be pretty obvious that web caches can reduce the load placed on origin servers, but it's quite difficult actually to say how much of an origin server's load is absorbed by caches. Both the site's popularity and cachability affect the percentage of requests satisfied as cache hits. A more popular site provides more opportunities for cache hits because more clients request its objects. An object that remains fresh for a long period of time also provides more opportunities for cache hits.

As fascinating as all this may be, should you really care about the load absorbed by web caches? Maybe not. Organizations that require heavy-duty web servers can usually afford to buy whatever they need. Smaller organizations can probably get by with inexpensive hardware and free software. The most important thing to remember is this: if you're thinking about making all your content uncachable one day, expect a very large increase in server load shortly thereafter. If you are not prepared to handle significantly more requests, you might lose your job!

6.2.2 Ten Ways to be Cache-Friendly

This "Top Ten list" describes the steps you can take to build a cache-friendly web site. Do not feel like you have to implement all of these. It is still beneficial if you put just one or two into practice. The most beneficial and practical ideas are listed first:

1. Avoid using CGI, ASP, and server-side includes (SSI) unless absolutely necessary. Generally, these techniques are bad for caches because they *usually* produce dynamic content. Dynamic content is not a bad thing per se, but it may be abused. CGI and ASP can also generate cache-friendly, static content, but this requires special effort by the author and seems to occur infrequently in practice.

   The main problem with CGI scripts is that many caches simply do not store a response when the URL includes *cgi-bin* or even *cgi*. The reason for this heuristic is perhaps historical. When caching was first in use, this was the easiest way to identify dynamic content. Today, with HTTP/1.1, we probably need to look at only the response headers to determine what may be cached. Even so, the heuristic remains, and some caches might be hard-wired never to store CGI responses.

   From a cache's point of view, Active Server Pages (ASP) are very similar to CGI scripts. Both are generated by the server, on the fly, for each request. As such, ASP responses usually have neither a `Last-modified` nor an `Expires` header. On the plus side, it is uncommon to find special cache heuristics for ASP (unlike CGI) probably because ASP was invented well after caching was in widespread use.

Finally, you should avoid server-side includes (SSI) for the same reasons. This is a feature of some HTTP servers to parse HTML at request time and replace certain markers with special text. For example, with Apache, you can insert the current date and time or the current file size into an HTML page. Because the server generates new content, the `Last-Modified` header is either absent in the response or set to the current time. Both cases are bad for caches.

2. Use the GET method instead of POST if possible. Both methods are used for HTML forms and query-type requests. With the POST method, query terms are transmitted in the request body. A GET request, on the other hand, puts the query terms in the URI. It's easy to see the difference in your browser's *Location* box. A GET query has all the terms in the box with lots of & and = characters. This means that POST is somewhat more secure because the query terms are hidden in the message body.

   However, this difference also means that POST responses cannot be cached unless specifically allowed. POST responses may have side effects on the server (e.g., updating a database), but those side effects aren't triggered if the cache gives back a cached response. Section 9.1 of RFC 2616 explains the important differences between GET and POST. In practice, it is quite rare to find a cachable POST response, so I would not be surprised if most caching products never cache any POST responses at all. If you want to have cachable query results, you certainly should use GET instead of POST.

3. Avoid renaming web site files; use unique filenames instead. This might be difficult or impossible in some situations, but consider this example: a web site lists a schedule of talks for a conference. For each talk there is an abstract, stored in a separate HTML file. These files are named in order of their presentation during the conference: *talk01.html, talk02.html, talk03.html,* etc. At some point, the schedule changes and the filenames are no longer in order. If the files are renamed to match the order of the presentation, web caches are likely to become confused. Renaming usually does not update the file modification time, so an `If-Modified-Since` request for a renamed file can have unpredictable consequences. Renaming files in this manner is similar to cache poisoning.

   In this example, it is better to use a file-naming scheme that does not depend on the presentation order; a scheme based on the presenter's name would be preferable. Then, if the order of presentation changes, the HTML file must be rewritten, but the other files can still be served from the cache. Another solution is to *touch* the files to adjust the timestamp.

4. Give your content a default expiration time, even if it is very short. If your content is relatively static, adding an `Expires` header can significantly speed up access to your site. The explicit expiration time means clients know exactly

when they should issue revalidation requests. An expiration-based cache hit is almost always faster than a validation-based near hit; see Section A.8, "Service Times." See Section 6.2.4, "How to Choose Expiration Times," for advice on choosing expiration values.

5. If you have a mixture of static and dynamic content, you might find it helpful to have a separate HTTP server for each. This way, you can set server-wide defaults to improve the cachability of your static content without affecting the dynamic data. Since the entire server is dedicated to static objects, you need to maintain only one configuration file. A number of large web sites have taken this approach. Yahoo! serves all of their images from a server at *images.yahoo.com*, as does CNN with *images.cnn.com*. Wired serves advertisements and other images from *static.wired.com*, and Hotbot uses a server named *static.hotbot.com*.

6. Don't use content negotiation. Occasionally, people like to create pages that are customized for the user's browser; for example, Netscape may have a nifty feature that Internet Explorer does not have. An origin server can examine the User-agent request header and generate special HTML to take advantage of a browser feature. To use the terminology from HTTP, an origin server may have any number of *variants* for a single URI. The mechanism for selecting the most appropriate variant is known as *content negotiation*, and it has negative consequences for web caches.

    First of all, if either the cache or the origin server does not correctly implement content negotiation, a cache client might receive the wrong response. For example, if an HTML page with content specific to Internet Explorer gets cached, the cache might send the page to a Netscape user. To prevent this from happening, the origin server is supposed to add a response header telling caches that the response varies on the User-agent value:

        Vary: User-agent

    If the cache ignores the Vary header, or if the origin server does not send it, cache users can get incorrect responses.

    Even when content negotiation is correctly implemented, it reduces the number of cache hits for the URL. If a response varies on the User-agent header, a cache must store a separate response for every User-agent it encounters. Note that the User-agent value is more than just *Netscape* or *MSIE*. Rather, it is a string such as *Mozilla/4.05 [en] (X11; I; FreeBSD 2.2.5-RELEASE i386; Nav)*. Thus, when a response varies on the User-agent header, we can get only a cache hit for clients running the same version of the browser on the same operating system.

7. Synchronize your system clocks with a reference clock. This ensures that your server sends accurate `Last-modified` and `Expires` timestamps in its responses. Even though newer versions of HTTP use techniques that are less susceptible to clock skew, many web clients and servers still rely on the absolute timestamps. *xntpd* implements the Network Time Protocol (NTP) and is widely used to keep clocks synchronized on Unix systems. You can get the software and installation tips from *http://www.ntp.org/*.

8. Avoid using address-based authentication. Recall that most proxy caches hide the addresses of clients. An origin server sees connections coming from the proxy's address, not the client's. Furthermore, there is no standard and safe way to convey the client's address in an HTTP request. Some of the consequences of address-based authentication are discussed in Section 2.2.5, "Authentication."

    Address-based authentication can also deny legitimate users access to protected information when they use a proxy cache. Many organizations use a DMZ network for the firewall between the Internet and their internal systems.* A cache that runs on the DMZ network is probably not allowed to access internal web servers. Thus, the users on the internal network cannot simply send all of their requests to a cache on the DMZ network. Instead, the browsers must be configured to make direct connections for the internal servers.

9. Think different! Sometimes, those of us in the United States forget about Internet users in other parts of the world. In some countries, Internet bandwidth is so constrained that we would find it appalling. What takes seconds or minutes to load in the U.S. may take hours or even days in some locations. I strongly encourage you to remember bandwidth-starved users when designing your web sites, and remember that improved cachability speeds up your web site for such users.

10. Even if you think shared proxy caches are evil, consider allowing single-user browser caches to store your pages. There is a simple way to accomplish this with HTTP/1.1. Just add the following header to your server's replies:

    ```
    Cache-control: private
    ```

    This header allows only browser caches to store responses. The browser may then perform a validation request on the cached object as necessary.

---

* DMZ stands for de-militarized zone. A DMZ network is considered to be "neutral territory" between your internal network and the outside world. See [Zwicky, Cooper and Chapman, 2000] for more information.

6.2.3 Apache

In the previous section, I gave you a number of recommendations for the responses generated by your web server. Now, we will see how you can implement those with the Apache server.

6.2.3.1 The Expires header

Apache has a couple of ways to include an `Expires` header in HTTP responses. The old way is actually a legacy from the CERN proxy. It uses *.meta* directories to hold the header information. For example, if you want to set a header value for the resource */foo/index.html*, create a file named */foo/.meta/index.html*, in which you put lines such as:

```
Expires: Wed, 28 Feb 2001 19:52:18 GMT
```

Before you can use meta files in Apache, you must include the *cern_meta* module when you compile the server. This is accomplished with Version 1.3 of Apache by giving the following command-line option to the *configure* script:

```
./configure --add-module=src/modules/extra/mod_cern_meta.c
```

The CERN meta file technique has a number of shortcomings. First of all, you have to create a separate meta file for every file on your server. Second, you must specify the headers exactly. If you do not remember to update the `Expires` time, responses are served with an expiration time in the past. It is not possible to have the server dynamically calculate the expiration time. For these reasons, I strongly discourage you from using the *.meta* technique.

Apache has a newer module, called *mod_expires*, that is easier to use and offers much more flexibility. This module is available in Version 1.3 of Apache and later. To add the module to your server binary, you need to use this command:

```
./configure --add-module=src/modules/standard/mod_expires.c
```

This module is nice because it sets the `max-age` cache control directive, in addition to the `Expires` header. Documentation from the Apache web site can be found at *http://www.apache.org/docs/mod/mod_expires.html*.

To use the expires module, you must first enable the option for your server with the `ExpiresActive` keyword. This option can be set either globally or for a specific subset of your document tree. The easiest technique is simply to enable it for your whole server by adding the following line to your *httpd.conf* file:

```
ExpiresActive on
```

If you want to use fine-grained controls with the *.htaccess* file, you must also add `Override Indexes` for the necessary directories in *httpd.conf*.

The expires module has two directives that specify which objects receive an `Expires` header. The `ExpiresDefault` directive applies to all responses, while `ExpiresByType` applies to objects of a specific content type, such as *text/html*. Unfortunately, you cannot use wildcards (*text/**) in the type specification. These directives may appear in a number of contexts. They can be applied to the entire server, a virtual domain name, or a subdirectory. Thus, you have a lot of control over which responses have an expiration time.

Expiration times can be calculated in two ways, based on either the object's modification time or its access time. In both cases, the `Expires` value is calculated as a fixed offset from the chosen time. For example, to specify an expiration time of one day after the time of access, you write:

```
access plus one day
```

More complex specifications are allowed:

```
access plus 1 week 2 days 4 hours 7 minutes
```

The expiration time can also be based on the modification time, using the `modification` keyword. For example:

```
modification plus 2 weeks
```

The latter approach should be used only for objects that definitely change at regular intervals. If the expiration time passes and the object does not get updated, any subsequent request for the object will result in a preexpired response. This hardly improves the cachability of the object! Furthermore, you should use the modification keyword only for disk files. When a response is generated dynamically (a CGI script, for example), it does not have a `Last-modified` time, and thus Apache cannot include an `Expires` header.

Now let's see how to put it all together. Let's say you want to turn on `Expires` headers for your web server. You want images to expire 3 days after being accessed and HTML pages to expire after 12 hours. All other content should expire one day after being accessed. The following configuration lines, placed in *httpd.conf*, do what you want:

```
ExpiresActive on
ExpiresByType image/jpeg "access plus 3 days"
ExpiresByType image/gif "access plus 3 days"
ExpiresByType text/html "access plus 12 hours"
ExpiresDefault "access plus 1 day"
```

If you have a subdirectory that requires special treatment, you can put similar commands in an *.htaccess* file. For example, let's say you have a directory called *weather* that holds current images from weather satellites. If the images are updated every hour, you can put these configuration lines in the file named *weather/.htaccess*:

```
ExpiresByType image/gif "modification plus 1 hour"
```

6.2.3.2 General header manipulation

Apache also has a module that allows you to add arbitrary headers to a response. This module is called *mod_headers*, and it is useful for setting headers such as Cache-control. To add the headers module to your Apache installation, use the following configure option:

```
./configure --add-module=src/modules/standard/mod_headers.c
```

The full documentation can be found at *http://www.apache.org/docs/mod/ mod_headers.html*.

With the headers module, you can easily add, remove, and append almost any HTTP header. If you are not familiar with the format and structure of HTTP headers, review Section 4.2 of RFC 2616. The general syntax for the headers module is:

```
Header <set|append|add> name value
Header unset name
```

If the *value* includes whitespace, it must be enclosed in double quotes. The set keyword overwrites any existing headers with the same *name*. The append and add keywords are similar. Neither overwrites an existing header. The append keyword inserts the value at the end of an existing header, while add adds a new, possibly duplicate header. The unset keyword removes the first header with the given *name*. You can delete only an entire header, not a single value within a header.

Now we'll see how to include a Cache-control header so some responses are cachable by browsers but not by shared proxy caches. You can apply header directives for an entire subdirectory by adding the following to an *.htaccess* file in that directory:

```
Header append Cache-control private
```

Note that we use append instead of set because we don't want to clobber any existing Cache-control directives in the response.

As an alternative to the expires module described previously, you can use the headers module to set an expiration time and the max-age directive to define an expiration time. For example:

```
Header append Cache-control "max-age=3600"
```

For HTTP/1.1, this is equivalent to using "access plus 1 hour" in the expires module. The difference is that here we use `Cache-control`. An HTTP/1.0 client (or cache) may not understand the `Cache-control` header.

6.2.3.3 Setting headers from CGI scripts

It is also possible to set headers from your CGI scripts without the headers or expires modules. In particular, you might want to set `Last-modified` and `Expires` headers, since these are normally absent from CGI script responses.

The output of a CGI program consists of reply headers, an empty line, and the reply body. Some of the reply headers (such as `Date` and `Server`) are supplied by the server and not by the CGI program. However, the CGI script must at least output a `Content-type` header. Apache also allows you to pass other reply headers from the script to the server.

I've already mentioned that Apache includes `Last-modified` only for disk files. CGI scripts are considered dynamic, so the server does not generate a `Last-modified` header for them. You can generate your own from a CGI script with relatively little trouble. While you're at it, you might as well send an expiration time too. The following Perl code demonstrates how to correctly generate these headers:

```
#!/usr/bin/perl -w
use POSIX;

$exp_delta = 300;        # 5 minutes
$lmt = strftime("%a, %d %b %Y %H:%M:%S GMT", gmtime(time));
$exp = strftime("%a, %d %b %Y %H:%M:%S GMT",
    gmtime(time+$exp_delta));

print "Content-type: text/plain\n";
print "Last-modified: $lmt\n";
print "Expires: $exp\n";
print "Cache-control: max-age=$exp_delta\n";
print "\n";
print "This demonstrates setting reply headers from a CGI script.\n";
```

The trickiest part is that we have to use Perl's *POSIX* module to get the `strftime()` function. The magical format string, passed as the first argument to `strftime()`, is the preferred date format for HTTP messages, as defined in RFCs 822 and 1123.

When the above script is placed on a server and requested, the output looks something like this:

```
HTTP/1.1 200 OK
Date: Wed, 10 Jan 2001 03:13:11 GMT
Server: Apache/1.3.3 (Unix)
Cache-control: max-age=300
```

```
Expires: Wed, 10 Jan 2001 03:18:11 GMT
Last-Modified: Wed, 10 Jan 2001 03:13:11 GMT
Connection: close
Content-Type: text/plain
```

This demonstrates setting reply headers from a CGI script.

Note that the server included all of the headers we added and even rearranged them a little bit. The server also added Date, Server, and Connection headers.

Note that the response does not have a Content-length header. This is because Apache does not know how long the reply body is going to be. You should output a Content-length header from your CGI scripts if the body length is easy to calculate. As mentioned in Section 6.1.5, "Content-length," a missing Content-length has certain negative consequences for persistent connections.

6.2.4 How to Choose Expiration Times

If I have managed to convince you that specific expiration times are a good thing, you might wonder what sorts of values you should use. Before we can answer that, you'll have to think about these related questions: how often does your content usually change? How important is it for your readers/viewers to have absolutely up-to-date content? The answers to the latter question might vary depending on the type of content.

Generally, people consider HTML pages to be more dynamic and critical than images. Thus, you can probably give images a longer expiration period than HTML files. This is a good tradeoff since images comprise about 70% of all web traffic, while HTML accounts for only 15%. For most web sites, I recommend an expiration period of between one hour and one day for HTML and between one day and one week for images. You may certainly use expiration times longer than one week, but unless the object is popular, many caches will delete it before then anyway.

If your HTML content changes daily at specific times (e.g., midnight), obviously you should use an expiration time of "modification time plus one day." However, if your content changes daily, but at random times, you'll probably want to use an expiration scheme such as "access time plus six hours." Then it will take no longer than six hours for your updated page to propagate through all web caches. If you have time-sensitive information, it is a good idea to include a timestamp somewhere on the page. For example:

This page was last modified Fri Mar 9 02:50:34 GMT 2001.

This gives your viewers important information when they wonder if the page is up-to-date. If they believe the page may have been changed, they can ask for the latest version by clicking on their browser's Reload button.

6.3 *Being Cache-Unfriendly*

What if you need (or want) to send cache-unfriendly, uncachable responses? To accomplish this, it's only a matter of adding a few specific headers.

If you just want to count the requests, you don't need to make the response uncachable. Instead, you can make caches revalidate the response for each client request. To do this, use the no-cache, max-age=0 or must-revalidate directives. Of these, no-cache is the strongest, max-age=0 is the weakest, and must-revalidate is somewhere in the middle. To insert the no-cache directive with Apache's *headers* module, use this configuration line:

```
Header: append Cache-control no-cache
```

If you just want to prevent users from sharing a cached response, you can use the private directive. That still allows the response to be stored in single-user caches.

If your goal is truly to defeat caching, you should use the no-store directive.

Cache-control is an HTTP/1.1 feature; how can you ensure that HTTP/1.0 agents do not store the response? Unfortunately, this is a little bit confusing, and both of the following techniques should probably be used.

According to the HTTP/1.0 specification RFC 1945, "If the [Expires] date given is equal to or earlier than the value of the Date header, the recipient must not cache the enclosed entity." This rule is unfortunate because expiration and cachability are really separate characteristics. Nonetheless, an HTTP/1.0-compliant cache should not cache a response if the date and expires values are identical or if the expires value is invalid. Many applications use the following:

```
Expires: 0
```

HTTP/1.0 also defines the Pragma header for both requests and responses. RFC 1945 specifically discusses no-cache for requests but not for responses. Even so, it is common practice to include this directive in a response to mark it as uncachable. So, if you really want to be sure, also add this header:

```
Pragma: no-cache
```

The techniques mentioned above may not be good enough for the really paranoid. Another way to defeat caching is to make each user's URIs unique. Usually, this approach also requires cookies to differentiate individual users. *www.global-computer.com* uses this technique. If you make a request that doesn't have a valid cookie, you get redirected to a unique URL such as:

```
HTTP/1.0 302 Moved Temporarily
Server: Netscape-FastTrack/2.01
Date: Fri, 02 Feb 2001 04:32:45 GMT
```

```
Set-Cookie: GlobalOrdernet=TXlN5ajd; expires=Fri, 02-Feb-2001 04:32:45
       GMT; path=/; domain=167.206.148.90
Location: /TXlN5ajd/
Content-Type: text/html
```

As you can see, the cookie and the URL both contain the string "TXlN5ajd." While this doesn't prevent caching, it does prevent sharing responses between users.

Finally, another way to prevent sharing is to use encrypted transfers, a la SSL/TLS. Caching proxies can only tunnel these responses. Only the client can decrypt the message. Once decrypted, the client can store and reuse the response, however. SSL/TLS requests are also interesting in that they cannot be diverted to interception caches.

6.4 Other Issues for Content Providers

As a content provider, you may have concerns regarding how caches deal with your site content. In particular, many people worry about dynamic responses, advertisements, and accurate access count statistics. While each of these usually result in uncachable content, some methods are worse than others. In this section, I talk about some of the tradeoffs and what you can do to minimize the wait times for users.

6.4.1 What About Dynamic Responses?

Dynamic responses are generally cache-unfriendly. This doesn't mean that dynamic content is bad. It does mean that caches cannot help to improve users' wait times for dynamic pages.

As a webmaster, this is a tradeoff you must carefully consider. How important is the dynamic aspect of your content? Is it worth making people wait for it? Is it worth losing some viewers/customers because the wait is too long? You might say that your customers won't have to wait because you can build a really big server with really fast hardware. However, your big, fast server does nothing to alleviate wide-area network congestion. Neither can it reduce network round-trip delays, nor make someone's dial-up connection faster. You'll have to decide on a balance between dynamic content and cachability.

6.4.2 What About Advertisements?

Advertisements, ad images in particular, are not necessarily at odds with web caching. It really depends on how the system is set up. A number of reasonable approaches are possible. For the following discussion, consider a typical web page with advertisements. Most likely, there are two or more ad images on the page, and the actual ad images change with each request.

One approach is to use fixed URLs in a static HTML page. The URLs for the ad images remain the same but return a different image each time. You can do this with a CGI script that opens a random image file and writes it to the server. For this to work properly, the image response must be uncachable. Otherwise, users of a shared cache will probably see the same advertisement whenever they access that page. Another reason to have the image uncachable is so it can be counted at the origin server. Then the server knows exactly how many times a particular ad image was downloaded. Assuming that only humans download the images, this also corresponds to the number of views of the advertisement. The content provider can then charge the advertiser based on how many people saw the ad. This technique is good in that it gives accurate view counts, but it's bad in that it makes people wait too long for images to download and wastes bandwidth by repeatedly transmitting the same images.

An improvement on the previous approach is to turn the ad image URL into a CGI script that returns an HTTP redirect message. The redirect can point to a static image URL. For example, the embedded URL might be *http://www.host.com/cgi-bin/ad*. When requested, the server returns an HTTP 302 redirect:

```
HTTP/1.1 302 Moved Temporarily
Location: /ad-images/ad1234.gif
```

When requested again, the redirect message has a different Location URL for a different ad image. This technique allows the actual images to be cachable because the dynamic aspects are handled by the redirect message, which is uncachable by default. It's better for the redirect message to be uncachable because it is probably about an order of magnitude smaller than the ad image. The origin server still gets an accurate view count because the CGI script is executed for every view. Also note that the HTML file can be static and cachable. Unfortunately, the CGI script and redirect message do add some latency to the overall page display time because the browser must make two HTTP requests for each image.

A third option is to make the HTML page dynamic and uncachable, while leaving the images static and cachable. Each time the HTML page is requested, links and URLs for advertisements are inserted on the fly. This approach is not a huge loss, because only 15% of all web requests are for HTML pages. Once again, this technique allows the origin server to accurately count views.

Note that each of the techniques that give origin servers accurate view counts rely on some aspect of the page to be uncachable. It could be the images themselves, the underlying HTML document, or the redirect messages. The best solution is the one which minimizes both network delays and bytes transferred. In other words, if you have a single small ad image in a large HTML file, it is better for the image to be uncachable.

6.4.3 Getting Accurate Access Counts

What can you do if you want to be cache-friendly but still want accurate access counts? One common approach is to insert a tiny, invisible, uncachable image in the HTML page that you want to count. Every time someone requests the page, even if they got it from a cache, they should also request the image. Since the image is very small and invisible, people should never realize it is there. When you insert the image in the HTML page, be sure to specify the image dimensions so the browser can render the area quickly. For example:

```
<IMG SRC="/images/counter.gif" WIDTH="1" HEIGHT="1">
```

Of course, one drawback is that not everyone who views the HTML file also requests the image. Some people (usually those with low-speed connections) disable the browser option to automatically load images. Also, not everyone uses graphical browsers; Lynx users will not get counted.

You might want to use the <OBJECT> tag instead of <IMG>. Both can be used to place images in an HTML document. However, browsers won't display the broken image icon when you use OBJECT and the file can't be loaded. The syntax is:

```
<OBJECT DATA="/images/counter.png" WIDTH="1" HEIGHT="1"
TYPE="image/png">
```

For my own web site, I added both cachable and uncachable (invisible) images to the top-level page. By counting the number of requests for both types, I can approximate the ratio of requests for cachable and uncachable objects. If I want to know how many people actually requested my pages, I simply multiply my server's count by the ratio. For my site, the ratio varies daily from anywhere between 1.5 and 2.5, as shown in Figure 6.1.

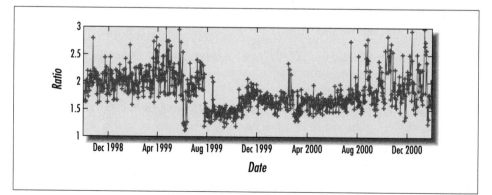

Figure 6.1. Ratio of uncachable-to-cachable requests

Finally, I want to mention hit metering. Some members of the IETF's HTTP working group spent a lot of time on a proposed standard for hit metering. This work has been published as RFC 2227. Hit metering has two components: limiting and reporting, both of which are optional.

The standard provides mechanisms for limiting how many times a response can be used as a cache hit until it must be revalidated with the origin server. For example, a server can say, "You may give out 20 cache hits for this document, but then you must contact me again after that." Alone, this is a simple scheme; things become complicated, however, with cache hierarchies (see Chapter 7). If the server gives a cache permission for 20 hits, it must share those hits with its neighbor caches. In other words, the first cache must delegate its hits down to lower-level caches in the hierarchy.

Hit metering also provides features for reporting cache hits back to origin servers. The next time the cache requests a metered resource, it uses the Meter header to report how many hits were given out. A cache has a number of reasons to re-request the resource from the origin server, including:

* It ran out of hits according to limits specified by the origin server.

* The response has become stale and the cache needs to revalidate it.

* A client generated a no-cache request, probably by clicking on the Reload button.

If none of those occur before the cache wants to remove the object, the cache is supposed to issue a HEAD request to report the hits to the origin server.

Hit reporting also becomes a little complicated with cache hierarchies. Lower layers of the tree are supposed to report their hits to the upper layers. The upper layers aggregate all the counts before reporting to the origin server.

While hit metering seems promising, the biggest problem at this time seems to be that no one is interested in implementing and using it. A chicken-and-egg situation exists, because neither origin server nor proxy cache developers seem to be willing to implement it unless the other does as well. Perhaps most importantly, though, the folks who operate origin servers are not demanding that their vendors implement hit metering.

7

Cache Hierarchies

A cache hierarchy is just what you might expect—an arrangement of caches that cooperate with each other. In a cache hierarchy, the lower layers forward cache misses up to the higher layers until a cache hit is found or the request is sent to the origin server. Cache hierarchies are attractive because they can offer performance improvements. Some of the requests that are misses in your cache will be hits in your neighbor's caches. This further reduces wide-area network bandwidth and improves download speeds.

However, you must carefully consider a number of important issues surrounding hierarchies, such as trust, freshness, scalability, and effects on routing. These are particularly important when the members of the hierarchy are controlled by different organizations. It's often awkward and difficult to participate in a hierarchy in the absence of an existing business relationship. Large organizations, especially, are more comfortable being self-sufficient rather than relying on others.

In this chapter, we'll talk about hierarchies in general, focusing on definitions and issues. In Chapter 8, we'll learn about the protocols that make meshes and hierarchies possible. Caching proxies use these protocols to decide which neighbor, if any, should be the next hop for a particular request.

7.1 How Hierarchies Work

Web cache hierarchies can be complicated and amorphous. We use the terms *parent*, *child*, and *sibling* to describe the relationship between any two caches. Sometimes *neighbor* or *peer* are used to refer to either a parent or a sibling relationship, just to confuse you.

A child cache forwards its cache misses to a parent. The parent cache then provides the child with a response from its own cache, the origin server, or another cache. A parent cache may use bandwidth to origin servers to satisfy a child cache's request.

Sibling relationships, on the other hand, are designed to prevent one cache from incurring costs on behalf of another. All requests sent to a sibling should result in cache hits. The sibling should never have to fetch an object requested by its peer. If the sibling doesn't have the object cached, it returns a message that indicates its unwillingness to forward the request. A cache communicates with its siblings using one of the intercache protocols described in the next chapter. These protocols allow a cache to find out whether the neighbors have a particular object in their caches. A request should only be sent to a sibling if the intercache protocol predicts it will be a cache hit. As we'll see later, hit predictions are not always accurate, so we need a way to deal with false predictions.

These relationships (parent-child, sibling-sibling) are not fixed. One cache might be a parent to some caches and a sibling to others. This type of configuration is sometimes used by large ISPs, which act as a parent for requests to their customer's origin servers and as a sibling for all other requests.

The terms parent and sibling map well into a hierarchical topology, as shown in Figure 7.1. Parents are considered to be one level up from their child caches. Sibling caches are on the same level with each other. The only way to go up the hierarchy is through a parent cache. Other topologies, such as the one in Figure 7.2, are not really hierarchical. For these, the term *mesh* may be used instead.

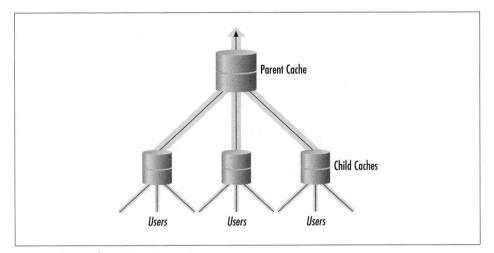

Figure 7.1. Parent-sibling hierarchy

The relationship between two caches is not necessarily symmetric. In other words, just because cache A sends requests to cache B, it does not mean that B can also send requests to A. If requests are to flow both ways, there should be a

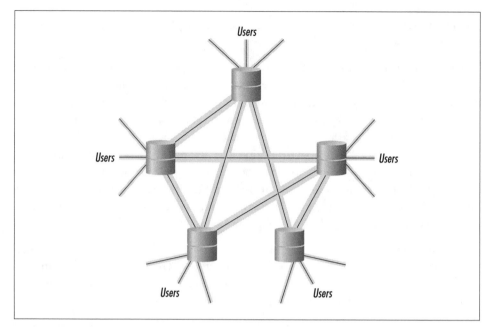

Figure 7.2. Sibling mesh

relationship defined for each direction. In practice, siblings usually have symmetric, bidirectional relationships. Parents and children, on the other hand, usually do not. Since there are no strict rules, it is possible to create some rather strange and complicated topologies. Two caches may have a sibling relationship in one direction but a parent relationship in the other. Of course, a child cache may have any number of parents.

7.2 Why Join a Hierarchy?

As a cache administrator, you might wonder if you should participate in a cache hierarchy. The decision is not always an obvious one; there are many factors and issues for you to consider. People are usually motivated to peer with other caches either for improved performance or to force traffic along a non-default path.

7.2.1 Performance

Performance often motivates people to join a cache hierarchy. However, hierarchical caching is not a magic bullet; it is not guaranteed to improve your performance. If you seek better performance, you must first decide what is most important to you. Reduced bandwidth? Lower latency? In some situations, you may be required to trade one for the other. You should establish a system for measuring your cache's performance so you can quantitatively compare one configuration to another.

To realize improved performance with a cache hierarchy, the following points should all be true:

- Some of the objects not found in your cache will be found in your neighbor caches. In other words, you can get cache hits from your neighbors.

- Cache hits from neighbors are delivered more quickly than misses from origin servers.

- Cache misses from parent caches are not significantly slower than responses from origin servers.

If any of these are false, then your cache performance may actually suffer. Whether they are true or false depends on a number of factors. For example, if a parent cache is heavily loaded, then it may be slower than a direct connection to the origin server. Also, if your neighbor cache is far away, then cache hits may not be significantly faster. Furthermore, the behavior can change over time. One day your parent cache can be very fast but the next day very slow. Don't assume that conditions will always remain the same. Install some monitoring tools that can notify you if performance does not stay within certain thresholds.

7.2.2 Nondefault Routing

Parent caches are useful when you need to force web traffic along a specific route in your network. A common example of this is to get through a firewall. Many corporations and other organizations use firewalls to protect their internal network from the rest of the Internet. There are a number of different ways to deploy a firewall. Some do not allow internal users to communicate directly with external servers; they block outgoing connections for most ports, including port 80. In this case, the only way to reach the outside servers is through the firewall proxy, which is probably also a cache. If you have another caching proxy on the inside, then the firewall proxy is a parent for all of your requests to the outside.

It is increasingly common for corporations and other organizations to use interception proxying. Client HTTP connections are automatically diverted to a caching proxy, rather than blocked. If the client is a caching proxy in this case, the firewall proxy is a parent even though the child proxy does not realize it.

Organizations that pay metered rates for Internet bandwidth sometimes use multiple parent caches to send traffic over specific connections. For example, one connection might be less expensive but more congested. Low-priority requests are sent over the cheap link, while high-priority traffic goes over the expensive one. In some cases, the rates change depending on the time of day. Some caches (e.g., Squid) let you forward requests to different locations based on the current time.

7.3 Why Not Join a Hierarchy?

Now that you know about the advantages of hierarchical caching, it is also important to consider carefully some of the disadvantages and potential problems. Any improvements in performance may be offset by one or more of the following issues.

Some of these issues are significant only when you establish a relationship with caches outside your own organization. For example, you probably trust a neighbor cache within your company more than you trust one that belongs to another company. The presence or absence of a business agreement between two organizations also affects many of these issues. For instance, when you pay another party for a service, it is much easier to get problems resolved quickly.

7.3.1 Trust

You may recall that we talked about trust in Chapter 3. That discussion focused on content integrity and privacy concerns with logfile information. These issues are even more important when you join a cache hierarchy. Not only must you trust your immediate neighbors, but you must also trust all of their neighbors, and so on. Again, you are trusting them to protect the privacy of your web requests and to deliver correct, unmodified documents. Hierarchies can be quite large. It's possible that your requests and responses pass through five or more caching proxies between you and the origin server.

When you get a web page, how can you tell if it is authentic? Currently, there is no good way. Such a scheme would most likely involve digital signatures and public encryption keys in the manner of PGP. Then it should be possible to prove the content originated with a certain entity and was not tampered with before reaching you. In practice, this can be very difficult to implement. Imagine needing to store a PGP-like public key for every web server you visit. Furthermore, the distribution of such keys requires secure channels of communication.

Since there is no end-to-end mechanism for verifying web content, clients usually have no choice but to trust that neighbor caches and origin servers deliver the correct data. If a web page becomes altered, either intentionally or not, it may go undetected. When combined with the fact that HTTP headers may be altered as well, an invalid response could remain fresh for a very long time. Since fresh objects are not normally revalidated, many people may receive the wrong page or incorrect information. Furthermore, this bogus content may spread through a cache hierarchy.

In Chapter 3, we also talked about the need to protect users' privacy. Of course, when you use neighbor caches, many of the requests from your users end up in the neighbor's log files. There are obvious privacy concerns here. The operators of the other cache may easily be able to determine something about your company or your users that you or your users would rather keep secret.

7.3.2 Low Hit Ratios

The hit ratios from parent and sibling caches are normally quite low when compared to a cache that services end users directly. For example, let's say you have a standalone cache that has a hit ratio of 35%. The other 65% of your requests are cache misses that must be forwarded to origin servers. If you establish a parent or sibling relationship with another cache, you can expect that about 5% of all requests would be found as hits in your neighbor cache. In other words, you would have 35% local hits, 5% remote hits, and 60% going to origin servers. There are two primary reasons for low neighbor hit ratios:

- A response that passes through two caches, such as a parent and a child, is usually cached by both. This means, of course, that some responses are duplicated in both caches. The degree of duplication depends on the size of each cache. If the two caches have the same size, then all cache hits are satisfied by the first cache. If, on the other hand, a parent cache is significantly larger than its child cache, objects that quickly get removed from the child may still be found in the parent.

- First-level caches (that service end users directly) usually have more clients than a parent cache does. A first-level cache may serve hundreds or thousands of users. A typical parent cache probably serves no more than 20 child caches. More clients means more cache hits, because there is a smaller probability that any single client is the first to request a particular URI.

In an ideal parent-child relationship, the parent cache would be about an order of magnitude larger than the child cache. In practice, it may not be possible to build or find such a large parent cache. At the minimum, the parent should be at least twice as large as the child. If the two caches are nearly the same size, then only a small percentage of requests result in cache hits at the parent.

7.3.3 Effects on Routing

We've already discussed the fact that proxy caches alter the flow of packets through a network (see Section 3.10, "Effects of Proxies"). In some cases, this can be advantageous, while at other times, it causes problems. As a rule of thumb, when neighbor caches are close, there are fewer problems. As the distance (router hops) increases, so do the effects of routing differences.

As an example, let's say you have a parent cache that has multiple connections to the Internet. Your own cache uses a different Internet connection. If one of the parent's connections goes down, it won't be able to reach some origin servers. Requests sent to the parent may result in "connection timed out" error messages. Since your own cache has a different route to the Internet, it may still be able to reach those origin servers. If the outage is severe enough, you may want to terminate the parent relationship, at least temporarily. Squid has some features that attempt to detect such failures automatically and work around the problem.

7.3.4 Freshness

Maintaining consistency and freshness between members of a hierarchy can be difficult. Consider a child cache with two parents where each cache has saved a copy of a particular URI and the cached response is still fresh. A user generates a no-cache request by clicking on her *Reload* button. This request goes through the child cache and the first parent cache. The resource has been modified recently, so the origin server returns a response with new content. The new response is saved in the child cache and the first parent. However, at this point in time, the second parent has an older version of the resource, which it believes is still fresh.

How can we avoid this situation? The best way is to use some sort of object invalidation process. When a cache discovers a resource has been updated, it "broadcasts" invalidation messages to its neighbors. Some of the protocols that we'll discuss in Chapter 8 have invalidation features. It seems that relatively few products support invalidation at this time, however. Mirror Image Internet has a caching service that makes use of invalidation between nodes. There is currently some interest within the IETF to create a standard invalidation protocol. You may want to search the IETF pages and databases for "RUP," which stands for Resource Update Protocol.

7.3.5 Large Families

If you consider a hierarchy like the one in Figure 7.1, you can see that the upper-layer nodes need to support all the traffic from the lower layers. This is the famous scaling issue found in many aspects of the Internet. The issue brings a number of questions to mind. Can a single parent cache support the load from hundreds, thousands, or even more child caches? How many levels deep should a hierarchy be? At what point do the uppermost nodes become a bottleneck? I do not have a simple answer to these questions. It will depend on many factors, such as the performance of your systems and the request rate. Every product and every architecture has its limits, but finding that limit may be hard. Most likely, you'll have to take a wait-and-see approach.

A caching proxy can become a bottleneck for a number of reasons. A caching system consists of many components, each of which has finite resources. Every product has its limits, but different products have different limits, due to either their design or their particular hardware. The common bottlenecks include network media bandwidth, disk drives, available memory, and network state information. (We'll talk more about performance in Chapter 12.)

When the incoming load exceeds a single proxy cache's resources and leads to performance degradation, steps must be taken to rectify the situation. Typically, you have three options: upgrade the cache, create a cluster of caches, or reduce the incoming load. Upgrading a cache may be as simple as adding disks or replacing a CPU. On the other hand, it may require the purchase of an entire new system. Cache clusters provide a scalable solution to this problem. (We'll talk more about clusters in Chapter 9.) Finally, you may want or need to decrease the load from lower layers. This involves asking the other administrators to stop using your cache as a parent and instead forward their requests directly to origin servers.

7.3.6 *Abuses, Real and Imagined*

I've already mentioned in Section 1.5.2, "Caching Proxies," how a caching proxy hides the client's IP address. Whenever a proxy forwards a request to an origin server, the server logs a connection from the proxy's IP address. If a content or service provider believes their resources are being abused, they almost always contact the person or organization associated with the source IP address. A parent cache that forwards traffic for thousands of users is likely to receive a few email messages from angry providers complaining about one thing or another. Sometimes the complaints are legitimate, but usually they are not.

Credit card fraud is a good example of a legitimate complaint. People who buy and sell lists of stolen credit card numbers use automated software to figure out which are still valid. It seems that they repeatedly submit orders for products via web sites. If the order is accepted, the card number is valid. By using a hierarchy of caching proxies, they hide from the merchant site and force the merchant to deal with the proxy administrator. A deeper hierarchy is better for the criminals because it's less likely they will be found.

Fortunately, almost all web sites use SSL encryption for credit card transactions. Since caching proxies cannot store encrypted responses anyway, parent caches should be configured to deny all SSL requests. The only reason for a caching proxy to tunnel SSL requests is when the users are behind a firewall. By denying SSL requests, we force users to connect directly to origin servers instead. If the users are doing something illegal, this makes it easier to identify them and take appropriate action.

Though it is obvious that cache administrators should intervene to stop illegal activities such as credit card fraud, there are cases where the appropriate course of action is less obvious. The example I am thinking of relates to freedom of speech.

Message boards and chat rooms abound on the Web, and many of them are unmoderated. Anyone can post or say whatever they like. When someone posts a message the other members find offensive, they may be able to find out that the message "originated" from your parent cache. They may ask you to do something to prevent further offensive messages. In some cases, they may block all accesses from your cache's IP address.

The fact that hierarchies aggregate traffic from lower layers is another source of potential problems. At the upper layers, the traffic intensity is significantly increased compared to a normal user. In other words, a top-level parent cache has a higher connection rate than we would expect for a single user. Some content providers interpret such traffic as web robots or even denial-of-service attacks. The *xxx.lanl.gov* site is famous for its anti-robot stance. If they detect apparent robot activity, all subsequent requests from that IP address are denied. Fortunately, the LANL folks understand caching proxies and are willing to make exceptions.

7.3.7 Error Messages

Proxy caches, by their nature, must occasionally generate error messages for the end user. There are some requests that a caching proxy cannot possibly satisfy, such as when the user enters an invalid hostname. In this case, the proxy returns an HTML page with an error message stating that the hostname could not be resolved. Unfortunately, the proxy can't always tell the difference between a DNS name that really doesn't exist and a temporary failure.

In most cases, neither the caching proxy nor the end user is really smart enough to identify the real cause of a particular error. If the user is to blame, we don't want them calling the support staff to complain that the proxy doesn't work. Conversely, we do want users to notify the support staff if the proxy is misconfigured or malfunctioning. Thus, error pages usually include an email address or other contact information so users can receive assistance if they need it.

A tricky situation arises when cache hierarchies cross organizational boundaries. Downstream users may receive an error message from an upstream cache. In the event of a problem, the downstream users may contact the upstream provider with support questions. The support staff from company A is probably not interested in providing assistance to the users or customers of company B, unless there is some kind of business relationship between the two.

7.3.8 False Hits

Recall that a sibling relationship requires a hit prediction mechanism, such as one or more of the intercache protocols described in the following chapter. These predictions are not always correct, due to various factors and characteristics of the intercache protocols. When a request is predicted to be a hit but turns out to be a miss, we call it a *false hit.*

False hits can be a serious problem for sibling relationships. By definition, the sibling relationship forbids the forwarding of cache misses. False hits are not a problem for parent relationships because the parent is willing to forward the request. Given that false hits are a reality, we have two ways to deal with them.

One way is to relax the requirements of a sibling relationship. That is, allow a small percentage of false hits to be forwarded anyway. This may require configuring the sibling to always allow misses to be forwarded. If so, the sibling is vulnerable to abuse by its neighbors.

HTTP/1.1 provides a significantly better solution to this problem. The `only-if-cached` cache-control directive is used on all requests sent to a sibling. If the request is a cache miss at the sibling, then it returns a 504 (Gateway Timeout) response. Upon receiving this response, the first cache knows that it should retry the request somewhere else.

A false hit followed by a 504 response adds a small delay to the user's request. Checking the cache for a particular URI should be almost instantaneous. Thus, most of the delay is due to network transmission and should be approximately equal to two round-trip times. In most situations, this corresponds to 100 milliseconds or less. Given that sibling hits are rare (say 5%) and among those, false hits are rare as well (say 10%), very few requests overall (0.5%) experience this delay.

7.3.9 *Forwarding Loops*

A *forwarding loop* occurs when a request is sent back and forth between two or more nodes. Looping also occurs in other systems such as email and IP routing. Normally, a well-behaved network is free of loops. They may appear, however, due to configuration mistakes or other errors.

In a proxy cache hierarchy (or a mesh), a forwarding loop can appear when two caches are configured such that each has a parent relationship with the other. For a request that is a cache miss, each cache forwards the request to the other. This configuration can result only from human error. Two caches must not be parents for each other. It is of course possible that loops appear for other reasons and in more complicated situations. For example, a group of three or more caches may have a forwarding loop. Loops with sibling caches were relatively common before the `only-if-cached` directive became widely used.

Fortunately, it is relatively easy for a proxy cache to detect a loop. The `Via` request header is a list of all proxy caches that a request has been forwarded through. By searching this list for its own hostname, a cache knows whether it has seen a particular request before. If a loop is detected, it is easily broken by sending the request to the origin server rather than to a parent cache. Of course, with interception proxying (see Chapter 5), it may not be possible to connect directly to the origin server. The request could be diverted to a caching proxy instead.

7.3.10 Failures and Service Denial

A proxy cache, and especially a parent cache, is potentially a single point of failure. There are a number of techniques designed to work around equipment failures transparently. Layer four switching products have the ability to bypass servers that become unavailable. Many organizations use dual servers in a redundant configuration such that, if one system fails, the second can take over. Also, applications themselves may be able to detect upstream failures and stop sending requests to caches that appear to be down.

There are some subtle problems that are more difficult to detect than a total failure. If your parent cache becomes heavily loaded, your response times increase, but all requests continue to be serviced. However, increased response times don't necessarily indicate a problem with your parent cache. It might instead be due to general Internet congestion or the failure of a major traffic exchange.

The DNS is another potential source of service denial. If your parent cache's DNS server fails, it is likely to cause an increase in response times for some of your requests. It may be enough to annoy a few of your users but not significant enough to detect and quickly diagnose, especially since failed DNS lookups are an everyday occurrence when surfing the Web anyway.

The bottom line is that you should carefully consider these and other possibilities when using a parent cache. If your parent cache is under the administration of a separate organization, there may be little you can do to get problems fixed quickly. Unless your caching product is good at detecting failures (and hopefully partial failures as well), you may find yourself disabling neighbor caches when you observe suspicious behavior or performance.

7.4 Optimizing Hierarchies

Remember that a primary motivation for cache hierarchies is to find cache hits in your neighbors. Usually, a cache uses one of the intercache protocols described in Chapter 8 to predict neighbor hits. In some cases, though, we can identify requests that could not possibly result in a cache hit. For these, it makes sense to immediately forward the request to the origin server rather than go through a neighbor cache. In most cases, a direct connection to the origin server is faster than a cache miss through a parent. In addition to reducing latency for end users, this technique also reduces the load placed on upper layers of a hierarchy.

Identifying requests that should bypass the hierarchy is relatively straightforward. The most common case is requests that have uncachable responses. An easy way to find uncachable responses is by looking at the request method. Recall from Section 2.2, "Is It Cachable?" that only GET method requests are cachable by default. Many of the other methods are never cachable, and POST is cachable only if specifically allowed. Thus, a common heuristic is to send all non-GET requests (with one exception) directly to origin servers.

The exception to this rule is the TRACE method. The purpose of the TRACE method is to enable someone to discover the sequence of caches (or proxies) between the user and an origin server. It is similar to the *traceroute* program used to show IP routing paths. Even though TRACE responses are not cachable, a proxy cache should forward a TRACE request as though it were a GET, so the proper forwarding path can be shown.

We saw additional heuristics for identifying uncachable requests in Section 2.2.7, "Dynamic Content." Perhaps the most common is to look for "cgi" or "?" in the URL. Even though there is some small probability that such a request can be cached, it's probably still better to bypass the hierarchy. You may lose one cache hit out of 1,000 requests, but you'll gain much more in better response times.

Requests that require authentication always have uncachable responses, unless the response includes the `proxy-revalidate` directive. At the present time, responses to authenticated requests almost never have the `proxy-revalidate` directive, so this is another good way to identify uncachable requests.

We might be tempted to bypass the hierarchy for requests that have a `no-cache` directive because they always force a cache miss. Bypassing the hierarchy for these requests is probably a bad idea. Let's assume that a parent cache has stored a response that is now out of date but is believed to be fresh. If a user clicks the *Reload* button, the browser includes the `no-cache` directive in its request. If this request doesn't go through the parent, then the out-of-date response does not get updated. Thus, a `no-cache` request should still go through a cache hierarchy, but it must never be sent to a sibling cache.

8

Intercache Protocols

In this chapter, I will cover four different intercache protocols. These specialized protocols are used between cooperating proxy caches for a number of reasons. Their most important function is to aid in forwarding decisions. That is, given a request and some number of neighbor caches, to which cache should the request be sent? Or should it be sent directly to the origin server? The intercache protocols provide information that a cache may use to minimize the time to retrieve an object. They may also be used to implement other features, such as prefetching and metadata updates.

The Internet Cache Protocol, or ICP, was the first intercache protocol invented. This lightweight query-response protocol probes neighbor caches for would-be hits. ICP is perhaps the most widely used of the protocols we will discuss in this chapter, mostly because it has been around the longest. All of the other protocols we will discuss were designed to improve upon ICP in one way or another. The most common complaint about ICP is the additional round-trip delay that every request incurs.

The Cache Array Routing Protocol, or CARP, is very different from ICP. It uses a deterministic algorithm, rather than a real-time query, to select a next-hop cache. CARP places emphasis on distributing load among a cache cluster rather than finding a cached copy of a given resource. Unlike some simpler load distribution techniques, CARP nicely accommodates changes in the number of cluster members. In theory, CARP can also be implemented in browsers or other user-agents—a proxy autoconfiguration script for example.

The Hypertext Caching Protocol, or HTCP, is similar to ICP in that it is also a UDP-based query-response protocol. One major difference is that HTCP uses much more information to determine whether a request would be a hit or a miss.

Another significant improvement is the addition of strong authentication. The downside is that the message format is significantly more complex.

Cache Digests are compact representations of a cache's contents. The digest provides a way for a cache to quickly look up an object in its neighbor's directory. Thus, the per-request delays of ICP and HTCP are eliminated. The tradeoff comes in the form of increased memory usage and some amount of inaccuracy in the predictions. Overall bandwidth utilization is probably similar to that of ICP but with different characteristics. Network traffic due to ICP is proportional to the cache request rate and is relatively smooth over time. Cache Digests, on the other hand, generate significant bursts in network utilization at regular intervals.

If you are looking for WCCP here, you won't find it. WCCP is not used between cooperating caches. Rather, it is a protocol that switches and routers use to divert traffic to a proxy cache. See Section 5.2.3, "WCCP," for the scoop.

8.1 ICP

ICP is the original intercache protocol. Its primary purpose is to discover whether any neighbor caches have a fresh copy of a particular object. The neighbor caches answer with either yes (HIT) or no (MISS). The querying cache collects a particular number of ICP replies and then makes a forwarding decision. Even if all neighbors reply with MISS, ICP may provide additional hints that help to choose the best parent cache.

ICP is far from perfect. But despite its shortcomings, it is still in widespread use today. In countries where wide-area network bandwidth is both expensive and fully utilized, informal cache hierarchies offer much better response time than standalone caches. ICP is supported by almost all of the major caching products. At the time of this writing, products from the following companies are known to implement ICP: Squid, Network Appliance, Cisco, CacheFlow, Novell, Netscape, InfoLibria, Inktomi, Novell, iMimic, and Lucent. (See Appendix B for the low-level details of ICP.)

8.1.1 History

ICP was invented during work on the Harvest project in 1994 [Bowman, Danzig, Hardy, Manber and Schwartz, 1994]. During that time, ICP became increasingly popular because it allowed people for the first time to create complicated web cache hierarchies. The CERN proxy supported simple hierarchies where all requests were forwarded to another proxy. With Harvest, however, you could have multiple parent and sibling caches as neighbors.

The original protocol design included features that were later dropped or never actually implemented. For example, the earliest surviving ICP documentation describes opcodes for transmitting cached objects and features that could multiplex numerous responses over a single TCP connection. Unfortunately, as often happens with research projects, the implementation changed, but the protocol documentation did not.

Towards the end of 1995, the Harvest project came to a premature end. It was at this time that the Harvest cache software spawned two new projects. Peter Danzig took the software and offered it commercially under the name Netcache, which later became a product of Network Appliance. I took a job with the National Laboratory for Applied Network Research and developed the Squid Cache as part of a project funded by the National Science Foundation. Both projects made some changes to ICP.

In the Harvest design, eight octets were to be used for authentication features. The Harvest code never made use of this field, however. Netcache decided to use this area to hold a pair of timestamps. My friends at Network Appliance told me that one timestamp is a last-modified value, and the other, an if-modified-since value. Netcache also decided to increment the version number for their implementation. To the best of my knowledge, the Netcache (Network Appliance) implementation is not formally documented.

Squid also takes advantage of the unused authentication field, but for a different purpose. The first four octets are option flags that indicate support for new features. The second four octets may contain option-specific data. On the Squid project, we added a couple of new features to ICP. (These are covered in the following section.) Squid still uses 2 for the version number, as did Harvest.

As the number of Squid and Netcache installations continued to increase, more and more people began to suggest documenting ICP as an Internet RFC. In September 1997, the IETF adopted two documents describing ICP Version 2 (ICPv2) under the Informational category. The first, RFC 2186, describes the ICP message format and structure. The second, RFC 2187, outlines the way that web caching applications should actually use the protocol. The Informational status of these documents carries no recommendation or endorsement by the IETF. In other words, people don't necessarily think ICP is a good protocol just because it has been published as an Informational RFC.

RFCs 2168 and 2187 essentially document the implementation of ICP in Squid Version 1.1.10 (April 1997). They are specific to ICPv2 and thus do not include any information about the Netcache implementation. Harvest, Netcache, and Squid were the only products to implement ICP when these documents were written.

8.1.2 Features

ICP has a number of interesting features, some of which were added after the initial design. This section covers only the features of ICPv2 as documented in RFCs
2168 and 2187. Some new and experimental features have been added since then.
These are described in Section B.4, "Experimental Features."

8.1.2.1 Hit prediction

As already mentioned, the primary purpose of ICP is to find out which, if any, of
your neighbor caches have a specific object. This feature is fundamental to the
idea of a sibling relationship. We can request only cache hits from a sibling, so we
need some way to predict whether a given request will be a hit or a miss. ICP's hit
predictions are useful for parent relationships as well. In most cases, a hit from
one parent should be faster than a miss from another.

8.1.2.2 Probing the network

ICP messages are normally sent as UDP packets, which have some useful side
effects. The delay that an ICP transaction experiences tells us something about the
status of the network and the remote cache. For example, if we don't receive a
reply message within a certain period of time, we can conclude that the remote
cache is offline or the network is severely congested. ICP can be used as a
tiebreaker when choosing between two or more equivalent parents. A parent that
is heavily loaded takes longer to process an ICP query, and the transaction experiences some delay. By selecting the first cache that responds, we do some basic
load balancing.

Even though UDP is used in practice, the protocol specification does not require
any particular transport protocol. In theory, TCP can be used, but it is probably
more of a hindrance. The fact that UDP is unreliable benefits ICP because we
don't really want the messages to be delivered if congestion occurs. Since ICP is
used only to provide hints and never for critical functions, UDP is an ideal choice.
I am not aware of any implementations that use TCP.

8.1.2.3 Object data with hits

While working on the Harvest project, we realized that a lot of cached objects
were small enough to fit inside a UDP packet. According to the statistics in Section
A.1, "Reply and Object Sizes," half of all web objects are smaller than 4 KB, and
about 75% are smaller than 9 KB.* In the case of an ICP hit reply, we can put the
actual object in the ICP message and avoid a subsequent HTTP request. Since the

---

* The maximum size of a UDP packet can vary greatly between systems. 9 KB is a conservative
  estimate.

HTTP request takes at least one or two round-trip times, this feature can significantly reduce response times for clients. This so-called "HIT_OBJ" feature was added to a beta version of Squid-1.0.

The initial response to HIT_OBJ was very good. Unfortunately, after a few months, we began to receive numerous problem reports. One problem is that ICPv2 has no support for object validation. A client's If-Modified-Since header is not sent in an ICP query, and a stale response may be sent in the ICP reply payload. Thus, HIT_OBJ results in a stale response when an HTTP request does not. Generally, the problem is that HTTP has many headers and features that cannot be conveyed in an ICP query message.

Another issue is the increased UDP packet size. HIT_OBJ messages are significantly larger than plain HIT messages. A congested network is more likely to drop a large UDP packet than a small one because the large one must be fragmented. UDP has no retransmission, so if just one fragment is lost, then the entire UDP packet must be dropped. In this case, it may be better to have plain HITs delivered rather than losing the HIT_OBJ replies.

For these reasons, I do not recommend the use of the HIT_OBJ feature. Squid has not supported HIT_OBJ since Version 2.0.

8.1.2.4 Source RTT measurements

Under Harvest, the next-hop cache was chosen based on which reply arrived first. This algorithm favors near caches over far ones because the near cache replies almost always arrive first. We address this problem in Squid by assigning weights to each cache. The measured delay is divided by the weight. Thus, faraway caches may be treated as though they were closer. Unfortunately, this is only a partial solution.

The Harvest algorithm considers only distance, not direction. To account for direction, we also need to know the proximity of each neighbor cache to the origin server. Given the choice between two parent caches, it makes sense to select the one closest to the origin server.

During the development of Squid Version 1.1, we added the *network measurement database*. Squid sends ICMP "pings" to origin servers and tracks their average round-trip times, aggregated by class C networks. Thus, when Squid sends an ICP miss reply, it may be able to include its estimated round-trip time to the origin server. This feature utilizes the ICP_SRC_RTT_FLAG (see Section B.3, "Option Flags").

8.1.3 Issues

Before rushing off to configure ICP on your caches, you need to be aware of certain issues and tradeoffs. ICP is not necessarily going to improve your cache's performance. If you're not careful, it can actually make things worse.

8.1.3.1 Delays

One of the benefits of caching is reduced wait time for web pages. A strange thing about ICP is that cache misses actually incur an additional delay during an ICP query/reply phase. The ICP transaction is very similar to gambling. If you get a HIT reply, then the gamble probably paid off. If, on the other hand, you get all MISS replies, then you lost the bet. The big question is: does ICP increase or decrease your overall object retrieval times in the long run? The answer depends on a number of factors, including the network distances to your neighbor caches and the speeds at which web objects are transferred from neighbors and origin servers.

If your neighbors are relatively close compared to the rest of the Internet, then the ICP delays represent a small gamble with a big payoff. If you win, you can perhaps download an object in 0.5 seconds instead of 5 seconds. If you lose, you've wasted perhaps only 0.05 seconds. Conversely, if your neighbor caches are not much closer than the rest of the Internet, ICP probably doesn't make sense. All downloads may still take 5 seconds on average, and the ICP misses probably add an additional 0.1- or 0.2-second delay.

Another important factor is the percentage of replies that are hits. In essence, this represents the probability of the gamble paying off. In practice, the ICP hit ratio is quite low—about 5%. Some caches achieve up to 10%, and some only get around 1%. The reason for this low percentage is that neighbor caches tend to store the same set of popular objects over time. The users of one cache request the same web pages as the users of another cache.

We can also approach this problem analytically. Given the following four variables, we can determine whether an ICP-based peering reduces average response times:

S_o

   Average HTTP service time from origin servers

S_n

   Average HTTP service time from neighbor caches

R_n

   Average ICP service time from neighbor caches

P

   ICP hit ratio

The average service time without ICP is simply:

$$S_o$$

The average service time with ICP is:

$$PS_n + (1 - P)S_o + R_n$$

We are interested in the case when:

$$PS_n + (1 - P)S_o + R_n < S_o$$

which reduces to:

$$P > \frac{R_n}{S_o - S_n}$$

In other words, when the ICP hit ratio is larger than the ratio of the ICP service time to the difference in the HTTP service times, then the benefits of the neighbor hits are greater than the costs of doing the ICP queries. If the ICP hit ratio is smaller than the service time ratio, using ICP does not reduce the overall service time for user requests.

Also note that some people use caches primarily for saving bandwidth, not for reducing service times. They probably don't mind the slight extra delay if it reduces their monthly bandwidth costs.

8.1.3.2 Bandwidth

Speaking of bandwidth, you may be wondering how much of it ICP consumes. It is quite easy to calculate the additional bandwidth ICP uses. The size of an ICP query is 24 bytes plus the length of the URL. The average URL length seems to be about 55 characters, so ICP queries average about 80 bytes. ICP replies are four bytes smaller than queries.

Taken together, an ICP query/reply transaction uses about 160 bytes per neighbor before including UDP and IP headers. A cache with 3 neighbors uses 480 bytes for each cache miss. To put this in perspective, consider that the average web object size is about 10 KB. Thus, a cache with three ICP neighbors increases its bandwidth consumption by about 5% on average. Note that this corresponds to a measurement made at the cache's network interface. Whether ICP increases your wide area bandwidth depends on the location of your neighbor caches.

8.1.3.3 False hits

Notice that an ICP query contains only a URL and none of the other HTTP headers from a client request. This is problematic because whether a given HTTP request is a hit or a miss depends on additional headers such as the `Cache-control: max-age`, `Accept-language`. ICP doesn't include enough information for a cache to make an accurate determination, which leads to false hits.

For example, consider two sibling caches and one object. The object does not exist in the first cache but has been cached by the second for the past two days. The following HTTP request arrives at the first cache:

```
GET http://www.foo.org/object.html HTTP/1.1
Cache-control: max-age=86400
```

The first cache sends an ICP query to the second for *http://www.foo.org/ object.html*. The second cache sends back an ICP HIT reply because it considers the object to be still fresh. When the first cache forwards the HTTP request to the second, there is a cache miss because of the `max-age` directive. The cached object is two days old, but the client is willing to accept only objects that have been cached for one day or less.

In addition to the solution outlined in Section 7.3.8, "False Hits," there are two ways to handle ICP-related false hits:

1. Configure the sibling cache to allow misses, even though it's not supposed to take them. This opens the door for potential abuse of the sibling cache.

2. Ensure that all sibling caches use the same configuration for determining whether a cached object is fresh or stale. This solution is not perfect, and it may work only with Squid, which sets the `max-age` value in outgoing requests based on its *refresh_pattern* configuration.

8.1.3.4 UDP

There are certain aspects of the User Datagram Protocol that make people uncomfortable. First of all, unlike TCP, UDP does not have any end-to-end congestion control. If TCP and UDP compete for bandwidth, UDP will win because TCP includes algorithms to back off. There is no built-in feedback mechanism to tell a UDP sender to slow down or stop. Using our previous example, 10 ICP messages per second to each of 3 neighbors generates about 38 Kbps (before UDP and IP headers). On medium- to high-capacity networks, ICP should cause no problems at all.

Another issue with UDP (and TCP) is datagram fragmentation. When a single IP packet exceeds a particular network's maximum transmission unit (MTU), it must be fragmented into smaller packets and then reassembled by the next hop or by the remote end. A well-known paper [Kent and Mogul, 1987] makes a strong case that fragmentation leads to inefficient use of resources such as bandwidth, memory, and processing power.

ICP messages are normally quite small, probably 80 bytes on average, which is well below any network's MTU size. When the HIT_OBJ feature is used, however, ICP replies may become quite large—up to 9 KB. With an MTU of 1,500 bytes, a 9 KB message is split into six fragments. If any one of these fragments is dropped, the entire ICP message is lost.

8.1.3.5 No request method

You may have noticed that ICP does not have a field for a request method. The GET method is implied for ICP queries. In other words, when a cache receives an ICP query for *http://www.web-cache.com*, it checks for a cached response from a "GET http://www.web-cache.com" request. This, of course, means that we cannot use ICP to query for cached responses from other request methods. At the present time, this is not a huge problem, because non-GET request methods are normally uncachable. If some new cachable request methods are invented in the future, we won't be able to use ICPv2 with them.

8.1.3.6 Queries for uncachable responses

Some people complain that ICP causes a lot of queries for uncachable objects. My data in Section A.7, "Cachability," shows that about 25% of web objects are uncachable. However, nothing about ICP requires a cache to make queries for these objects. The problem is that the cache doesn't always know which URLs are cachable and which are not.

Squid's implementation of ICP doesn't make queries for objects it knows are uncachable. Usually, this includes URLs with "cgi" or "?" in them. If the administrator has configured other uncachable rules, requests matching these won't be queried either. This is an easy thing to implement, but it catches only a subset of uncachable responses.

To prevent queries for other uncachable URLs, the cache could remember something about previously seen objects—in other words, an "uncachable cache." Thus, the cache remembers which URLs weren't cached before and doesn't make ICP queries for those URLs again.

Queries for uncachable objects may be desirable in some situations. In addition to providing hit/miss information, ICP can also help make forwarding decisions, even for uncachable objects. The source RTT measurement feature can tell a child cache which parent is the best choice for a given URL.

8.1.3.7 *Interoperation*

For the most part, different ICP implementations interoperate very well. The only exception is with a version that Network Appliance used in their products from 1996 to 2000. Whereas the majority of caching products use ICPv2 as described in the RFCs, Network Appliance's implementation was a little different. Primarily, they used 3 for the version number. In addition, they used the *Options* and *Option Data* fields for timestamps. Finally, Network Appliance's ICP messages always had the *Reqnum* field set to 0. These differences can significantly affect interoperation. Even though Network Appliance's current products use ICPv2, I'll describe how Squid interoperates with their version in case the older products are still in use.

Dealing with Network Appliance's timestamp fields is very easy. Squid knows those octets are not *Options* and *Option Data*, so it simply ignores them. This probably means that a Squid cache occasionally returns an ICP_OP_HIT when another Network Appliance cache would return an ICP_OP_MISS instead. For a parent relationship, that is not a big deal, but for a sibling relationship, it may cause some problems. Sibling relationships rely on accurate hit predictions to be effective. Returning an ICP hit instead of a miss in this case leads to false hits, which we discussed in Section 7.3.8, "False Hits."

The 0 *Reqnum* field turns out to be more of a problem for Squid. This is due to how Squid internally indexes its cache objects. In Squid, an object is either *public* or *private*. A public object has a key that can be found by any cache client, while a private object's key is known only to a single client. A key is made private by prepending a unique 32-bit integer to the URL. Only the client that originates the request knows that 32-bit identifier. An object always starts its life with a private key, but the key is changed to a public key if the response is cachable. The change is made when we receive the complete response headers. This scheme prevents a second client from getting a cache hit on a private, uncachable response while that response is being retrieved.

At the time when an ICP query is sent and the reply received, the cache key is still private. It won't be changed until after the HTTP request is sent. When the ICP reply arrives, we need to find the pending cache object to which it belongs. If the object key is private, then we need to know the 32-bit number to locate it. Not coincidentally, we put the identifier into the *Reqnum* field. Thus, a valid ICP reply has both the URL and the private identifier, which allows us to locate the pending cache entry.

If our cache neighbor is a Network Appliance box, however, the *Reqnum* is 0 in the ICP reply. This means Squid cannot find the cache entry corresponding to the reply message because the 32-bit identifier is missing. Squid has a workaround for this ugly problem. If it ever receives an ICP reply with a 0 *Reqnum*, then pending objects start out with a public cache key. Unfortunately, this means that two or more clients could receive a single response that should have been sent to only the first client.

8.1.3.8 Unwanted queries

When other people discover (or are under the false impression) that you have a caching proxy listening for ICP queries, they may configure your site as a neighbor without your permission. Your site is now subject to a constant stream of ICP queries from an unknown neighbor. This traffic is annoying because it consumes your bandwidth and CPU cycles. In some cases, getting it to stop can be quite difficult.

If you don't want to receive queries from unknown sites, you should configure your cache to respond with ICP_OP_DENIED messages. RFC 2187 recommends that caches stop sending queries to a neighbor when 95% or more of the replies are ICP_OP_DENIED. Unfortunately, it seems that some products do not have this safeguard and continue sending queries regardless.

You'll certainly know the IP address originating the queries. But how do you get in touch with a person at that site who will help you out? On most Unix systems, you can use the *host* command to find out if the IP address is associated with a hostname. Then you can send email to the *root* account at that host or domain. Unfortunately, many addresses don't resolve to hostnames. Furthermore, many individually run Unix sites aren't configured properly and *root*'s mail goes unread. You may need to use tools such as *traceroute* and the databases from ARIN (*http://www.arin.net*), RIPE (*http://www.ripe.net*), and APNIC (*http://www.apnic.net*) to track down persons responsible for that IP address.

If you get desperate, you can try blocking the queries with a filter on your router or an IP firewall rule on the host. Unfortunately, because ICP uses UDP, the sending site can't tell the difference between a blocked packet at your end and a network failure somewhere in the middle. The ICP client will probably continue sending queries under the assumption that the network is down. It expects the network to be repaired and wants to know immediately when it can talk to your cache again. In retrospect, the ICP RFCs should have mandated an exponential backoff algorithm in the event of packet loss.

8.1.4 Multicast ICP

Multicast ICP is a technique for efficient delivery of multireceiver traffic. Its development has been driven largely by the desire to support multimedia broadcasts on the Internet. Consider what happens with 100 people listening to an Internet radio station. If the station has to send data directly to each listener, each packet is transmitted 100 times. The station's bandwidth requirements increase in proportion to the number of listeners. But if the station uses multicast, each packet is sent only

once on any particular link. The packets are "copied" and replicated as necessary
by the routers between the sender and the receivers.

It turns out that we can use multicast with ICP. You may have noticed that nothing
in an ICP query message depends on the message's destination. A cache with four
neighbors sends the exact same query to each one. Although ICP messages are not
particularly large, some people would like to eliminate this redundancy. Multicast
offers a way for us to reach multiple neighbors by sending only one message.
However, multicasting ICP messages is not as straightforward as we would like. To
better understand how multicast ICP works, let's consider a group of six caches.
Instead of unicasting queries to each other, we want to use multicast.

One of the first things to do is select a multicast address for the group. The IANA
has reserved a large block of the IPv4 address space (224.0.0.0–239.255.255.255)
for multicast. Some care must be taken when selecting an address because we do
not want to select one already being used by some other application(s) on the
global Internet. Unfortunately, it is currently difficult, if not impossible, to find out
which addresses are being used at any given time. The IETF's Multicast Address
Allocation (MALLOC) working group is developing protocols and procedures to
address this issue. Until then, the best approach is to randomly select an address
from the multicast space. Given that there are 2^{28} multicast addresses, the probability of a collision is quite low. Once an address has been selected, we must configure the cache software to listen to that address so it receives multicast ICP
queries.

The next step is to configure the caches to send ICP queries to the multicast
group. We already know the IP address we send messages to. In addition, we
need to think about a multicast time-to-live (TTL) value. This parameter determines how far away our queries can travel. We'll see why this is important in just
a bit. Every multicast link in the Internet has a nonzero threshold. If a multicast
packet's TTL is greater than or equal to a link's threshold, then the packet may be
sent over that link. After a packet is sent, its TTL value is decremented by 1. Obviously, large TTL values allow packets to travel further than small ones. A small
value, such as 4 or 8, should keep all multicast queries within your organization's
network. The maximum possible TTL value is 128 and probably allows your
queries to be delivered to any host on the Internet that has joined your multicast
group. You can use the *mtrace* program to see the threshold values for a specific
multicast path. In the following example, a TTL of at least 10 hops is required to
reach the destination:

```
% mtrace -s uc
Mtrace from 141.142.121.5 to 132.249.40.200 via group 224.2.0.1
Querying full reverse path...
  0  oceana.sdsc.edu (132.249.40.200)
 -1  tigerfish.sdsc.edu (132.249.40.11)  PIM  thresh^ 1   [default]
```

```
  -2   medusa.sdsc.edu (132.249.30.10)  PIM/Special  thresh^ 6
  -3   cs-f-vbns.sdsc.edu (198.17.46.43)  Unknown protocol code 8  thresh^ 0
  -4   cs-atm0-0-2.ncsa.vbns.net (204.147.129.70)  PIM/Static  thresh^ 0
  -5   charlie-atm0-5.ncsa.uiuc.edu (141.142.11.2)  No route
  -6   uc.cache.nlanr.net (141.142.121.5)
Round trip time 502 ms; total ttl of 10 required.
```

Only ICP queries are sent via multicast. ICP replies are sent to unicast addresses for a couple of reasons. First, multicasting ICP replies does not reduce the amount of traffic in the network. ICP queries have a one-to-many property that fits nicely into IP multicast. Replies, however, are many-to-one, and multicast is of no help. Second, we sometimes rely on ICP to test the unicast path between a cache and a neighbor cache. Multicast and unicast routing paths may be significantly different. If there is a unicast routing problem, we would rather have the reply packet dropped so the neighbor cache is automatically eliminated from the selection process.

IP multicast does not have any built-in security mechanisms. Anyone connected to the Internet is allowed to send and receive multicast messages on any group. This has some interesting consequences for ICP. If your caches send ICP queries with a large TTL value, and if I know your multicast group address, I may be able to passively "snoop" on your cache traffic. By receiving all of your ICP queries, I know which web sites your users are visiting. If my application only receives and never responds, you will probably never know that I am listening. If I also respond to the multicast queries, then another problem arises. The cache that originates a query suddenly receives a reply from an unknown neighbor. A cache should not implicitly trust any host that sends ICP replies; the unknown neighbor's intentions may be malicious. Caches must accept ICP replies only from known and trusted neighbors.

Because of the above problems, I usually discourage people from using multicast ICP. Multicast itself is often difficult to work with. In my experience, the infrastructure is fragile; it works one day but not the next. Debugging is time-consuming. The privacy and security issues are significant and probably outweigh the bandwidth you'll save. To the best of my knowledge, multicast ICP is rarely used today.

8.2 CARP

CARP is an algorithm and not a protocol per se. It was designed to address a particular problem: how to achieve efficient and scalable load balancing while maximizing hit ratios and minimizing latency. It is useful in situations where a proxy caching service consists of a number of machines tightly clustered together. For example, a large ISP may need five web caches to handle all the traffic from their customers. Given a cache cluster or array, how can we distribute the load among the members?

One technique is known as DNS round-robin. Each cache has its own IP address, but all are listed under a single hostname. For example:

```
$ORIGIN us.ircache.net.
bo                    IN      A       192.52.106.30
                      IN      A       192.52.106.31
```

A DNS server, such as BIND, cycles the order of the addresses for every lookup. When one client asks for *bo.us.ircache.net*, it receives the answer (192.52.106.30, 192.52.106.31). The next client that asks gets the same addresses in a different order: (192.52.106.31, 192.52.106.30).* Clients normally try the first IP address in the list. They'll try the next address only if there is a failure with the first. With this technique, each cache should receive about half of the the requests.

The drawback to this approach is that client requests are randomly assigned among the member caches. One client may request *http://www.web-cache.com* from cache A, while another requests the same URL from cache B, thereby missing the opportunity for a cache hit. Of course, the caches can use ICP among themselves to get cache hits from each other, but this adds some delay. Furthermore, the member caches become nearly identical over time.

URL hashing, as described in Section 4.3.2, "Sample PAC Scripts," is better than DNS round-robin because it deterministically partitions all URLs among the set of caches. However, it also has a couple of annoying problems. It is easy to split the load equally among all caches, but anything more sophisticated (such as 10%/30%/60%) is awkward to implement. Second, adding or removing a group member causes a significant readjustment of the URL-to-cache mapping. Because of the modulo function, adding one cache to a set of N means that the mapping changes for N out of each N+1 URLs. Increasing the number of caches from four to five members displaces 80% of all cached objects.

CARP addresses this last problem with a creative, if not complicated, algorithm. For a given request, CARP calculates a score for every proxy cache. The request is forwarded to the proxy with the highest score. If this fails, then the second-highest scoring cache is tried. The score is a calculation based on a hash of the URL, a hash of the cache's name, and weights assigned to each cache. The important characteristic is that adding a new cache to the array does not change the relative ranking of the scores for the other caches; instead, the new cache creates new scores. Statistically, the new scores will be higher than the existing caches' scores for a fraction of the URLs that is proportional to the cache's weight within the array.

---

* You can see this for yourself by running *host www.cnn.com* on your Unix system.

CARP also specifies a file format for a *Proxy Array Membership Table.* This table allows clients to figure out which caches belong to a group. The table may be accessed via web protocols (HTTP) so many clients can easily retrieve the information.

The CARP algorithm may be used by any web client, such as a browser or proxy cache, that needs to choose among a set of caches. Note, however, that it only works for parent relationships because CARP does not predict cache hits. Another minor problem with CARP is related to persistent HTTP connections. A client that makes four requests may use more TCP connections with CARP than it would without. Finally, also note that CARP has linear scaling properties (similar to ICP) because a score must be calculated for every group member.

At the time of this writing, CARP is documented only as an Internet draft, which is now expired. The details of this document are included in Appendix C. Whether CARP advances to become a more formal standard remains to be seen. The document authors, Vinod Valloppillil of Microsoft and Keith W. Ross of the University of Pennsylvania, have not been actively pushing for its adoption recently. Both Squid and the Microsoft Proxy products implement CARP. The draft document mentions that CARP can be implemented as a proxy autoconfiguration script (see Section 4.3, "Proxy Auto-Configuration Script"), but none is provided.

8.3 HTCP

CARP addresses some of ICP's problems, but it is not an option for everyone. If you want to have sibling relationships, or even parent relationships with loosely-defined groups, you still need a way to predict cache hits. HTCP was designed to improve upon ICP's weaknesses. Both are per-request query/response protocols, and both use UDP for transport. This, however, is where the similarities end.

Recall from Section 8.1.3.3, "False hits," that false hits can be a serious problem for ICP, especially in sibling relationships. HTCP solves this problem by sending full HTTP headers (not just the URI) in requests and responses. Thus, if the client's HTTP request includes headers such as Cache-control: max-age, the HTCP server is able to reply correctly with a hit or miss.

HTCP also includes most of the features that are experimental in ICP. For example, with HTCP one cache can ask another to delete or update a particular object. It also has a monitoring feature whereby one cache tells another (in real time) about objects added, refreshed, replaced, and deleted. Unlike ICP, HTCP supports relatively strong authentication by use of a shared secret key and MD5 hashing. This allows a receiver to be confident that a message was actually sent by the correct party.

HTCP is documented as an experimental RFC (2756). It is also described in Appendix D.

8.3.1 Issues

If you look at the HTCP specification, you'll see that it is significantly more complex than ICP. The message structure is relatively rich, and there are numerous variable-size fields in any given message. The complex message structure necessitates additional system resources, namely processing power. This may effectively limit the rate at which a cache can send and receive HTCP queries.

Another potential problem is that an HTCP TST response should include the HTTP response and entity headers. Unless the headers are stored in memory, it may take a significant amount of time to read them from disk. An HTCP server implementation must therefore choose to either return partial headers quickly or full headers with a much higher latency. Which is more important: accuracy or speed?

Because HTCP also uses UDP for transport, it shares some problems with ICP. UDP is not congestion-controlled. Small UDP messages cause certain inefficiencies in the network. Large messages are undesirable too because we don't want them to be fragmented. In measurements with Squid, the mean size of an HTCP query is 520 bytes, while the median is 475 bytes. HTCP replies, on the other hand, are almost always 20 bytes because Squid does not store headers in memory. Recall from the previous section that ICP queries and replies average about 80 bytes.

8.4 Cache Digests

Two of the protocols discussed so far, ICP and HTCP, incur a lookup delay for every cache miss. Before a cache miss can be forwarded, the selection process takes about one network round-trip time to query the neighbor caches. Depending on the proximity of the neighbor caches, this could take anywhere from 10 to 300 milliseconds. Such a delay can be significant, especially for a web page with many embedded images.

The lookup delay exists because a cache doesn't know a priori which neighbors hold a particular object. Furthermore, it cannot predict which, if any, would return a cache hit for the object. If we can give a cache this advance knowledge about its neighbors, then we can eliminate the delays. We want the best of both worlds: hit predictions without delays.

As mentioned previously, CARP has no forwarding delays. However, it does not meet our requirements because the next-hop cache is chosen based solely on the requested URL. CARP does not care whether the request will be a cache hit or miss. This means, for example, that CARP is not usable in a sibling relationship.

To predict hits in a neighbor, a cache needs to know which objects are stored there. A neighbor's cache contents can be represented as a database or directory. These directories must be exchanged between neighbors. By looking up objects in the directory, we can predict cache hits. Since a cache's content changes over time, the directories must also be updated. A primary goal of our new protocol is to make the transmission and storage of this directory as efficient as possible.

Probably the worst we could do is use a plain list of cached URLs. The average URL length is about 55 bytes, or 440 bits. The URL list is poor choice for a directory because URLs are an inefficient representation—they use only printable characters, and some sequences appear very frequently. In information theory terms, URLs have a low amount of entropy. A better option is to use a list of hash values of the URLs. With hash values, we may have collisions where two or more URLs have the same hash value. A collision's probability is related to the hash value range and the number of URLs in the list. For a cache of about one million objects, we probably need 24 to 32 bits per object. That's a significant reduction in directory size compared with 440 bits per object in a URL list. Believe it or not, we can do even better. With an algorithm known as a *Bloom filter*, storage is reduced to only a few bits per object.

8.4.1 Bloom Filters

The Bloom filter algorithm, first described by Burton Bloom in 1970, encodes a set of input keys with the help of some hash functions. Recall that a hash function is simply an algorithm that takes a chunk of data as input (the *key*) and produces an integer as output. A good hash function has the characteristic of being random. That is, given a sufficiently large number of input keys, the output values should have an apparently random distribution. Another hash function characteristic is the range of its output. Often, the range is expressed as a power of 2, such as 32 bits or 2^{32}. One of the most often used hash functions is called *MD5*, which is short for Message Digest (Version 5) [Rivest, 1992]. The MD5 hash function outputs 128-bit values and is used extensively in the current Cache Digest implementation.

A Bloom filter is defined by two parameters, K independent hash functions and an array of M bits. The bits of the filter are used to efficiently encode a collection of N items. For a Cache Digest, the collection is the set of object keys (URIs or URLs) stored in a cache. To construct a Bloom filter, we iterate over the items in the collection. Applying the K hash functions to each item gives us K hash values. Each hash value represents a bit position in the filter that should be turned on. If a hash value is larger than M, we apply the modulus operator to keep it in range. Note that M should be less than the hash function range; otherwise, some bits can never be turned on.

After all items have been added, the filter should consist of approximately equal numbers of 1's and 0's. Note that more than one key can turn on the same bit. (Of course, a bit can only be turned on once. In other words, once a bit is turned on, it remains on.) This property means that it is not possible to delete an item from the filter. A given bit may be on due to multiple items. Clearing the bit removes all of these items from the filter.

Let's look at a simple example to get a better handle on Bloom filters. Assume that we have four hash functions called H1, H2, H3, and H4, and a filter size of 2^{20} bits. We want to add an object, in this case a URL, to the filter. Our sample URL is *http://www.squid-cache.org*. Step one is to apply our four hash functions to the URL. Step two is to take the modulus of each value by 1,048,576. Finally, step three is just to turn on the bits in the corresponding positions. Table 8.1 shows the values for this example.

Table 8.1. Bloom Filter Example

Hash Function	Step 1 Value	Step 2 Value
H1	4,107,498,967	226,775
H2	2,692,669,443	974,851
H3	3,532,948,500	295,956
H4	991,683,655	779,335

After the filter has been populated, we can look up specific objects using the same procedure. We apply the same four hash functions to the URI in question and end up with four bit positions. If at least one of these bits is off, we know the URI is not present. If all of the bits are on, then there is some probability that the URI is present.

We cannot conclude that an item is present even though all K bits are on. Consider the following contrived example: the key "A" turns on bits 1, 2, 5, and 9. The key "B" turns on bits 3, 6, 7, and 11. Now we test for the presence of key "C," which corresponds to bits 2, 5, 6, and 11. Even though "C" was not added to the filter, we will find all of C's bits on. This occurrence, known as a *false positive*, is the price we pay for the Bloom filter's compact representation. The probability that a lookup will be a false positive depends on the size of the filter, the number of hash functions, and the number of items in the collection. Bloom's paper [Bloom, 1970] gives some formulas that relate all of these parameters. In particular, this probability is:

$$\left(1 - \left(1 - \frac{K}{M} \right)^N \right)^K$$

For large values of M, this simplifies to:

$$\left(1 - e^{\frac{-KN}{M}}\right)^K$$

For example, with $K = 4$, and $\dfrac{N}{M} = 0.2$, the false positive probability is 9.2%.*

8.4.2 Comparing Digests and ICP

How do Cache Digests and ICP compare in terms of network bandwidth? We know that a Cache Digest is a very efficient encoding of a cache's contents, but that doesn't mean it uses less bandwidth. The Cache Digest protocol uses bandwidth in proportion to the size of a cache. ICP, on the other hand, uses bandwidth in proportion to the rate of cache requests. This means, for example, that ICP uses less bandwidth during idle periods, whereas Cache Digests probably use the same amount during idle and busy times.

We can do some simple calculations to estimate when it makes sense to switch from ICP to Cache Digests. First, let's define our parameters: S is the cache size in gigabytes, L is the mean object size in kilobytes, T is the digest update period in hours, and R is the average ICP query rate *per peer* in queries per second. Let's also assume the cache digest is sized at 5 bits per cache object, and the average ICP message size is 80 bytes. Then, the bandwidth that Cache Digests uses is given in bytes/second as:

$$\frac{5}{8} \times \frac{S}{L} \times \frac{2^{20}}{3600T}$$

The ICP bandwidth is:

$$2 \times 80 \times R$$

Equating these two, substituting 10 KB for L, and solving for R, we get:

$$R = \frac{S}{8.8T}$$

Given a cache size S and digest update period T, we can now calculate the ICP query rate that uses the same amount of bandwidth. For example, a 20 GB cache

---

* Bloom's formula requires that K distinct bits are turned on for each input key. In Cache Digests, two or more hash functions could have the same value for a single input key, and thus fewer than K bits could be turned on. The probability of this occurring is the inverse of the filter size, i.e., on the order of 10^{-6} for a typical cache.

with a 1-hour digest update period uses the same bandwidth as 2.3 ICP queries per second. If the query rate exceeds 2.3 ICP queries per second, then Cache Digests uses less bandwidth than ICP.

ICP and Cache Digests also differ significantly in their usage of system resources. For the most part, ICP requires little CPU processing, except for copying buffers and building packets. Cache Digests, on the other hand, may require more of the CPU because of the hash function calculations. The major difference, however, is in memory usage. ICP is stateless and therefore uses no memory. Digests, of course, require a moderate amount of memory. A cache may store its own digest on disk, but it must keep all of its neighbors' digests in memory for fast lookups. Cache Digest memory usage scales linearly with the number of neighbors.

Cache Digests eliminate the annoying per-request delays from ICP but introduce another potential source of delay. A sibling relationship that uses Cache Digests experiences some fraction of false hits. In these cases, the first cache must re-forward its request to another server. Most likely, the delays due to cache digest false hits are negligible compared to ICP delays. It may be difficult to quantify the delay caused by a false hit, but we can assume it is on the order of one network round-trip, just like an ICP query. Since false hits occur in a small percentage of cases, whereas ICP delays every request, we're already ahead by using digests. Furthermore, since ICP also may cause false hits, we're even better off with digests. Finally, remember that digest false hits cause a delay only for sibling relationships.

8.5 *Which Protocol to Use*

The four protocols and algorithms presented here each have unique features and characteristics. Which one you should use depends on numerous factors. The following guidelines may help to determine the best protocol for your particular situation.

ICP may be a good choice if you need to interoperate with products from different vendors. Since ICP has been around longer than the others, it is supported in most caching products. It is also a reasonable choice if you want to build or connect into a small mesh of caches. You want to avoid having too many neighbors with ICP; try to limit yourself to no more than five or six. ICP may not be a good choice if you are very concerned about security, and it may be all but useless on networks with high delays and/or a large amount of congestion. The protocol has no authentication mechanisms and may be susceptible to address spoofing. Finally, you probably cannot use ICP if there is a firewall between you and your neighbor caches because firewalls typically block UDP traffic by default.

CARP is a logical choice if you have multiple parent caches administered by a single organization. For example, some large service providers may have a cluster of proxy caches located where they connect to the rest of the Internet. If this applies to you, make sure you always have up-to-date configuration information. CARP is the only protocol that does not allow you to create sibling relationships.

HTCP has characteristics similar to ICP. You can use HTCP for small cache meshes and where network conditions are good. Unlike ICP, HTCP has relatively strong authentication. This may be particularly important if you need the object deletion features. HTCP should cause fewer false hits than ICP because hit/miss decisions are based on full HTTP headers rather than only the URI. Note that HTCP messages are about five times larger than ICP, so it uses more bandwidth.

You should use Cache Digests if you can afford to trade increased memory usage for lower forwarding delays. The bandwidth tradeoffs of Cache Digests versus ICP depend on many factors. You should apply the formulas in Section 8.4.2, "Comparing Digests and ICP," to your particular situation. You cannot really use Cache Digests over slow network connections because the transfer of a large digest saturates the link. Cache Digests probably result in a higher percentage of false hits compared to ICP. Even so, overall client response times should be lower, and false hits are only a concern for sibling relationships.

9

Cache Clusters

A *cache cluster* is a group of separate caching proxies configured to act like a single server. In other words, even though there are many machines in the cluster, clients and users perceive it as a single unit.

A cluster is different from a hierarchy or mesh in some subtle ways. Primarily, the members of a cluster are typically located together, both physically and topologically, for example, with servers in the same room and on the same subnet. Since a cluster appears as a single system, a single organization has administrative control over all the machines. A hierarchy, on the other hand, often involves multiple locations and multiple organizations.

Why would you need a cluster? Many companies use cache clusters to serve or cache more pages and provide redundant service. Let's say you're already using a certain caching product you really like, but your traffic load is increasing, and the service is becoming slow. You need to upgrade, but you don't want to discard your current product. You can double your capacity if you buy a second server and create a small cluster. As mentioned earlier, if a cache is down, users may not be able to surf the Web. In a cache cluster, if one server fails unexpectedly, the other(s) can absorb the additional load.

This chapter covers three different reasons for clustering. We'll start with ways to provide redundancy and not worry about additional capacity. Then we'll focus on techniques for distributing load among multiple machines. Some of the load-sharing methods waste bandwidth, so we'll also look at ways to optimize a cluster for bandwidth savings.

9.1 The Hot Spare

One way to provide redundancy is to have a second cache available on standby. In normal operation, all the traffic goes to the primary cache; if the primary fails, the secondary takes over. This arrangement is not exactly a cluster, since just one of the caches is active at any one time. However, the techniques for clustering and redundancy are similar.

You can use the DNS to support a hot spare. Your users configure their browsers with a hostname for the caching proxy service. You specify the primary cache's IP address in the DNS zone file. If the primary fails, simply change the DNS file to use the secondary's IP address. Manually updating the DNS zone files is a big drawback to this technique. If you're brave enough, you might be able to automate the process with some scripts. For example, if the primary cache doesn't respond to pings, swap zone files and restart *named*. Any DNS-based technique also requires relatively low TTL values (e.g., five minutes) for the cache's address record. Some user agents will continue using the old address until its TTL expires. Another drawback is that some users might enter the cache's IP address rather than the hostname. Those users' traffic always goes to one of the caches, regardless of the DNS configuration.

Another simple approach is to give two caches the same IP address, but connect only one at a time to the network. If the primary fails, just unplug its network cable and replace it with the secondary. Alternatively, for a Unix-based system, you can use *ifconfig* to enable and disable interfaces without touching network cables. Again, this method requires manual intervention or, in the case of *ifconfig*, some carefully written scripts. There is also an issue with ARP—the protocol that maps IP addresses to Ethernet addresses. When you enable the secondary machine, other devices on the subnet won't be able to talk to it until their ARP caches time out, which usually takes a minute or so.

A number of products are available that can automatically provide faster and smoother failover to backup systems. These are the same products listed in Table 5.1 (i.e., layer four switches). You can configure them for interception or with a *virtual server* address. You also tell the switch the real IP addresses for the primary and backup caches. Normally, it forwards all connections to the primary. If the switch determines that the primary is down, it uses the backup instead. Since users always talk to the virtual server, there are no issues with the DNS or ARP cache timeouts.

The hot spare technique has some characteristics that make it unpopular. Primarily, the secondary system probably sits idle most of the time. Those resources (CPU, disk, memory) are hardly being utilized at all. It's somewhat wasteful to have the box powered up but not doing anything useful. Another concern is that the secondary cache could fail and the failure go unnoticed until the secondary was actually needed. For these reasons, many people prefer a load sharing configuration rather than a hot standby. The remainder of this chapter talks about load sharing configurations.

9.2 Throughput and Load Sharing

A cache cluster with load sharing can improve both throughput and reliability. Throughput is increased because N caches can handle more traffic than just one. Reliability is increased because when one cache fails, the other cluster members absorb the increased load.

The really cheap way to implement load sharing is with the DNS. You simply list the IP addresses of all members under a single host name. Most DNS resolver libraries change the order of the addresses for each lookup. Thus, requests are sent to the caches in a round-robin fashion. This technique provides very rudimentary failover when one cache goes down. When a browser cannot connect to one of the IP addresses, it should try the next one in the list. Unfortunately, this can take a long time (up to two minutes), and browsers don't usually remember which addresses don't work.

A more robust approach, if you can afford it, is to use a layer four switch or dedicated load balancing product (see Table 5.1). These products have a number of load sharing algorithms (see Section 5.2.2, "Layer Four Switches") and generally do a better job of spreading the load among cluster members. Furthermore, users are less likely to experience delays or other problems if one member fails.

You may notice that I am intentionally avoiding the word *balance*. Some of the load sharing techniques may not distribute the load evenly among caches. The DNS-based approach is difficult to predict and control. One or two really busy clients could send all their requests to one of the caches, possibly overloading it. Layer four switches can be configured to partition requests based on IP addresses—either the source or the destination. A busy client or popular server can cause one cache to receive many more requests than the others.

Random mapping between clients and caches also causes some problems for session tracking. A number of web services (origin servers) assume that all requests from a single user come from the same IP address. They get confused if different HTTP requests that belong to a single session come from multiple addresses. It seems that these origin servers are clustered as well. A layer four switch sits in front of them and distributes requests based on the client's IP address. When the user logs in, its authentication request is sent to one of the origin servers. This sets up some state information on that server so subsequent requests are allowed. But if the subsequent requests go to a different server, they are denied. To accommodate client-side clustering, the server-side layer four switch needs to be aware of the session information (i.e., cookies). This type of so-called *layer seven* switching is increasingly common for distributed servers. However, you may still encounter a service that uses address-based distribution and won't work with your cache cluster.

9.3 *Bandwidth*

Note that with the configurations discussed so far, we haven't talked about sending specific requests to specific caches. We also haven't talked about using an inter-cache protocol to search for cache hits. A simple load sharing configuration results in wasted disk space and bandwidth. Space is wasted because the same response can be stored in multiple caches. Bandwidth is wasted because we don't always need to forward a cache miss if we know one of the other members has a particular response saved.

There are two ways to improve the disk and bandwidth utilization of a cache cluster. One is to partition requests before they enter the cluster. That is, some device or algorithm makes sure that the same request always goes to the same member. The second way is to create sibling relationships between the caches and use an intercache protocol to locate previously cached responses. In this case, we don't really care which cache initially receives a particular request.

Recall from Chapter 8 that ICP and HTCP are UDP-based, per-query object location protocols. They work well for a small cluster with five or fewer members. ICP uses smaller packets than HTCP at the expense of being less accurate. Both ICP and HTCP add some latency to cache misses while querying the neighbors. However, this should not be a significant problem for a highly localized cluster with plenty of local-area bandwidth.

Cache digests are an alternative to ICP and HTCP. They eliminate per-request delays but require more memory. In a sibling relationship, digests probably consume more local area bandwidth than ICP, but this is not an issue for most environments.

Note that the intercache protocols do not address the problem of storing a response in more than one cache. By default, when one cache gets a response from its sibling, the response is saved in both caches. Some products, such as Squid, have the option never to store responses received through a sibling or parent.

There are a number of techniques and products that partition requests and assign them to specific cluster members. Cisco's WCCP is designed to do this. The router applies a hash function to the destination IP address; the hash value corresponds to one of 256 buckets, which specifies the cluster member for that address. If the member happens to be down, the router forwards the request directly to the origin server.

Layer four switches have similar functionality. The destination address is hashed, and the resulting value is used to select one of the real cache servers. If one of the caches goes down, the switch can either bypass it or redistribute the load among the remaining caches. Many products also have *URL switching* features. Rather than use the destination address, the switch calculates the hash function over the URL or some other part of an HTTP request. URL switching should result in a more evenly balanced distribution of load. It also allows you to bypass the cache cluster for uncachable responses, such as *cgi-bin* requests. Since URL hashing requires more of the switch's resources than address hashing, the peak throughput for URL hashing may be lower.

CARP is another good way to partition requests throughout a cluster. The best thing about CARP is that it minimizes the reallocation of requests when you add or subtract a cluster member. One of the difficult things about CARP is deciding where to implement it. Browsers can implement CARP directly, with a proxy auto-configuration script, for example. In this case, only the properly configured JavaScript-capable browsers forward requests based on CARP. HTTP requests from nonbrowser clients won't know about the cache array. Another option is to have a number of first-level caching proxies that intercept HTTP connections. These can forward requests to a cluster of parent caches using CARP.

10

Design Considerations for Caching Services

As someone looking to design or purchase a caching system for your organization, you have many options and many decisions to make. Numerous companies now offer caching products, and all of them would love to sell you theirs. The purpose of this chapter is to help you pick a product that meets your needs. We'll focus on hardware configurations and product features rather than specific products and vendors.

10.1 Appliance or Software Solution

For the most part, caching products can be classified into appliances and software solutions. Choosing an appliance means that the hardware and software come bundled together as a single product. With a software solution, on the other hand, you buy the hardware from a different company or perhaps use some equipment you already have. Appliances are usually designed to run just one application— the web cache. Both types have their advantages and disadvantages.

10.1.1 Appliances

Many people are attracted to appliances because they tend to be easier to install and maintain. The software comes preloaded on the hardware. You don't have to think about disk space, file permissions, startup scripts, etc. Often, the product is up and running after you provide a few basic configuration details, such as the box's IP address, hostname, default route, and DNS server.

Appliances usually have a nice graphical interface for administration. That is, you simply use your web browser to configure and administer the cache. The interface probably also includes real-time graphs that show you current load, disk usage, and other useful metrics.

Another benefit of an appliance is that you don't have to worry about hardware compatibility or drivers. You can be sure that all components of the system work together. When buying your own system, you might end up with the wrong type of memory, for example, or the operating system may not support your particular network card.

Often, an appliance's operating system is optimized and customized for its particular hardware or task. For example, the product may use a specialized filesystem specifically designed for 9 GB SCSI LVD disks. Another likely optimization is to have a tighter integration between the network and the application. Copying data buffers between layers is a potential source of delay. Eliminating those copies improves the product's performance.

Until recently, it was rare to find an appliance that used *ssh* for remote access. Telnet was the only option for a long time. Now it seems like most of the appliance products have adopted *ssh* as well. Even so, a general-purpose operating system may give you more security features than an appliance. With *ssh* on Unix, for example, you can require or deny certain types of encryption, key formats, and so on. Additionally, most Unix systems now have extensive packet filtering capabilities not likely to be found on appliances. On the plus side, appliance vendors should be very responsive to known security problems. You may not be able to receive software updates without a support contract, however.

In general, an appliance is more difficult to customize. You won't have access to the operating system or be able to run additional services on the cache machine.

You might have a difficult time upgrading an appliance. If you need more disk space, for instance, any number of problems might surface. Higher capacity disks may not be available for your particular model. Some appliances are designed to be very small and may not have open slots for additional network or disk controllers. If you need more processing power, you may not be able to upgrade just the CPU. Also note that your warranty or license may not allow you to upgrade the hardware yourself, even if you know how. These issues are perhaps less important for small, cheap appliances because you can simply add more units to expand your capacity.

The following companies offer appliances: Network Appliance, InfoLibria, Cisco, CacheFlow, Lucent, iMimic, IBM, Dell, Compaq, and Inktomi. A number of companies sell appliance products based on Squid. For a current listing, visit *http://www.squid-cache.org/products.html*.

10.1.2 Software

If you decide on a software solution, then you must buy the necessary hardware on your own. If you're lucky, you may already have some hardware you can use. When buying your own hardware, there is a risk that some of the components are not well matched. For example, you might get too much disk space and not enough memory, or you may spend too much money on an overly powerful CPU. There is also some risk of incompatibility. Your operating system might not support Gigabit Ethernet cards, or you might get the wrong type of memory.

The software solution allows you to reuse your hardware for other purposes. If you invest a lot of money in appliances and later decide you don't like them, you may be stuck with unusable equipment. Your general-purpose hardware retains some value even if you don't use it for caching. Also, it might make sense for you to run additional services, such as DNS and email, on your caching hardware. This reduces the number of boxes you have to administer.

The software approach allows you to choose hardware and operating systems that you are comfortable with. Your company may have invested a lot of time and expertise in a specific platform, such as Digital Unix or Solaris. Furthermore, you may have a good business relationship with certain vendors. If your company is large enough, then you probably get good discounts on hardware and support contracts.

A software solution allows you to customize many aspects of the system. For example, you can write your own scripts to analyze and archive log files. For additional security, you can utilize packet filtering features of the operating system or use third-party applications.

Open source products such as Squid offer another level of customization. If you are so inclined, you can add your own features, change some hardcoded values, and even fix some bugs.

On the other hand, a general-purpose operating system is probably not tuned and optimized for proxy caching. Historically, proxy caches that run on Windows or Unix have used the native filesystems (i.e., NTFS, UFS). Soon we will see more software solutions that have their own filesystems. Even so, general-purpose operating systems have a lot of code, including drivers, that could be optimized or simply removed for a system dedicated to proxy caching.

A software solution may be easier to debug because you have full access to the operating system. You can use native tools to monitor disk performance, CPU utilization, memory usage, etc. For example, you might find it useful to run *tcpdump* when debugging network problems.

You are likely to spend more time administering a software solution than an appliance. With an appliance, the operating system basically takes care of itself. A software product, on the other hand, requires you to create users, monitor disk usage, write *cron* jobs, etc. You also need to stay up-to-date with bug fixes and security patches from the operating system provider.

Finally, software products may be easier to expand and upgrade, especially if you use inexpensive PC hardware. You should have few problems upgrading to a faster CPU, getting more memory, and adding additional disk drives.

Squid is available as software (source code , although a number of companies sell Squid-based appliances. The following companies sell software products: Netscape, Microsoft, Novell (Border Manager), and Inktomi.

10.2 Disk Space

When buying or building a proxy cache, it is important to have enough disk space. If your disk size is too small, then your cache replaces valuable objects that otherwise would result in cache hits. It's okay to have too much disk space, but after some point, adding more space does not significantly increase your hit ratio. Figuring out the right amount of disk space is complicated because you must consider a number of parameters and overheads. The following advice should help you get started.

As a rule of thumb, your cache should take at least three days to fill up. This magic number of three days comes from empirical observations and analysis of real Web traffic. It is essentially the average time that particular web objects remain popular and valuable. To find out how much disk space we can fill in three days, we need to perform a number of calculations, beginning with the rate that HTTP traffic enters your organization's network.

Ideally, you already have a sense of how much HTTP traffic comes into your network. We're looking for a number with units of bytes per second, averaged over a 24-hour period. Any network measurement tool should be able to give you a breakdown by port number. Here, we're mostly interested in port 80 traffic, although there is likely to be a small amount of HTTP traffic on other ports as well. If you have no idea, you can use your network connection speed as an upper limit. For example, lets say that your company has two T1 connections to the Internet. Together, these can carry about 3 Mbps, or 375 KB per second. If your company is typical, then 60% of your total traffic is HTTP. If you suspect your company is not typical in this regard, then adjust accordingly. Given two (saturated!) T1s, we can assume a 24-hour average HTTP traffic rate of 225 KB/second.

Remember that we're interested in how quickly the cache fills up. Thus, we have to account for cache hits, which do not cause objects to be written to disk. If your organization is small, you can expect a 25% byte hit ratio. Medium-sized organizations can expect 35%, and large ones can expect 45% or higher. To get the HTTP miss traffic rate, we multiply the total rate by the miss ratio, which is the opposite of the hit ratio. Let's say our two T1s service a medium-sized organization. Our HTTP miss rate is 225 × 65%, or about 150 KB/second.

Next, we also need to account for the fact that some HTTP requests are not cachable. On an average site, roughly 20% of cache misses are not cachable. Thus, we subtract that 20% from the HTTP miss rate. In our example, we now have 117 KB/second.

Now we know the HTTP cachable miss rate, or the cache fill rate, in terms of bytes/sec. To find out how much space we need, we simply multiply by 3 days. Continuing our example, 117 KB/second × 3 days × 86,400 seconds/day comes out to about 30 GB.

If you are specifying a cache for the first time, you probably want to add some extra capacity for future growth. In most cases, doubling the size estimate based on three days of current traffic should provide you with plenty of capacity for the next year or two.

Keep in mind that the formula calculates cache storage size, not physical disk size. This is particularly important if you are using a software solution. Your software solution may use the operating system's favorite filesystem, and some of the disk space is lost to overheads such as inodes, directories, file allocation tables, etc. It's a good idea to increase your estimate by 25% for these overheads. Also remember that hard drive vendors cheat when they tell you about disk sizes. The vendor may say 20 GB, but your operating system reports 18 GB, even before formatting.

Finally, keep these points in mind when going through this calculation:

- Bandwidth estimates are averaged over a 24-hour period, which is probably different from your peak utilization.

- These are only guidelines, not requirements. If you can't afford a huge amount of disk space, a smaller cache is still useful.

- Any of the preceding numbers (e.g., hit ratio, cachable ratio) are probably different for your organization. Unfortunately, you won't have exact figures until you install a proxy cache and take your own measurements.

10.3 *Memory*

Caching products vary greatly in how they use RAM. Some caches, notably Squid, keep a number of indexes in memory. The indexes have an entry for every cache object, such that index memory requirements are proportional to cache size. Most caching products also use memory to store popular or recently requested objects. Storing popular objects entirely in memory results in a performance improvement. Caches also use memory to pass data to and from the network. The amount of memory used for network buffers is proportional to the load on the system.

Memory starvation can be a serious problem. It is certainly serious for Unix-based solutions, such as Squid. When the application needs more memory than is physically available, some of the process memory is written to disk. Performance degrades very quickly when swapping occurs.

If you're thinking about an appliance-based solution, you probably don't have to worry about memory configurations. The product should come with an appropriate amount of memory, based on the particular software and other hardware components. If additional memory is available for your product, it may boost the cache's performance by holding extra objects in memory.

If you're using a software-based product, you'll need to find out the amount of memory the vendor recommends. Current versions of Squid require a lot of memory compared to other products (including appliances). For Squid, I typically recommend 1 MB of RAM for every 32 MB of disk capacity. A significant amount of Squid's memory usage is for storing pointers in an index. Some CPUs, such as the DEC Alpha, have 64-bit pointers, which further increases memory requirements.

10.4 *Network Interfaces*

These days, 100-megabit Ethernet is the most common network media in use. Every caching product supports 100-megabit Ethernet, and it is probably sufficient for most situations. In tests that I have done, 100baseTX achieves about 90 Mbps in both directions (full duplex). For typical web traffic, this corresponds to a request rate of about 1,000 per second. A 100-megabit network interface is not going to be a bottleneck for speeds up to dual T3's.

Gigabit Ethernet is available with many caching products as well. In a few years, Gigabit Ethernet is likely to replace 100-megabit Ethernet as the de facto standard.

Less popular network interfaces, such as FDDI and ATM, may be available as well. If you're thinking of a software solution, then certainly you can make your own choices for networking hardware. If you're looking at appliances and don't want to use Ethernet, check with the vendor to see what else is available.

10.5 Operating Systems

The operating system may or may not be a deciding factor in your particular situation. With an appliance, you don't have to worry about the operating system at all. A software product, however, requires that you manage the operating system yourself. This probably includes tasks such as adding users, monitoring disk usage, and applying security patches.

Some organizations start with the operating system as a requirement and then look for products that run on it. For example, if you run Windows NT on all of your systems, you probably want to find an NT-based caching proxy. In other cases, your hardware determines your operating system. Sun hardware almost always runs Solaris, SGI hardware runs IRIX, and so on. A number of choices exist for Intel-based systems, however. You can run one of many freely available Unix systems, such as FreeBSD, OpenBSD, NetBSD, and Linux. There are a number of commercial PC Unix systems also, including BSD/OS, SCO, and Solaris. And, of course, there's always Microsoft Windows.

If you do have a number of operating system choices, you may want to consider some of the following characteristics:

Robustness
> Since your cache is a production service, you don't want the machine to crash at random times. However, it may be hard to find quantitative robustness data for various operating systems. Coworkers and mailing lists are a good source for this information.

Security
> It goes without saying that your proxy must be as secure as possible at all times. All operating-system vendors should be good at providing security fixes in a timely manner. You may want to browse or search the *Bugtraq* archives (*http://www.securityfocus.com/bugtraq/archive*) to see if one is better than the other. OpenBSD (*http://www.openbsd.org*) has a strong focus on building a very secure operating system.

Manageability
> You should select an operating system that you find easy to administer. Some people prefer to use point-and-click tools, while others are perfectly comfortable with command lines.

Support
> You might want to think about how you'll get support for your operating system, such as answers to technical questions, bug fixes, and updates. In some cases, the operating system may be sold without any form of support. Freely available operating systems tend to have self-supporting user communities, but a number of companies provide support for Linux and BSD variants as well.

Performance

Operating systems may have slightly different performance characteristics, especially regarding file systems.

10.6 High Availability

Unfortunately, computer systems do occasionally fail. If 100% availability is important, you should build some redundancy into your caching service. Redundancy can be a complicated business, and many organizations take it to extremes. Because computer systems have so many different ways to fail, you'll be faced with numerous options.

Power is one of the most obvious and common causes of failure. An uninterruptible power supply (UPS) is a good idea and relatively inexpensive. Even a small UPS that provides enough power for a few minutes will get you through most power outages. Many caching products and general-purpose servers have the option of redundant power supplies. These help guard against failure of the power supply itself and against power outages if you have separate power feeds.

Disk drives are also prone to failures. This is especially true for caching proxies that are busy 24 hours a day, 7 days a week. Some people like to use RAID systems to provide high-availability storage. In my experience, caches perform noticeably worse with RAID than without. If you really want to use RAID, you should probably use mirroring (RAID level 1) only. The importance of reliable storage depends on your location and the quality of your Internet connection. If your connection is good, the loss of a disk is not a big deal. However, if your connection is poor, the data on disk is very valuable, and RAID makes more sense.

In Chapter 9, I mentioned a number of ways that clusters can improve reliability. These range from simple DNS tricks to complicated load-balancing configurations. In general, cost is an important factor here. You can implement DNS-based failover and balancing for free, but you'll probably spend a lot of time working on it. The layer four switches and related products are expensive, but they provide better failure detection.

Once you insert a device like a layer four switch into your architecture, you also need to consider the reliability of that device. What happens if the layer four switch stops working? Some organizations use multiple switches in complex, cross-connected configurations, such as the one shown in Figure 10.1. In addition to providing fault tolerance, they also allow you to upgrade individual components without affecting the overall service. However, the complexities of these topologies makes them difficult to get "just right." You may find yourself spending a lot of time working on the configuration, especially when adding or removing servers.

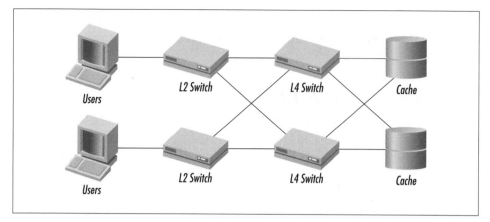

Figure 10.1. Redundant layer four switches

If you're using interception caching, you can still provide robustness without redundancy in everything. Recall that with interception, a network device diverts packets to the cache instead of sending them to the origin server. If the cache fails, the device can simply send them to the origin server and pretend the cache doesn't exist. Most of the layer four switching products (see Table 5.1) have this bypass feature, as does Cisco's WCCP. InfoLibria's products use a device called the DynaLink that bypasses the cache in the event of a failure, including power loss. It has physical relays that essentially couple two cables together in the absence of electrical power.

If you choose one of these techniques to provide high availability, remember to think through the consequences of a failure. For example, if you have a cluster of caches and one goes down, can the remaining systems handle the full load? If not, you're likely to see cascading failures. The failure of one machine may cause another to fail, and so on. If you plan to use the bypass feature, think about the capacity of your Internet connection. Is there enough bandwidth to handle all the requests that would normally be served from the cache? Even if the network becomes severely congested, it's probably better than a complete denial of service for your users.

10.7 Intercepting Traffic

I covered the pros and cons of interception caching in Chapter 5. Most, if not all, of the caching products on the market support interception proxying. Of course, you also need a network device to divert TCP connections to the cache. For that you can use a router (with or without WCCP), a layer four switch, or even an inexpensive PC running Unix.

Interception caching offers many benefits. You don't need to configure browsers at all, and you maximize the amount of traffic that goes through the cache. As described previously, many of the network devices that support interception caching handle cache failures without a disruption of service.

The downside is that interception caching may cause problems for some origin servers. Users who experience problems are usually unable to fix them. You need to configure the network device to bypass the cache for problem cases.

10.8 Load Sharing

I covered load sharing in Chapter 9. There are several ways to split the load between multiple servers:

DNS round-robin
> This brute force approach relies on DNS servers to randomize IP addresses in lookup replies. It is somewhat inefficient because requests are randomly assigned to individual proxies.

Layer four switches
> These products usually have a number of balancing algorithms available (number of connections, response time, etc.). Alternatively, requests can be partitioned by origin server IP address.

CARP
> CARP partitions requests with a sophisticated algorithm that allows members to be weighted unequally. It also minimizes the disturbance to the partitioning when members are added or removed.

ICP and HTCP
> These protocols are only used between caches. They can be used to maximize cache hits within a cluster. This is particularly useful if clients send requests to caches randomly, as with DNS round-robin.

WCCP
> In Cisco's WCCP implementation, the master cache builds an origin server-based partition and sends it to the router. The router uses the partition to divide the load among all member caches.

Given these choices, which one should you use? If you're comfortable with traffic interception, then layer four switches and WCCP are good options. Between the two, it depends on what type and manufacturer of equipment you are familiar with. Organizations that already have an investment in Cisco routers are likely to use WCCP. Some organizations prefer the features offered by layer four switches.

Without traffic interception, you'll probably have to use DNS round-robin or CARP. To implement CARP, you'll need either CARP-aware user-agents or a hierarchy of caches. Perhaps the easiest configuration is DNS round-robin for cache selection, with ICP/HTCP between proxies to maximize cache hits.

10.9 Location

Where should you place a cache or caches within your network? The answer, of course, depends on your particular network. Most likely, you should locate your cache near your firewall or border router—in other words, near the last piece of equipment that you manage as packets from your network head out to the Internet. This maximizes the number of people who can use the cache.

With the above approach, the cache does not reduce bandwidth on your internal network. Both cache hits and misses use internal bandwidth between users and the cache. Also, response-time benefits from cache hits may be lost if the internal network is congested. If you have a large internal network, then you may want to build an internal cache hierarchy. Place child caches on department-level networks and configure them to forward cache misses to a company-wide parent cache. With caches closer to users, you should observe reduced internal bandwidth and fast response times for cache hits.

ISPs often have points-of-presence (POPs) in different cities or locations. To reduce wide-area bandwidth usage, it's a good idea to put a cache in each POP.

10.10 Using a Hierarchy

I covered the advantages and disadvantages of hierarchical caching in Chapter 7. Though a hierarchy can improve your cache's performance, it can also create some new problems. In most cases, the performance improvements are marginal, affecting 5–10% of requests. The nature and extent of any problems depend mostly on who is operating the other caches. If all caches in the hierarchy are managed by a single organization, the potential for problems is significantly diminished. Interorganizational hierarchies, on the other hand, are more susceptible to issues that outweigh any performance gains.

Performance improvements come in the form of additional cache hits and lower average response times. The percentage of requests that are hits in neighbor caches depends on the size of the hierarchy. Cache hits become more common as the hierarchy membership grows. Hierarchies and meshes also offer better scaling characteristics, which can be critical for organizations with large networks. In other words, an intraorganizational hierarchy may not perform significantly better but may be easier to manage.

If you feel that a cache hierarchy will benefit your service, be sure to find out which intercache protocols the candidate products support. Most products support ICP, which is good if the other caches in a hierarchy are made by different companies. Don't forget to consider the effects of the different intercache protocols. ICP and HTCP add delays to cache misses. Cache Digests may end up using more bandwidth than you save from the extra cache hits.

When it comes to cache hierarchies, especially those among different organizations, I usually advise people to be cautious. Carefully consider the issues described in Chapter 7. To what extent are you willing to rely on your neighbor caches? What if they fail or become compromised? Do you trust the organizations who operate those caches? What is your backup plan in case something goes wrong?

11

Monitoring the Health of Your Caches

Active monitoring of your cache is one of the most important steps you can take to providing a first-rate service. Most caching products provide statistics in real time via SNMP, a web browser, or some other specific interface. This data is extremely valuable in quickly diagnosing problems and complaints. When a user calls to complain that the cache is making things slow, you can tell if it's a real problem or an isolated incident.

I also feel it is important to keep a long history of measurements. If one day you suddenly notice that your CPU utilization is 80%, you'll wonder if it's always been that way, or if it's a sudden problem you should investigate. Having a long-term view also makes capacity planning for the future much easier. By extrapolating bandwidth usage data, you can decide when to upgrade your Internet connection capacity. Similarly, a long-term analysis of cache request rates and response times may tell you when your existing solution reaches its performance limits.

In this chapter, I'll talk about the statistics you should monitor and why you should monitor them. In addition to the standard measurements, such as request rate and response time, I'll explain how tracking some of the less obvious parameters can help you diagnose problems quickly. If you're on a tight budget, you can build a very nice monitoring system with freely available Unix software. I like to use UCD-SNMP and RRDTool. I'll help you get started along those lines with some installation tips and quick examples.

11.1 *What to Monitor?*

Different caching products provide different statistics and measurements for monitoring purposes. In general, you should collect as much information as you can. It's better to be on the safe side, since you never know when some information may come in handy. The following list describes the parameters you should collect and monitor, if possible.

Client request rate

> This is the rate at which clients issue HTTP requests to the cache. In a corporate environment, you'll probably observe a daily peak that begins in the morning when people arrive at work and ends when people leave in the evening. ISPs with dial-up customers usually see an evening peak. University traffic usually has both trends combined, with one long peak from early morning until late at night.

> The shape of the request rate data is less important than how it differs from the normal pattern. As the administrator, you should be familiar with how the request rate changes over the course of a day. If you notice a significant change, you should probably investigate the cause. Less traffic than usual can indicate local network problems. More requests than usual could mean someone is using prefetching or web crawling software.

Bandwidth

> There is normally a strong correlation between bandwidth and request rate. However, you may want to monitor it separately. If bandwidth becomes a bottleneck, it might be more obvious in this data. Also, large file downloads, such as MP3s, show up as spikes on a bandwidth plot but do not stand out on a request rate plot.

> If your cache doesn't give you bandwidth measurements, you can probably get it from other sources. In fact, you might prefer to take readings from a switch or router. These should enable you to separate out the internal and external traffic as well.

Client-side response time

> Response time is the most important way to measure how well the cache serves your users. A normal value probably means your users are happy. A high response time means your users are upset and are probably calling you to complain about it. Any number of things can affect response time, including upstream network congestion, an overloaded cache server, a broken DNS server, etc.

Server-side response time

> You should monitor server-side response times separately from the client side, if possible. Server-side requests are sent to origin servers or upstream caches for cache misses. If you notice an increase in client response times, but no change in server response times, it probably indicates a local problem. On the other hand, if both measurements increase, then you can blame the slowness on upstream Internet delays.

DNS lookup response time

> Resolution of DNS names to addresses is a critical aspect of web caching. Some caching products have an internal "DNS cache" but use an external DNS server to resolve unknown names. Tracking the response time for DNS lookups is a good way to monitor the status of the external DNS server. Because internal DNS caches have very high hit ratios, a DNS server failure may not show up in the client-side response time data.

Hit ratio

> Monitoring your cache's hit ratio tells you how much bandwidth is being saved. Don't be too surprised if the hit ratio varies significantly over the course of the day.

Memory usage

> If you have an appliance-based product, you may not have access to memory-usage information. For software products, however, it is important to understand how much memory the application is using. If it's near the limit, then you'll need to buy more memory or change the configuration to use less of it. Monitoring memory usage is also a good way to find some software bugs, such as memory leaks.

Disk usage

> Normally, your cache should use a constant amount of disk space. If you notice it changing significantly over time, then something interesting may be going on. Some caches may lose their disk contents if the system crashes. Such an event would show up in this data. Also, it is interesting to see how quickly the disk fills up. As I mentioned in Section 10.2, "Disk Space", a cache that fills very quickly (in less than three days) can benefit from having more disk space.

CPU usage

> Monitoring the system's CPU usage tells you if the CPU is becoming a bottleneck. CPU usage can be tricky because a high amount of utilization isn't necessarily bad. For example, if your caching proxy is blocking on disk I/O, the CPU utilization may be quite low. Removing the disk bottleneck allows the cache to support higher throughput, which should result in higher CPU utiliza-

tion as well. I wouldn't worry about upgrading the CPU until utilization reaches 75% for hours at a time.

Another thing to keep in mind is that some products may use spare CPU cycles to poll for events more frequently. Even though the CPU appears to be really busy, the application isn't working as hard as it can. CPU utilization doesn't necessarily increase in proportion to supported load. Although the system reports 100% utilization, the cache may be able to handle additional load without negatively affecting overall performance.

File descriptor usage

Unix-based caches, such as Squid, use file descriptors to read and write disk files and network sockets. Each file descriptor identifies a different file or TCP connection that is currently open for reading or writing. Usually, a Unix system places limits on the number of file descriptors available to a single process and to the system as a whole. Running out of file descriptors results in service denial for your users, so you probably want to track the usage. All modern Unix systems let you raise the per-process and systemwide limits. It's a good idea to be conservative here. Give yourself plenty of extra descriptors and familiarize yourself with the procedure.

The number of file descriptors in use at any given time is approximately equal to the average request rate multiplied by the average response time. For most locations, both request rate and response time increase during the middle of the day. If your Internet connection goes down, response time becomes essentially infinite, and your cache is likely to reach its file descriptor limit. Thus, when you see a huge spike in file descriptor usage, it's usually due to an upstream network failure.

Abnormal requests

My definition of an abnormal request is one that results in an error, is denied access, or is aborted by the user. You should always expect to see a small percentage of errors, due to transient network errors, broken origin servers, etc. However, a significant increase in errors probably indicates a local problem that requires your attention.

Changes in the percentage of requests that are denied access may require investigation as well. If you normally deny a lot of requests due to request filtering, this data can assure you it's working properly. A sudden drop in the percentage of denied requests could mean that the filtering software is broken, and users are visiting sites that should be blocked. On the other hand, if you usually deny only a small number of requests, an increase may indicate that outsiders are trying to send requests through your proxy to hide their tracks.

ICP/HTCP query rate

If you're using ICP or HTCP and acting as a parent or sibling for others, it's a good idea to track the query rate as well. Often, it's helpful to look at the ratio of HTCP to ICP requests. A sharp change in this ratio can indicate that your neighbor changed its configuration. Perhaps it went from a parent-child to a sibling relationship, or maybe it turned ICP on or off.

TCP connection states

TCP ports are another limited resource, especially for busy servers. If you've ever looked at *netstat* output on a Unix system, you probably remember seeing connections in various states such as *ESTABLISHED*, *FIN_WAIT_1*, and *TIME_WAIT*. Monitoring connection states can provide you with important information. For example, your system may be configured with a relatively small number of ephemeral ports. These are the local port numbers for outgoing connections. If too many of the ephemeral ports are in the *TIME_WAIT* state, your cache won't be able to open new connections to origin servers. In the rare event that you're the target of a "SYN flood" attack, this would appear as a spike in the number of connections in the *SYN_RCVD* state. It's also interesting to see how enabling or disabling HTTP persistent connections affects these statistics.

Some caching programs and appliances may not make TCP state information available. If you're running on Unix, you can get it with a simple shell script. The following command should be enough to get you started:

```
netstat -n | awk '/^tcp/ {++S[$NF]} END {for(a in S) print a, S[a]}'
```

11.2 Monitoring Tools

Most caching products provide both custom interfaces and monitoring via SNMP (Simple Network Monitoring Protocol). The custom interfaces are typically web-based and often use Java. While these tools can display graphs for some of the parameters just described, they usually have only volatile storage. When the proxy cache restarts, the historical data is lost.

Although most products support SNMP, there is no standard SNMP proxy MIB (Management Information Base). Instead, each vendor or product has its own MIB with product-specific information. If enough customers complain about the lack of a standard MIB, vendors are likely to develop one within the IETF.

In theory, monitoring a network device via SNMP is relatively simple. You make the MIB file available to your network management application and tell it which variables to collect and display. In practice, however, it's often a frustrating process. There are a number of management applications available for all types of operating systems. As a relatively simple example, the remainder of this section describes how to install and configure UCD-SNMP and RRDTool to monitor a Squid cache. To monitor another SNMP-addressable caching product, you'll need to use its MIB.

11.2.1 UCD-SNMP

The University of California at Davis distributes a suite of SNMP tools for Unix. You can download the software from their home page, *http://ucd-snmp.ucdavis.edu,* or one of the mirror sites. Hopefully, you'll find the software easy to compile and install. It should be as easy as this:

```
% gzip -dc ucd-snmp.tar.gz | tar xf -
% cd ucd-snmp-4.1.1
% ./configure
% make
% su
# make install
```

During the *configure* phase, you'll be prompted to enter some information. This information is used only when you run the *snmpd* daemon. The *snmpd* program is not needed to monitor Squid or any other proxy cache. We are only interested in the *snmpget* command.

If you watched the install process closely, you noticed that SNMP MIB files are placed in */usr/local/share/snmp/mibs/* by default. We'll need to copy the Squid MIB to this location:

```
# cp squid/src/mib.txt /usr/local/share/snmp/mibs/SQUID-MIB.txt
# chmod 644 /usr/local/share/snmp/mibs/SQUID-MIB.txt
```

Once the MIB has been installed, we can test everything with the following *snmpget* command:

```
% snmpget -m SQUID-MIB -p 3401 -R webcache.isp.net public \
    squid.cacheConfig.cacheAdmin
```

The -m option tells *snmpget* to load the SQUID-MIB file. This is needed to translate the long identifier name into a sequence of numbers. The -p option specifies the destination port number for the SNMP query. Squid uses port 3401 by default. The -R option allows us to use short variable names. Without it, the last argument would need to be much longer. You should replace *webcache.isp.net* with the hostname of your own proxy cache. The next argument, public, specifies the SNMP community string. Essentially, this is a password. Many applications use public as the default but should allow you to change it if you like. Finally, squid.cacheConfig.cacheAdmin specifies the MIB variable we want to get. In this case, we're asking for the email address of the cache administrator. If successful, the result comes back like this:

```
enterprises.nlanr.squid.cacheConfig.cacheAdmin = wessels@web-cache.net
```

If you get an error message, *snmpget* may not be able to locate the Squid MIB file. If you get no response or a timeout, Squid might not be configured for SNMP. You'll also get a timeout if your network has a firewall that blocks UDP packets.

11.2.2 RRDTool

RRDTool is a successor to the highly popular MRTG (Multi Router Traffic Grapher) software. RRDTool manages data in the form of a *round-robin database* (RRD). The idea is that data is archived over time, at different granularities. A database stores the same measurements consolidated over various time intervals. For example, you can have 24 hours' worth of measurements taken at 5-minute intervals, a month's worth of measurements consolidated into 1-hour intervals, and so on. With this structure, RRDTool can store many years' worth of measurements in a relatively small amount of space. Of course, some information is lost as old measurements are consolidated over time. You won't be able to go back and compare two five-minute intervals from a year ago.

You can get the RRDTool software from *http://ee-staff.ethz.ch/˜oetiker/webtools/rrd-tool/*. After downloading, it should compile and install easily:

```
% gzip -dc rrdtool-1.0.13.tar.gz | tar xf -
% cd rrdtool-1.0.13
% ./configure
% make
# make install
```

The next step is to create a round-robin database to hold and manage the measurements. To do this, we need to know which values we'll store, their types, and for how long. The syntax for *rrdtool create* is somewhat confusing. Since I can't explain everything here, you may want to read the RRDTool manual before proceeding.

For this example, we'll create a database to hold HTTP and DNS median service times. The *gauge* data type is used for values that go up and down, such as temperature:

```
% rrdtool create svctime.rrd \
    --step 300 \
    DS:http:GAUGE:600:U:U \
    DS:dns:GAUGE:600:U:U \
    RRA:AVERAGE:0.99:1:288 \
    RRA:AVERAGE:0.99:6:336 \
    RRA:AVERAGE:0.99:12:744
```

The `step` argument specifies the default interval (in seconds) at which measurements are collected. The `DS` lines define the data sources. In this case we have HTTP and DNS request counters. The `RRA` lines specify how the data is archived and consolidated.

To collect the data, we use a shell script that runs as a cron job every 5 minutes. The script uses *snmpget* to get the data and stores the values with *rrdtool update*:

```
#!/bin/sh
SNMPGET="snmpget -q -R -s -m SQUID-MIB -p 3401 webcache.isp.net public"
cd /where/rrd/files/live

http=`$SNMPGET cacheHttpAllSvcTime.5 | awk '{print $2}'`
dns=`$SNMPGET cacheDnsSvcTime.5 | awk '{print $2}'`

rrdtool update svctime.rrd --template http:dns N:$http:$dns
```

Squid calculates service times averaged over 1-, 5-, and 60-minute time intervals. This example uses the 5-minute interval, which is what the the `.5` following both names refers to. The `N` in the last argument of the *rrdtool update* command stands for the current time (i.e., "now").

Finally, let's see how *rrdgraph* is used to make a graph of the data:

```
% rrdtool graph svctime.day.png \
    --start -1day \
    --title "Service times" \
    --vertical-label "seconds" \
    --imgformat PNG \
    DEF:http=/where/rrd/files/live/svctime.rrd:http:AVERAGE \
    DEF:dns=/where/rrd/files/live/svctime.rrd:dns:AVERAGE \
    AREA:http#0000FF:HTTP \
    LINE2:dns#00FF00:DNS
```

The `--start -1day` option instructs *rrdgraph* to show the previous 24 hours' worth of data. The `AREA` argument draws the HTTP service time as a filled area with color #0000FF (blue). The `LINE2` argument draws the DNS service time as a solid line with double thickness in green. Figure 11.1 shows the resulting image.

The RRDTool package also includes a program called *rrdcgi*. It parses HTML files with special embedded tags that look like *rrdgraph* commands. Using *rrdcgi*, you can write HTML pages that generate RRD graphs on the fly. Unfortunately, setting up *rrdcgi* is somewhat complicated. You'll need to refer to the RRDTool documentation for syntax and examples.

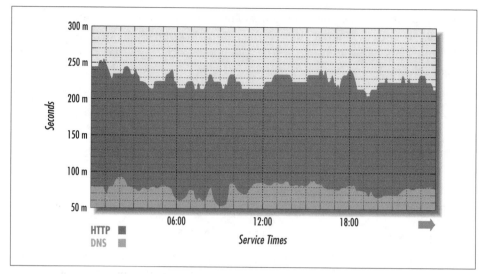

Figure 11.1. Sample RRD graph

11.2.3 Other Tools

Many people use MRTG to collect and display their cache statistics. MRTG is perhaps easier to install and configure, but it's not nearly as flexible as RRDTool. MRTG also has a number of performance problems. You can download MRTG from *http://www.mrtg.org*.

In addition to real-time monitoring, you'll probably want to use some scripts or tools to analyze your access log files. These can tell you how many requests were served, the cache hit ratio, bandwidth utilization, and more. Again, I recommend keeping an archive of these reports and statistics for planning and troubleshooting.

Any program that analyzes access log files needs to understand the file format. Many caching products support the HTTP common logfile format. A number of products also support Squid's format, probably to take advantage of the preexisting analysis tools. Calamaris (*http://calamaris.cord.de*) and Webalyzer (*http://www.mrunix.net/webalizer/*) are perhaps the most widely used programs. You can find additional tools listed at *http://www.squid-cache.org/Scripts/*.

12

Benchmarking Proxy Caches

Benchmarking is the process of measuring the performance of a product or service. Benchmarks are used for many different computer systems and components, such as CPUs, disk drives, Ethernet switches, and databases. A good benchmark must be stressful, reproducible, and meaningful. A test or workload that doesn't stress the device under test is not very interesting. Reproducibility is important for tests that compare different products or slightly different configurations under the same conditions. A meaningful benchmark is one that accurately predicts the performance of the device or system under real-world conditions.

Benchmarks are used by engineers, marketers, and customers alike. Product engineers use benchmarks to evaluate design choices and overall system performance. A good benchmark identifies bottlenecks and tells them if changing a certain component improves or worsens the product's performance. Benchmarking results are often used in marketing literature, especially when one company claims to have a superior product. Even when a particular product does poorly, marketing departments find some way to put a positive spin on the results.

Customers use benchmarking results to make buying decisions. Good benchmarks enable customers to compare different products with each other, find the one that best suits their needs, and understand the price versus performance tradeoffs. Without published, audited benchmark results, customers have no way to verify performance claims made by individual vendors. If you are considering the purchase of a particular product, I highly recommend asking the vendor for recent published and audited benchmark results first.

In this chapter, I'll talk about benchmarking for caching products. First, I'll introduce you to the metrics that are important for web caches. Understanding the metrics and how they are related enables you to interpret published results quickly and correctly. I'll also tell you about some of the tools you can use to run your own benchmarks. Since executing a benchmark on a web cache is somewhat complicated, we'll also talk about the common pitfalls and difficulties others have encountered. The final section provides a basic recipe for how to benchmark a web cache.

Note that I am heavily involved in benchmarking caching products through my company, The Measurement Factory (*http://www.measurement-factory.com*). We organize the industry "Cache-Offs" and perform private tests for both vendors and customers. We have been fortunate enough to work with most, but not all, of the companies that sell caching products.

12.1 Metrics

There are a number of measurements that relate to proxy cache performance. The most common are throughput, response time, and hit ratio. For web caches, these metrics are related and tend to influence each other. For example, a decrease in hit ratio usually results in an increase in mean response time. To fully understand a benchmark result, you need to consider all the metrics. Don't look at just the throughput. It's quite possible that two products can achieve the same throughput but with much different hit ratios.

Some people find multiple metrics confusing because they complicate product comparisons. Is a product with high throughput and high response time better than one with low throughput and low response time? The answer depends on individual circumstances and the attributes most valued by the user. Other types of benchmarks report a single measurement or combine many measurements into a single value. While this makes it possible to easily rank products, I feel that doing so for proxy caches does more harm than good. Combining multiple measurements into a single value makes it difficult for people to evaluate products in the areas they feel are the most important.

12.1.1 Throughput

Throughput is a metric common to many types of benchmarks. Database benchmarks report throughput as transactions per second. CPU benchmarks measure instructions per second. For web caches, it's HTTP responses per second. Some people say "requests per second" or even "URLs per second" instead. The three phrases are equivalent for most purposes.

Throughput is not always a measured value. For some tests, it is an input parameter. That is, the workload specifies a particular offered request rate. Instead of asking, "What's the maximum throughput this product can support?" the question becomes, "What is this product's response time and hit ratio at X requests per second?"

Peak throughput varies significantly among products. In recent industry Cache-Off tests [Rousskov and Wessels, 2000], the lowest was 115 responses per second, while the maximum was about 3,300. A cache's peak throughput determines how much bandwidth and how many simultaneous users it can support. If you have more traffic than one box can handle, you can scale the peak throughput linearly by adding additional boxes.

Some network administrators are more comfortable thinking in terms of bandwidth—megabits per second—rather than responses per second. To convert from response rate to bandwidth, simply multiply by the mean response size. For example, in the Cache-Off tests mentioned earlier, the mean response size is 10.9 KB. Thus, the lowest tested throughput was 9.7 Mbps, while the highest was 281 Mbps. Real traffic reply size distributions vary from location to location. If you're not sure what to use, 10 KB is probably a good approximation. Note that responses, flowing from servers to clients, account for the majority of bandwidth. Requests also consume some bandwidth in the other direction, but the amount is almost insignificant since requests are typically 50 times smaller than responses.

12.1.2 Response Time

Response time measures how quickly a cache responds to requests. For a single request, it's the amount of time elapsed between sending the request and receiving the end of the response. Since individual response times vary greatly, it's useful to keep a histogram of them. From the histogram we can report the mean, median, percentiles, and other statistical measures.

Response times for cache misses depend largely on network and origin server delays. The mean response time for real web traffic is typically 2–3 seconds. Cache hits, on the other hand, have very small response times, usually a few hundred milliseconds. Thus, the cache hit ratio affects the overall response time. As the hit ratio goes down, more requests result in cache misses, which drives up the mean response time.

If a proxy cache becomes overloaded, both cache hits and misses can experience additional delays. In some cases, a cache becomes so busy that hits take longer than misses. When this happens, you would get better response time with no caching at all. However, even a slow and busy cache can reduce your network bandwidth usage.

12.1.3 Hit Ratio

Hit ratio measures the effectiveness of the cache and the amount of bandwidth saved. Recall that there are two hit ratio measurements: cache hit ratio and byte hit ratio. The first refers to the number of requests made, the latter to the number of bytes transferred. Since small objects are more popular than large ones, byte hit ratio is normally smaller than cache hit ratio. When a result says just "hit ratio," it probably refers to cache hit ratio.

A particular workload in a test environment has an upper bound on achievable hit ratio, based on an ideal cache. An ideal cache has an infinite size, stores all cachable responses, and returns a hit whenever possible. Of course, real caches are not quite ideal and may not achieve the maximum hit ratio for a number of reasons. The disk capacity may not be large enough. The product's rules for caching may be different from what the benchmark software expects. Some caching products are able to bypass their disk storage (for both reads and writes) when faced with high loads. A cachable response that doesn't get stored results in a missed opportunity for a cache hit later on.

12.1.4 Connection Capacity

You might be interested to know how many simultaneous connections a product can handle. To get an approximation, simply multiply the throughput by the response time. Connection capacity is usually not reported as a separate metric because it is rarely a limiting factor.

12.1.5 Cost

It may seem strange to include cost as a metric. However, the cliché "you get what you pay for" is true for web caches. Certainly, you would expect a $50,000 solution to perform better than one costing $5,000. The cost of a product is a good way to normalize the performance metrics, such as throughput. By including cost, you can calculate how many cheap boxes you need to get the same performance as one expensive box. Some benchmarks, such as the Transaction Processing Performance Council (TPC) (*http://www.tpc.org*), which tests databases, take this a step further and report long-term cost of ownership information. For example, how much does a support contract cost? What about power and cooling requirements? How much space does the product need?

12.2 Performance Bottlenecks

The performance of a proxy cache system depends on numerous factors. Any one of the system components can become a bottleneck. In some cases, it's possible to use benchmarking tools to identify the bottlenecks. For example, you can benchmark two different hardware configurations and compare their results. Does a faster CPU improve response time? How much does your hit ratio improve if you double the disk space?

12.2.1 Disk Throughput

Disk I/O is often a bottleneck for web caches. Due to the nature of web traffic, web caches make very heavy use of their disk drives. If you've ever looked at the disk lights on a busy cache, you probably noticed the lights are almost constantly on.

The performance of disk systems varies greatly between products, and a number of factors are involved. First, the controller's bus speed limits how quickly chunks of data move from memory to the disk controller. For SCSI, this limit is usually 20, 40, or 80 MB per second. For IDE controllers, the limit is either 33, 66, or 100 MB per second. These rates correspond to theoretical upper limits. It's rare for a controller to sustain its maximum rate for any length of time, partly because individual disk drives have much lower limits. When multiple devices are connected to the bus, as is common with SCSI, then the bus bandwidth limit becomes more relevant.

Another, and more realistic, limit is how quickly an individual drive can transfer data to and from its magnetic media. This limit relates to the drive's rotational speed and other mechanical properties. For most drives, this limit is on the order of 10–20 MB per second. Note that 20 MB per second corresponds to about the same as an OC-3 network link (155 megabits/sec). Again, this rate is achievable only under ideal conditions when the disk can write large chunks of data continuously.

Due the nature of web traffic, cache disk drives are unlikely to achieve sustained data transfer rates as high as 10 MB per second. Cached objects are relatively small (about 10 KB), so a disk spends a lot of time seeking back and forth to different positions. While some caching products are able to optimize writes into large, contiguous chunks, it's harder to optimize reads for cache hits. In most cases, the real limit for disk performance is the rate of disk accesses. In other words, how many reads and writes can the disk handle per second? The maximum rate for most disks available today is about 100 operations per second. The determining factor is usually the seek time. To maximize your disk performance, use hard drives with low average seek times.

It's relatively easy to find out if your disk system is a bottleneck. First, benchmark the cache with a 100% cachable workload. This should cause the cache to store every response, thereby stressing the disks. Next, run another benchmark with 0% cachable responses. Since disks are probably the slowest devices in the system, chances are you'll see a big difference in performance.

12.2.2 CPU Power

For the most part, web caches don't require really powerful CPUs. However, an underpowered CPU can limit a cache's performance. Caching and proxying involves the movement of data buffers from one place to another (e.g., network and disk). Copying buffers and scanning for string patterns probably accounts for the majority of CPU time.

One exception is caches that encrypt or decrypt HTTP/TLS traffic. The encryption algorithms are very CPU-intensive. A number of companies sell "SSL accelerator" cards or devices that offload encryption processing from the CPU onto a dedicated processor.

Testing for CPU bottlenecks can be difficult. It's probably easiest to use system tools (e.g., *top* and *vmstat* on Unix) to watch the CPU usage while running the benchmark. Other than that, you may need simply to try different CPUs in the system with the same workload.

12.2.3 NIC Bandwidth

A cache's network interface may be a limiting factor, although this is unlikely as long as the NIC is configured properly. Fast Ethernet is quite common today and sufficient for most available products. A single 100baseTX interface can usually handle 900–1,000 HTTP requests per second. Products that support higher request rates have Gigabit Ethernet or multiple 100baseTX interfaces.

To find out if your network interface is a bottleneck, look for a large percentage of collisions. Many Ethernet hubs and switches have lights on the front that indicate utilization or collisions. On Unix systems, the *netstat -i* command reports collision and error counters for each interface.

12.2.4 Memory

Memory is a precious resource for web caches. It's used to buffer data, index cached objects, store popular objects, and more. A caching application has two ways to deal with a memory shortage: swap some pages to disk or postpone certain actions until memory becomes available. In either case, running out of memory results in a very sudden performance degradation.

To find out if memory is limiting your performance, you can use system tools (e.g., *top* and *vmstat* on Unix) to monitor memory usage. Alternatively, you may be able to adjust how the application uses memory. For example, Squid uses less memory if you decrease the cache size. Lowering Squid's *cache_mem* parameter may help as well.

12.2.5 Network State

TCP ports are a limited resource people sometimes forget about. A TCP connection is defined by a pair of IP addresses and port numbers. Since the TCP port number is a 16-bit field, there are 65,536 ports available. When a system initiates a new TCP connection, it must first find an unused port number. When a connection is closed, the endpoint that did not initiate the close must keep the port in a *TIME_WAIT* state for a certain amount of time. Most implementations use one minute, even though the standards specify four minutes.

The number of ports in the *TIME_WAIT* state is roughly equal to the rate of connection establishment multiplied by the timeout value. Thus, with 65,536 ports and a 60-second timeout, a proxy cache can establish no more than about 1,000 connections per second. In fact, the situation may be worse because some operating systems have fewer ephemeral ports by default. On FreeBSD, for example, the ephemeral port range is 1,024–5,000. You can easily increase the limit with the *sysctl* program.

Persistent HTTP connections may help to achieve a higher throughput if this limit is reached. However, persistent connections also tie up resources when the connection is idle. Very busy servers should use a low timeout (such as 1–2 seconds) for idle persistent connections.

Generally, there are three ways to avoid running out of ports: increase the ephemeral port range, decrease the TCP MSL value, or use additional IP addresses. Decreasing the MSL value reduces the time spent in the *TIME_WAIT* state and recycles ports faster, but you probably shouldn't use an MSL value smaller than 15 seconds on a production server. Adding more IP addresses effectively increases the number of available ports because sockets are bound to address/port tuples. Thus, two connections can use the same TCP port as long as they use different IP addresses. On Unix systems you can use *ifconfig* to add IP aliases to an interface.

12.3 Benchmarking Tools

A number of tools are available for benchmarking proxy caches. Some are self-contained because they generate all requests and responses internally. Others rely on trace log files for requests and on live origin servers for responses. Each technique has advantages and disadvantages.

Using trace files is attractive because the client and server programs are simpler to implement. A self-contained benchmark is more complicated because it uses mathematical formulas to generate new requests and responses. For example, a particular request has some probability of being a cache hit, of being cachable, and of being a certain size. With trace files, instead of managing complex workload parameters, the client just reads a file of URLs and sends HTTP requests. In essence, the workload parameters are embedded in the log files. Another problem is that trace files don't normally record all the information needed to correctly play back the requests. For example, a log file doesn't normally say if a particular request was on a persistent connection. It's also unlikely to indicate certain request headers, such as `Cache-control` and `If-Modified-Since`.

Trace log files are usually taken from production proxy caches. This is good because the trace represents real web traffic on your network, generated by real users. If you want to run a trace-based benchmark or simulation but don't have any log files, you might be out of luck. Log files are not usually shared between organizations because of privacy issues.

A benchmark that uses real URLs requested from live origin servers is likely to give inconsistent and unreproducible results. For example, if you run the same test on two different days, you may get significantly different results. Live origin servers have different performance characteristics depending on the time of day, day of the week, and unpredictable network conditions.

A self-contained benchmark has the advantage of being configurable, and it's also reproducible when run on dedicated systems. For example, it's easy to change a workload's hit ratio and other parameters as needed. However, some people find the myriad of workload parameters daunting. If your goal is to simulate the real traffic on your network, it's less work to take a trace file than to characterize the traffic and enter the parameters into a configuration file. Investing the time to characterize your traffic gives you many more options. Since simulated data sets are essentially infinite, you can run tests for as long as you like. You don't need to worry if your trace file has enough URLs for the test you want to run.

Another distinguishing feature of benchmarking tools is how they submit new requests. Two techniques are commonly used: best-effort and constant rate. The best-effort method uses a finite number of simultaneous client agents. Each agent sends one request at a time, waiting for the current request to complete before sending the next one. As the name implies, the constant rate method submits new requests at a constant, average rate, regardless of the number of active requests.

The best-effort technique is usually easier to implement. Often, each agent is a separate thread or process. This leads to a natural feedback mechanism: once all threads become busy, no new requests are submitted. New requests are sent only as fast as the cache responds to them. A fixed number of agents may not sufficiently stress a proxy cache. Furthermore, using too few agents leads to very misleading throughput measurements. For example, consider a caching proxy that, for whatever reason, delays every request by at least 100 milliseconds. A test with 10 threads can produce no more than 100 requests per second. However, a test with 100 threads can generate up to 1,000 requests per second.

The constant rate method usually results in a better workload. Even if the cache starts to slow down (i.e., response time increases), new requests continue to arrive at the same rate. Note that *constant* doesn't necessarily mean that requests arrive at perfectly spaced time intervals (e.g., one request every 10 milliseconds). Real Internet traffic is bursty, with a lot of variation between consecutive interarrival times. Some benchmarks model interarrival times with Poisson distributions or self-similar models that have constant average request rates. This technique also provides a better simulation of real traffic because the total number of users is usually much larger than the number of concurrent connections. When my browser submits requests, it doesn't care how many other browsers already have requests pending.

12.3.1 Web Polygraph

Web Polygraph (*http://www.web-polygraph.org*) is a comprehensive cache benchmarking tool. It's freely available and distributed as source code that runs on both Unix and Microsoft Windows. Polygraph is designed to be high-performance and very flexible. It simulates both HTTP clients and servers based on a rich specification language. (I have a personal preference for Polygraph because I am involved in its development.)

Polygraph is high-performance because it makes very efficient use of system resources. A single midrange PC system can easily saturate a fast Ethernet segment, which corresponds to about 1,000 requests per second. A lot of attention is given to optimizing the Polygraph source code. You can scale the offered load to very high rates by running Polygraph on many systems in parallel.

Simulating both clients and servers gives Polygraph a lot of flexibility. For example, clients and servers can exchange certain state information with each other via custom HTTP headers. This allows Polygraph to know whether a specific response was generated by the server or served from the cache. Polygraph can detect false hits, foreign requests, foreign responses, and other errors.

Polygraph's configuration language allows users to customize the simulated workload. For example, you can specify mathematical distributions for reply sizes, request popularity, think time delays, and more.

Another important part of Web Polygraph is the development of standard workloads. These workloads allow anyone to run their own tests and compare the results with previously published data. Workloads are developed and evolved with input from users, caching vendors, and other interested parties. The standard workloads mimic real web traffic as closely as possible. The parameters are taken from analyses of real systems, log files, and published research results.

Polygraph models the following web traffic characteristics:

Request submission

Polygraph supports both constant rate and best-effort request submission. In the best-effort approach, a finite number of agents each submit one request at a time. When the agent receives the complete response, it immediately submits another request. The constant rate model, on the other hand, submits new requests at a constant average rate. Polygraph allows you to specify an interarrival distribution for the constant rate model.

As I mentioned previously, the best-effort method may not put much stress on a proxy cache, especially if a small number of agents are used. New requests are submitted only as fast as the cache can respond to them. Constant rate submission is more likely to test the cache under stressful conditions. If the cache cannot keep up with the client, a significant backlog develops. Polygraph continues to submit new requests until it reaches a configurable limit or runs out of unused file descriptors.

Popularity

Popularity is an important aspect of web traffic. It determines how often some objects get requested relative to others. Numerous studies have shown that web access patterns are best described by a Zipf-like distribution [Breslau, Cao, Fan, Phillips and Shenker, 1999].

Among other things, the popularity distribution affects memory hit ratios. If the popular objects are too popular, then too many cache hits are served from memory. In this case, the workload does not sufficiently exercise the disk system, and the product achieves better performance than it does with live traffic. Getting the popularity model and memory hit ratio "just right" is one of the hardest aspects of proxy cache benchmarking.

Recurrence

The recurrence parameter also determines the hit ratio. It specifies the probability that a given request is for an object that was previously requested. Recurrence applies both to cachable and uncachable responses. Repeated requests for uncachable objects do not contribute to the hit ratio. Note that recurrence determines only whether a particular request is for a previously requested object. The popularity model actually determines *which* object gets requested.

Server delays

Polygraph supports server-side think time delays as a way to approximate server and network latencies. Such delays are important because they simulate busy servers and, to some extent, congested networks. They increase response times and cause the proxy cache to maintain a large number of open connections.

Content types

Polygraph allows you to specify a distribution of different content types. For example, you can say that 70% are images, 20% are HTML, and 10% are "other." Each content type can have different characteristics, such as reply size, cachability, and last-modified timestamps.

Reply sizes

It's very important to use a realistic distribution of reply sizes. In particular, a product's disk performance is probably sensitive to the reply size distribution. If the sizes are too small, the benchmark underestimates the actual performance. As mentioned previously, Polygraph allows you to assign different reply size distributions to different content types.

Object lifecycles

In this context, *lifecycle* refers to the times at which objects are created, modified, and destroyed. The lifecycle model determines values for a response's `Expires` and `Last-modified` headers and whether these headers are present at all. These parameters determine how caches and simulated clients revalidate cached responses. Unfortunately, the lifecycle characteristics of real web content are quite difficult to characterize.

Persistent connections

HTTP/1.1 defines persistent connections, which enable a client to make multiple requests over a single TCP connection. Polygraph supports sending a different number of requests over a connection, as occurs in real traffic.

Embedded objects

The bulk of web traffic consists of images embedded in HTML pages. Although Polygraph doesn't currently generate HTML, it can model pages with embedded objects. Furthermore, Polygraph clients mimic graphical browsers by immediately requesting a small number of embedded objects in parallel.

Uncachable responses

Polygraph marks some percentage of responses as uncachable with the `no-cache` and other `Cache-control` directives. Of course, uncachable responses affect response time, as well as hit ratio. Polygraph reports an error if it detects a cache hit for an uncachable response.

During an experiment, Polygraph measures the following at regular intervals:

- Client- and server-side throughput

- Cache hit ratio and byte hit ratio

- The distribution of response times, separately for hits and misses

- The distribution of reply sizes, separately for hits, misses, cachable responses, and uncachable responses

- Persistent connection usage

- Number and type of errors

- Number of requests and bytes for hits, misses, cachable responses, and uncachable responses

12.3.2 Blast

The blast software, developed by Jens-S. Vöckler, replays trace log files. Blast launches a number of child processes in parallel, each one handling one request at a time. In this way, it's similar to Polygraph's best-effort request submission model.

Blast also includes a simple program called junker that simulates an origin server. Junker supports the GET method, HTTP/1.1 persistent connections, and If-Modi-fied-Since validation requests.

You can get Blaster, in the form of Unix source code, from *http://www.cache.dfn.de/DFN-Cache/Development/blast.html.*

12.3.3 Wisconsin Proxy Benchmark

WPB was developed at the University of Wisconsin, Madison. Like Polygraph, WPB generates requests and responses on demand (versus from trace files). As with Blaster, WPB uses a one-request-per-process approach, which makes it similar to Polygraph's best-effort mode. WPB supports a configurable think time delay in its server. Many other workload characteristics, such as popularity and hit ratio, appear to be hardcoded.

You can download the Unix source code for WPB from *http://www.cs.wisc.edu/~cao/wpb1.0.html.* Since the project leader recently left the University of Wisconsin, it is unlikely that WPB development will continue.

12.3.4 WebJamma

WebJamma is similar to Blaster in that it plays back trace log files and uses best-effort request submission. One unique feature is the ability to distribute requests to multiple proxy caches. This allows you to evaluate more than one product at the same time and under the same conditions. The WebJamma home page is *http://www.cs.vt.edu/~nrg/webjamma.html.*

12.3.5 Other Benchmarks

A number of other benchmarks, such as WebStone, SPECweb99, WebBench, and httperf, have been designed to test origin servers. Although it may be possible to use them with proxy caches (via layer four redirection, for example), I do not recommend it. The workload for a single origin server is much different from the workload for a proxy cache.

12.4 Benchmarking Gotchas

Benchmarking a proxy cache is a complicated endeavor. Problems arise at all layers of the networking model, from the physical to the application. Bottlenecks or inefficiencies can appear in many places. The following sections describe some common problems I have observed while performing benchmarks.

12.4.1 TCP Delayed ACKs

TCP includes a mechanism known as *delayed ACKs* [Clark, 1982; IETF, 1989]. The idea is to not immediately acknowledge every data packet. ACK-only packets are very small and thus not particularly efficient. If the TCP stack waits a little while, there is a chance that a data packet is headed in the same direction. Piggybacking the ACK with the data is much more efficient. Most TCP implementations delay ACKs for up to 200 milliseconds. For some, the timeout is configurable.

Delayed ACKs are a big win for interactive flows (e.g., telnet) where small packets flow in both directions in bursts. HTTP, however, is largely unidirectional. HTTP requests normally fit inside a single TCP packet and, therefore, they are not affected by delayed ACKs. Responses, however, typically require many packets. At the beginning of the transfer, TCP slow start is also in effect. This means the sender won't transmit the second packet until the first one is acknowledged. Thus, clients that use delayed ACKs increase the response time of each request by about 100–200 milliseconds.

Most operating systems allow you to disable delayed ACKs. There is a tradeoff in doing so, however. Response times improve, but the number of packets in the network increases. I have seen caching products that achieve a higher throughput (responses per second) with delayed ACKs enabled because the network interface was handling fewer packets.

In 1999, a magazine attempted to benchmark a handful of proxy caches with a best-effort workload. They used only 20 agents. Because they did not consider TCP delayed ACKs, the mean response time was approximately 200 milliseconds. In this environment, none of the products could achieve higher than 100 requests per second. Many of the same products had been previously benchmarked at higher than 1,000 requests per second. Even worse, the delayed ACKs affected different products differently. Slower products actually appeared to perform better than faster ones.

For more information on TCP delayed ACKs, refer to Section 19.3 of [Stevens, 1994].

12.4.2 Port Number Exhaustion

Port numbers are a limited resource for busy clients and servers. When an application closes a connection, TCP requires the host to keep the socket in the *TIME_WAIT* state for some amount of time [Stevens, 1994, Section 18.6]. The *TIME_WAIT* duration is defined as twice the Maximum Segment Lifetime (MSL). For most TCP implementations, MSL is set to 30 seconds, so the *TIME_WAIT* value is 60 seconds. During this time, the same port number cannot be used for a new connection, although Stevens notes some exceptions.

When benchmarking, we usually want to push the limits of our load-generating machines. For example, a reasonable goal is to have the machine generate 1000 HTTP requests per second. At this rate, with a 60-second *TIME_WAIT*, we'll have 60,000 ports in that state after running for just a minute or so. TCP has only 65,536 ports, some of which we can't use, so this is dangerously close to the limit. In order to support high request rates, we need to decrease the Maximum Segment Lifetime (MSL) value on the load-generating hosts. It's probably safe to use an MSL value as low as three seconds, but only on the load-generating machines and only in a lab environment. If you change the MSL value on a production system, you risk receiving incorrect data. TCP may get confused and believe that packets from an old connection belong to a new connection.

12.4.3 NIC Duplex Mode

Many Ethernet interfaces and switches available today support both 10baseT and 100BaseTX. Furthermore, 100BaseTX supports both half- and full-duplex modes. These devices tend to have autonegotiation features that automatically determine the speed and duplex setting. However, autonegotiation doesn't always work as advertised, especially when it comes to the duplex mode.

A duplex mismatch can be tricky to detect because it probably works properly for very low bandwidth uses such as *telnet* and *ping*. As the bandwidth increases, however, a large number of errors and/or collisions occur. This is one of the reasons why running simple TCP throughput tests is very important.

12.4.4 Bad Ethernet Cables

100BaseTX requires high-quality, well-made Ethernet cables. A poorly made cable is likely to cause problems such as poor throughput, errors, and collisions. Remember that *netstat -i* shows error and collision counters on Unix systems. If you observe these conditions on an interface, replace the cables and try again. Bidirectional TCP throughput tests are useful for identifying bad cables.

12.4.5 Full Caches

To be really useful, measurements must be made on full caches. A cache that is not full has a performance advantage because it does not delete old objects. Furthermore, it is able to write data faster because the filesystem has large amounts of contiguous free space.

Once the disk becomes full, the cache replaces old objects to make room for new ones. This affects performance in two ways. The act of deleting an object typically has some impact, for example, updating a directory to indicate that certain disk blocks are now free. Object removal also leads to fragmentation; thus, when writing new objects, there are fewer contiguous free blocks available.

Some products have smarter filesystems than others. Those that have filesystems optimized for web caching might show roughly similar performance for empty and full caches. However, many products do exhibit a significant performance decrease over time.

12.4.6 Test Duration

It takes a long time to properly benchmark a proxy cache. Measurements should be taken when the cache has reached a steady state. Proxy caches usually have very good performance at the start of a test. As the test progresses, performance decreases slowly. The longer you run a test, the closer you get to the steady-state conditions. A production cache handling live traffic can take days or weeks to stabilize. A week-long benchmark is not usually an option, so we must settle for shorter tests. Personally, I recommend running benchmarks for at least six hours after the cache is full.

12.4.7 Long-Lived Connections

Long-lived connections are important because they tie up valuable resources in the proxy. By long-lived, I mean a few seconds, not hours or days. It's easy for a proxy to achieve 1000 requests per second when the mean response time is just 10 milliseconds. Achieving the same rate when the response time is three seconds is significantly harder. The reason for simulating long connections is because they exist in real web traffic. Slow modem speeds, wide area network delays, and loaded servers all contribute to response time.

12.4.8 Small Working Sets

Small working sets overestimate performance. The *working set* is the set of all objects that clients can request at any given time. The size of the working set affects memory hit ratios. Note that the contents of the working set can change over time, but the size remains approximately the same.

The working set is too small if it can fit entirely in the cache's memory. Since the cache doesn't need to read from the disk for memory hits, it achieves a higher performance. Similarly, a working set that is too large results in a very low memory hit ratio and worse performance.

For a cache to achieve the maximum possible hit ratio for a given workload, the working set size must be less than the cache size. Otherwise, the cache replaces some objects that are requested later, resulting in a cache miss.

12.4.9 Clock Sync

All systems involved in a benchmark should have their clocks synchronized to a single source. On more than one occasion, I have seen systems clocks differ by more than a year. Such a difference can cause unexpected behavior. HTTP's date-related headers affect validation and may affect cachability as well. Thus, clock skew can result in no cache hits or a decrease in performance due to excessive validations.

12.4.10 MSL (TIME_WAIT) Values

As I described previously, a TCP stack's MSL determines how quickly port numbers are recycled. When comparing different caching products, you should make sure they all use the same reasonable MSL values. Web Polygraph includes a program called *msl_test* that reports the MSL setting for a remote host.

12.5 How to Benchmark a Proxy Cache

Proxy cache benchmarking is tricky because many systems are involved, and many things can go wrong. To ensure we're really measuring the proxy's performance, we need to eliminate other devices and systems as potential bottlenecks and sources of uncertainty. For example, all computer systems used to drive the benchmark should be identically configured. Also, we need to test the networking equipment to guarantee that it's up to the task.

12.5.1 Configure Systems

The first step is to select and configure a number of systems for use as clients and servers. The number of machines you need depends on the total throughput you intend to achieve. For Web Polygraph, you can plan on 400–500 requests per second for each client-server pair. Other benchmarks may have different characteristics. Later, I'll describe how to run a test that proves your systems can adequately generate the load.

Benchmarking systems should be dedicated to their task. You don't want other processes running that can interfere with the measurements. For example, a busy server running on the same machine can use up significant amounts of bandwidth. Even worse, a runaway program can use significant amounts of memory or CPU time, starving the benchmarking processes and adversely affecting your results.

Continuing along these lines, any unneeded services or processes should be disabled. For example, don't run *lpd, cron, sendmail, portmap,* or even *inetd.* The standard FreeBSD installation, as an example, has a nightly cron job that runs *find* on all mounted filesystems. This I/O intensive process takes resources away from the benchmark and leads to unreproducible results.

Be sure to configure and run *xntpd* on all systems. Having clocks synchronized avoids certain problems interpreting HTTP headers that have dates. Additionally, it's much easier to correlate logfiles written on different systems. You might feel it is sufficient to simply synchronize clocks once, before a test starts, but some system clocks drift significantly over time. If your test is very long, there is a chance that one system will finish before or after the others.

Because a benchmark uses a lot of networking resources, you may need to tune your system or build a new kernel. It's likely you'll need to increase or change the following parameters:

- Open file descriptor limit
- Maximum number of threads
- TCP delayed ACKs
- Socket listen queue length
- Number of mbufs or mbuf clusters
- Ephemeral port range

12.5.2 Test the Network

Testing and benchmarking the network is critical. You don't want to spend a lot of time measuring cache performance only to discover later that a NIC was in half-duplex mode or your switch is a bottleneck.

First of all, use *ping* to make sure all systems can talk to each other. If you're using a routed environment, this also ensures you have the routes configured correctly. It's a good idea to let *ping* run for a while so it sends 10–20 packets. If you observe any packet loss, investigate the problem. Bad Ethernet cables are a likely culprit.

Next, run some TCP throughput tests. Good tools for this are *netperf* (*http://www.netperf.org*) and *nttcp* (*http://users.leo.org/~bartel/nttcp/*). Be sure to run throughput tests in both directions on each host at the same time. In other words, make sure each host is both sending and receiving traffic. I recommend running the throughput test for about five minutes. For a full-duplex, switched network, each host should achieve 88–94 Mbps in each direction. If you're using a hub instead of a switch, the peak throughput will be much less, because every host must compete for 100 Mbps total bandwidth, and each NIC runs in half-duplex mode. A test between two hosts should result in about 37 Mbps in each direction. If you get significantly lower throughput than you expect, it probably means one of your Ethernet cables is bad. A measurement slightly lower than expected is more difficult to diagnose. It may be due to an inefficient NIC driver, inadequate CPU power, or a switch or router that cannot support the full network bandwidth.

12.5.3 No-Proxy Test

By this point, you should be confident that your network can support a lot of TCP traffic. The next step is to make sure that the benchmarking systems can generate enough load to drive the proxy cache under test. To do this, I recommend running a no-proxy test. The no-proxy test is important for testing the system as a whole, minus the proxy cache. If successful, it helps to eliminate the client/server machines and networking equipment as a potential bottleneck. It also helps to establish a worst-case measurement you can use in a before-and-after comparison. If this test fails, then you know any measurements made against the proxy cache would be useless.

The no-proxy test uses the same workload you will use on the proxy cache. However, instead of sending requests to the proxy, they are sent directly from clients to servers. Some benchmarking software may not support this mode of operation. With Polygraph, you just comment out the ``--proxy`` command-line option. If you're using a layer four switch to divert traffic, simply disable the redirection temporarily. The no-proxy test should run for at least 30 minutes. Be sure to save the log files and other results from this test for later comparison with the proxy cache results.

12.5.4 Fill the Cache

We're almost ready to measure the proxy cache's performance. Before doing that, however, make sure the cache's disks are full. If the cache is already full, you may be able to skip this step. However, if reproducible results are really important, you should flush the cache and fill it again. I have seen considerable evidence that the method used to fill a cache affects subsequent results.

Ideally, you should fill the cache the same workload characteristics you are measuring with. A cache filled with really large objects, for example, leads to too few delete operations during the measurement phase. During the first industry Cache-Off, caches were filled with a best-effort workload, and the participants were allowed to choose the number of agents to use. One participant discovered that their product achieved higher throughput during the measurement phase when the cache was filled with one best-effort agent, while multiple agents resulted in lower throughput. This is probably because files are written to disk sequentially under the single-agent workload. When these files are later removed, the disk is left with relatively large sections of contiguous free space, which in turn results in faster write times for new objects.

12.5.5 Run the Benchmark

Finally, we're ready to actually benchmark the proxy cache. As I've already mentioned, this test should run for at least six hours. Longer tests are more likely to achieve, and thus measure, steady-state conditions.

The benchmark should record performance data as it runs. You may also want to collect your own statistics from the cache during the benchmark. For example, you can probably use SNMP tools as described in Chapter 11. It's possible, but unlikely in my experience, that such SNMP monitoring can adversely affect the cache's performance; if you're planning to use SNMP on your production caches, you'd probably like to know about this anyway.

Once the test completes, you'll want to analyze the results. Usually this means plotting graphs of various measurements versus time. By looking at the graphs, you should be able to tell whether the product's performance meets your expectations. If you observe spikes or very sudden changes, you may want to investigate these further. Most likely, you'll see something that's not quite right and will want to run another test after making an adjustment.

12.6 Sample Benchmark Results

This section contains results from a Web Polygraph benchmark of a Squid cache. The data shown here is not an official Polygraph result, but it uses the same *PolyMix-3* workload that we used for the third industry Cache-Off.

For this test, Squid is running on a Compaq Proliant system with an Intel Pentium III/450 processor, 1 GB of RAM, six 9 GB SCSI disks, and an Intel fast Ethernet interface. The operating system is FreeBSD-4.1 with a kernel specifically tuned for Squid. The Squid version is 2.4.DEVEL4.

PolyMix-3 has three input parameters: cache size, peak throughput, and fill rate. For this test, the cache size is 41 GB, the peak throughput is 130 requests per second, and the fill rate is 115 requests per second. Another characteristic of the workload is its different phases. *PolyMix-3* has three interesting phases: *fill*, *top1*, and *top2*. There are actually transitional phases in between, but we won't discuss them. The fill rate is the request rate during the *fill* phase, which can be different from the peak throughput for the top phases. During the *fill* phase, the hit ratio is only 5%, whereas it is about 57% during the top phases. During the *fill* phase, the cache is mostly writing objects to disk, with relatively few reads. Thus, a cache may be able to support a higher throughput during the *top2* phase, when it is reading more and writing less than it was during the *fill* phase.

These results were created by running Polygraph's *ReportGen* scripts. Rather than show all of the details that *ReportGen* provides, we'll look only at the three most interesting metrics: throughput, response time, and hit ratio. If we want to compare this result to another *PolyMix-3* run, we usually look at the metrics averaged during the *top2* phase. The *ReportGen* script puts this information in an executive summary table as shown in Table 12.1.

Table 12.1. Summary of Polygraph Results

Metric	Value
Throughput	130.36 req/sec
Hit response time	0.303 sec
Miss response time	2.802 sec
Overall response time	1.443 sec
Cache hit ratio	57.26%

12.6.1 Throughput

First, let's look at the throughput. Remember that this is an input parameter; that is, I told Polygraph what throughput to use. In Figure 12.1, you can see the three phases clearly: first is the long *fill* phase followed by the *top1* and *top2* phases. The *PolyMix-3* workload is designed to fill the cache twice. In other words, it would require twice the cache size to store every cachable response transferred during the fill phase. In this case, it takes about 25 hours to reach that point.

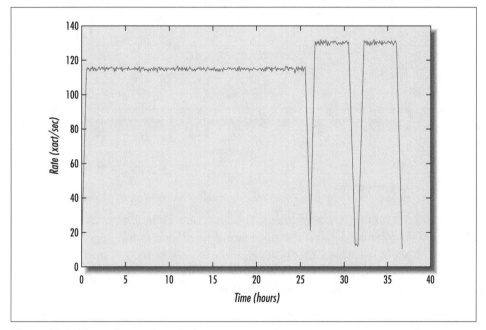

Figure 12.1. Throughput versus time

You can see that the throughput during the fill phase is 115 requests per second. During the *top1* and *top2* phases, Polygraph uses the peak throughput, which is 130 requests per second. Each top phase lasts for four hours. In between are some short *idle* phases.

12.6.2 Response Time

The response time trace is shown in Figure 12.2. One of the first things you notice about this graph is the spikes that occur every four hours. Initially the spikes are small, but they increase with time. They are caused by a cron job on the Squid box that prevents certain log files from growing too large. While Squid is cleaning up the logs, it has a hard time keeping up and some requests are delayed. After about a minute, Squid catches up and response time returns to normal levels.

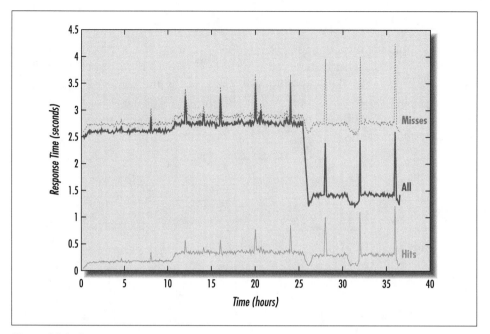

Figure 12.2. Response time versus time

The three lines on the response time graph represent cache hits, cache misses, and all requests combined. During the fill phase, the *All* line is just slightly below the *Miss* line. This is because 95% of all requests are cache misses, and only 5% are hits. During the top phases, you can see that the *All* line drops significantly because about 57% of requests are now cache hits.

Notice the slight increase in *All* response times after 10 hours. This corresponds to the point in time when Squid begins removing cached objects. The delete operations increase disk activity and affect the time to read and write object data.

12.6.3 Hit Ratio

Figure 12.3 shows the cache hit ratio trace. Here we see both the offered and actual hit ratios. A particular product may not achieve the ideal hit ratio for any number of reasons, such as insufficient disk space, overload conditions, and lack of support for certain HTTP features. In this case, Squid gets pretty close to the offered hit ratio, but not quite. During the *fill* phase the two are very close. However, you can see a gap when the hit ratio jumps to 57%. It looks like the gap gets smaller as the test continues after that point.

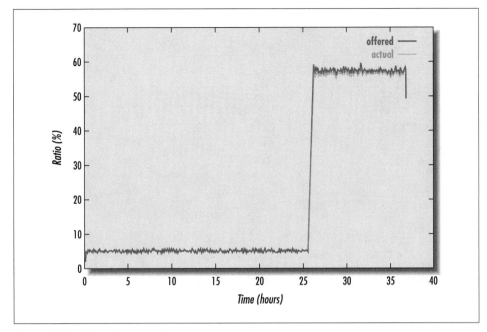

Figure 12.3. Hit ratio versus time

12.6.4 Other Results

Most caching vendors recognize the value in publishing benchmark results for their products. You can find publicly available Polygraph results by visiting *http://www.web-polygraph.org* and *http://www.measurement-factory.com.*

A

Analysis of Production Cache Trace Data

In this appendix, we'll look at some interesting characteristics of web traffic, such as reply size distributions, HTTP headers, and expiration times. Such data is useful for a number of reasons. First, the information in this appendix backs up some of the statements I made earlier in the book. For example, when I said that small files are more more popular than large ones, I wasn't just making that up. Second, this data can help you make decisions regarding your own caching proxies. The hit ratio analysis demonstrates how increasing your cache size may result in higher hit ratios.

For these analyses, I use data from two different sources. One is the NLANR/ IRCache project, consisting of nine caches I maintain throughout the U.S.* The other is a proxy cache located at a U.S. university, which I'll call Anon-U. All data comes from production Squid caches with real users.

I use the IRCache data for most analyses because it is significantly larger and includes more information. The IRCache set includes client access logs, cache "store" logs, and HTTP header logs. The access logs are from March 5–25, 2000 and contain 216 million responses. The store logs are from March 8–25, 2000, and contain 71 million entries. The header logs are from April 2–29, 2000, and contain 268 million request and response entries.

The IRCache proxies are unique in certain ways that can skew the data. In other words, the data collected from these proxies does not necessarily represent typical

---

* The NLANR/IRCache project is funded by the National Science Foundation, grants NCR-9616602 and NCR-9521745.

web traffic. In particular, keep the following points in mind while reading this appendix:

- Most of the IRCache clients are other caches. In some cases, there are three or more caches between the user and my cache. Many requests that would be hits are filtered out by the lower-layer caches. This tends to reduce the caches' hit ratios.

- Many clients use ICP or Cache Digests, so they request only cache hits. This tends to increase the caches' hit ratios.

- A number of clients use the IRCache proxies to bypass filtering in their own organization. Thus, these caches may see a higher percentage of pornography, etc., than a typical cache does.

The Anon-U data consists of 21 million access log entries from May 1–31, 1999. To protect the privacy of that cache's users, both the URLs and client IP addresses have been randomized. The URLs are sanitized in a way that removes information such as hostnames, protocols, port numbers, and filename extension.

When the analysis results in a distribution (e.g., reply sizes), I report both mean and median values. Many of the distributions have heavy tails that make mean values less interesting. In these cases, median is a better representation of the average.

When looking at traffic statistics collected from web caches, it's important to understand where the data comes from and what it represents. I can think of at least four different ways to collect and analyze caching proxy data:

- Per request, as seen on the network between the cache and its clients
- Per object (URL) stored in the cache
- Per request, as seen on the network between the cache and origin servers
- Per object (URL) stored at origin servers

Most of the analyses in this appendix use the first technique: per request between the cache and its clients. The exceptions are object sizes and cachability, both of which are per object. In each of the following subsections, I'll explain a little about the procedures used to generate the results.

A.1 Reply and Object Sizes

Figure A.1 and Figure A.2 show two size distributions, the first for objects and the second for reply sizes. The reply size distribution includes all responses sent to clients, and repeated URLs are counted each time. The object size distribution is meant to represent the size of objects stored on origin servers. Thus, repeated URLs are filtered out for the object size data so that each URL is counted just once.

The reply size distribution has a mean of 8,419 bytes, and the median is 1,266 bytes. The object size distribution is quite different, with a mean of 22,499 bytes and a median of 3,372 bytes.

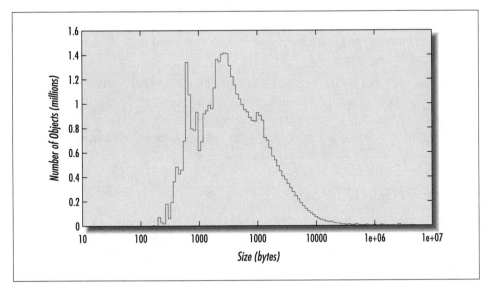

Figure A.1. Distribution of object sizes (IRCache data)

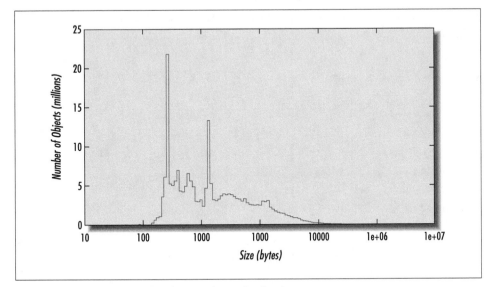

Figure A.2. Distribution of reply sizes (IRCache data)

Both distributions are derived from the fifth field of Squid's *access.log* file. For reply sizes, I include almost every response. I filter out TCP_DENIED responses and certain other Squid-specific responses (e.g., Cache Digests). After that, I take all the size values and calculate the mean, median, and a histogram. Calculating the object size distribution is a little trickier. First, I filter out non-GET requests and non-200 status responses. This is cheating a little bit because POST requests, for example, have origin server objects, or resources, that aren't included in this analysis. Second, I filter out repeated URLs. For each URL, I keep the largest size value seen in the access log. Finally, these values are used to calculate the mean, median, and histogram.

As you can see, reply sizes tend to be smaller than object sizes. This is because a significant percentage of the responses in the reply size distribution don't have an HTTP message body—for example, 304 (Not Modified) responses and 404 (Not Found) error messages. As we'll see later, about 20% of all responses in the IRCache traces are 304 messages.

A.2 Content Types

Table A.1 shows the breakdown of responses by content type. As you can see, images make up about 60% of all web requests by count and 40% by volume. The top three content types—GIFs, JPEGs, and HTML—account for 95% of all requests and 63% of all traffic volume.

Table A.1. The Most Popular Content Types (IRCache Data)

Content Type	Count %	Volume %	Mean Size, KB
image/gif	40.8	16.6	3.75
text/html	35.1	23.1	6.07
image/jpeg	19.0	22.9	11.12
text/plain	1.7	2.5	13.45
application/x-javascript	1.5	0.2	1.45
application/octet-stream	0.5	10.2	179.22
application/zip	0.1	8.0	684.14
video/mpeg	0.0	3.4	761.90
application/pdf	0.0	1.3	336.30
audio/mpeg	0.0	2.5	1707.70
video/quicktime	0.0	1.2	1205.42
All others	1.1	8.1	69.60

This data is derived from the fifth and tenth fields of Squid's *access.log* file. The logs include many responses without a content type, such as 302 (Found) and 304 (Not Modified). All non-200 status responses without a content type have been filtered out. I have not eliminated the effects of popularity. Thus, these numbers represent the percentage of requests made by clients rather than the percentage of content that lives at origin servers.

Figure A.3 shows some long-term trends of the three most popular content types and JavaScript. The percentage of JPEG images remains more or less constant at about 20%. GIF requests seem to have a decreasing trend, and HTML has a corresponding increasing trend. The GIF and JPEG traces are very periodic. The peaks and valleys correspond to weekends and weekdays. On weekends, JPEG counts are higher and GIF counts are lower. A possible explanation is that pornographic images are usually JPEG files, and people view pornography more on weekends than on weekdays. The JavaScript trace shows a very slight increasing trend, although it comprises a very small fraction of total traffic.

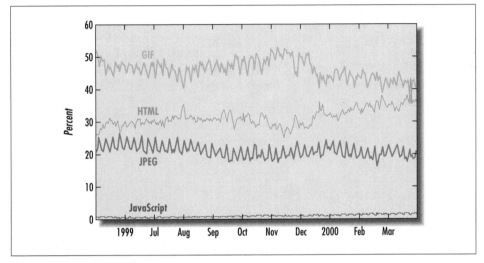

Figure A.3. Content-type trends over time (IRCache data)

This data is also derived from Squid's *access.log* file. To determine the content type, I look at the `Content-type` header and, if that's not present, the filename extension. I ignore responses for which the content type cannot be determined.

A.3 HTTP Headers

It is interesting to examine the HTTP headers of requests and responses flowing through the caches. To get this information, I temporarily modified Squid to write a short binary record that indicates which headers are present. I also tracked the `Cache-control` directives.

The headers log file does not include URLs, so I cannot eliminate the popularity effects. There is one entry for each request from and each response to a client, so this data is from the client's point of view.

A.3.1 Client Request Headers

Table A.2 lists the request headers and their frequency of occurrence. It's important to keep in mind that most of these requests come from child caches, not from
web browsers. Furthermore, most of the child caches are also running Squid. Evidence of this is seen in the occurrence of Via and X-Forwarded-For headers. Both
of these are added by proxies, and the latter is an extension header used by Squid.
According to this data, around 99% of all requests come from child caches.

Table A.2. Client Request Headers (IRCache Data)

Header	% Occurrence	Header	% Occurrence
Host	99.91	Range	0.46
User-Agent	99.21	Connection	0.26
Via	98.90	From	0.24
Accept	98.84	Date	0.18
Cache-Control	98.34	Proxy-Authorization	0.07
X-Forwarded-For	98.19	Request-Range	0.06
Accept-Language	91.33	If-Range	0.05
Referer	85.00	Expires	0.02
Accept-Encoding	82.60	Mime-Version	0.01
Proxy-Connection	78.46	Content-Encoding	0.00
Cookie	39.18	Location	0.00
Accept-Charset	28.77	If-Match	0.00
If-Modified-Since	24.83	X-Cache	0.00
Pragma	13.18	Age	0.00
Other	5.82	Last-Modified	0.00
Authorization	1.41	Server	0.00
Content-Type	1.00	ETag	0.00
Content-Length	0.84	Accept-Ranges	0.00
If-None-Match	0.61	Set-Cookie	0.00

The Referer and From headers are interesting for their privacy implications. Fortunately, very few requests include the From header. Referer is quite common, but it
is less of a threat to privacy.

The data indicates that about 25% of all requests are cache validations. Most of
these are If-Modified-Since requests, and a small amount are If-None-Match. Note
that Squid does not support ETag-based validation at this time.

Table A.3 lists the Cache-control directives found in the same set of requests. The
max-age directive occurs often because Squid always adds this header when

forwarding a request to a neighbor cache. The `only-if-cached` directives come from caches configured in a sibling relationship. (The `only-if-cached` directive instructs the sibling not to forward the request if it is a cache miss.)

Table A.3. Cache-control Request Directives (IRCache Data)

Directive	% Occurrence
max-age	98.01
only-if-cached	9.63
no-cache	0.09

A.3.2 *Client Reply Headers*

Table A.4 lists the HTTP reply headers. `X-Cache` is an extension header that Squid uses for debugging. Its value is either HIT or MISS to indicate whether the reply came from a cached response.

Table A.4. Client Reply Headers (IRCache Data)

Header	% Occurrence	Header	% Occurrence
X-Cache	100.00	Warning	0.03
Proxy-Connection	99.88	Content-Language	0.02
Date	95.20	WWW-Authenticate	0.02
Content-Type	84.94	Title	0.01
Server	82.49	Content-Base	0.01
Content-Length	65.67	Location	0.00
Last-Modified	65.61	Referer	0.00
ETag	53.07	Content-MD5	0.00
Accept-Ranges	48.06	From	0.00
Age	24.28	Host	0.00
Cache-Control	10.36	Public	0.00
Expires	10.30	Upgrade	0.00
Pragma	3.13	X-Request-URI	0.00
Set-Cookie	3.04	Cookie	0.00
Other	2.99	Accept-Charset	0.00
Mime-Version	1.62	User-Agent	0.00
Via	0.80	Retry-After	0.00
Vary	0.66	Accept-Language	0.00
Link	0.53	Authorization	0.00
Content-Location	0.28	Range	0.00

Table A.4. Client Reply Headers (IRCache Data) (continued)

Header	% Occurrence	Header	% Occurrence
Content-Encoding	0.28	Accept-Encoding	0.00
Allow	0.19	X-Forwarded-For	0.00
Connection	0.12	If-Modified-Since	0.00
Accept	0.04	Content-Range	0.00

The Date header is important for caching. RFC 2616 says that every response must have a Date header, with few exceptions. Here we see it in about 95% of replies, which is pretty good.

Content-length occurs in only 65% of responses. This is unfortunate, because when a client (including proxies) doesn't know how long the message should be, it's difficult to detect partial responses due to network problems. The missing Content-length header also prevents a connection from being persistent, unless the agents use chunked encoding.

Table A.5 lists the Cache-control reply directives present in the responses sent to cache clients. As you can see, no-cache and private are the most popular directives. The fact that both occur in 4.6% of responses leads me to believe they probably always occur together. max-age is the only other directive that occurs in more than 1% of responses. The "Other" entry refers to unknown or nonstandard directives.

Table A.5. Cache-control Reply Directives (IRCache Data)

Directive	% Occurrence	Directive	% Occurrence
no-cache	4.60	no-store	0.06
private	4.60	no-transform	0.02
max-age	2.69	s-maxage	0.00
must-revalidate	0.23	proxy-revalidate	0.00
Other	0.11	only-if-cached	0.00
public	0.09		

If we want to find the percentage of responses that have an expiration time, we need to know how often the Expires header and max-age directive occur separately and together. Table A.6 shows the percentage of responses that have one, the other, neither, and both of these headers. In these traces, 89.65% of responses have neither header, which means that only 10.35% have an expiration value. You can see that the Expires header is still more popular than the max-age directive, and that max-age almost never appears alone.

Table A.6. Responses with Explicit Expiration Times (IRCache Data)

Header/Directive	% Occurrence
Neither Expires nor max-age	89.65
Expires only	7.65
Both	2.64
max-age only	0.05

The analysis is similar for cache validators, although the results in Table A.7 are more encouraging. 77.04% of all responses sent to clients have a cache validator. Last-modified is still more popular than the ETag header, although a significant percentage (11.43%) of responses carry only the ETag validator.

Table A.7. Responses with Cache Validators (IRCache Data)

Header/Directive	% Occurrence
Both	41.64
Last-modified only	23.97
Neither Last-modified nor ETag	22.96
ETag only	11.43

A.4 Protocols

Table A.8 shows the distribution of the most popular transfer protocols, HTTP and FTP. Not surprisingly, you can see that on average FTP is used to transfer larger files. Note that this certainly does not represent the distribution of HTTP and FTP traffic on the Internet as a whole. This data comes only from proxy cache logs. Many people configure proxying for HTTP only and connect to FTP servers directly. Furthermore, most FTP clients cannot use HTTP proxies.

Table A.8. Transfer Protocol Usage (IRCache Data)

Protocol	% Requests	% Bytes
HTTP	99.9	95.9
FTP	0.1	4.1

This data is derived from a simple analysis of Squid's *access.log* file. The protocol is taken from the URL and the size from the fifth field.

A.5 Port Numbers

Recall that interception caching (Chapter 5) usually diverts only port 80 connections. However, some HTTP servers use other ports for various reasons. The IRCache data in Table A.9 shows that only 0.3% of HTTP traffic is not on port 80. However, this is an underestimation if we assume that many of the IRCache clients use interception proxying to begin with. The non-port 80 requests won't be intercepted and hence won't reach these caches.

Table A.9. Server Port Numbers (IRCache Data)

Port	% Servers	% Requests	% Bytes
80	99.705	99.610	99.619
8080	0.003	0.088	0.094
8000	0.003	0.039	0.040
All others	0.289	0.262	0.247

A.6 Popularity

Figure A.4 shows the Zipf-like distribution of object popularity. The X-axis is the popularity rank. The most popular object has a rank of 1, the second most popular object a rank of 2, and so on. The Y-axis is the number of requests for each object. Note that both axes have a logarithmic scale.

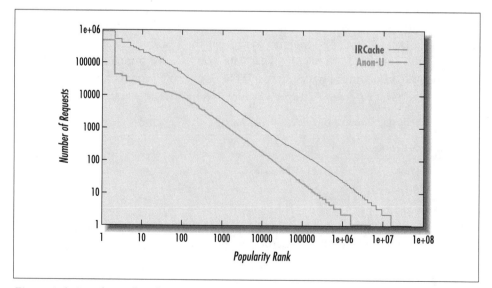

Figure A.4. Popularity distributions (IRCache and Anon-U data)

We say the distribution is Zipf-like because it almost follows Zipf's law. This law, named after George Kingsley Zipf, describes things such as the frequency of words in English texts and the populations of cities. It is also useful for characterizing the popularity of web objects. Specifically, the probability of access for the ith most popular object is proportional to i^{-a}. In Zipf's law, the exponent a is close to 1. For web traffic, the exponent is typically between 0.6 and 0.8.

This data is derived by counting the number of times each URL occurs in Squid's *access.log*. After getting these counts, the particular URLs are unimportant. The values are sorted and plotted against their rank in the list.

For comparison, I show curves for both the IRCache and Anon-U data sets. The Anon-U plot is below the IRCache plot because it has significantly fewer accesses. The two appear to be similar, except that the Anon-U line slopes down much more for the 100 most popular objects.

A.6.1 Size and Popularity

Back in Section 2.4, "Hit Ratios," and Section 12.1.3, "Hit Ratio," I mentioned that byte hit ratios are typically lower than cache hit ratios because small files are more popular than large ones. Here, I back up that assertion by analyzing the IRCache access logs. We'll look at the data in two slightly different ways.

Figure A.5 shows the mean number of requests for objects of different sizes. This is a histogram where the bin number is proportional to the logarithm of the object size. The histogram value is the mean number of requests for all objects in that bin. In other words, it is the number of requests divided by the number of unique objects in each bin. Although there are peaks and valleys, the mean number of requests generally decreases as object size increases. For example, the largest objects were requested about two times on average, while the smallest objects were requested hundreds and thousands of times.

Figure A.6 is a little more complicated. First, the Y-axis is the total number of requests, rather than the mean. Second, the bins are constant size. Third, in order to see all of the data, the plot has three views of the data at three different scales. The first trace is with a bin size of 1 byte, the second with 100-byte bins, and the third with 10 KB bins. In other words, the first trace shows file sizes up to 1 KB, the second up to 100 KB, and the third up to 10 MB.

In the "1 byte bin" trace, you can see that popularity increases with object size for objects between 0 and 400 bytes. From 400–600 bytes, the curve is relatively flat, but keep in mind that the Y-axis is logarithmic. In the other traces with larger bin sizes, the decreasing trend is quite obvious.

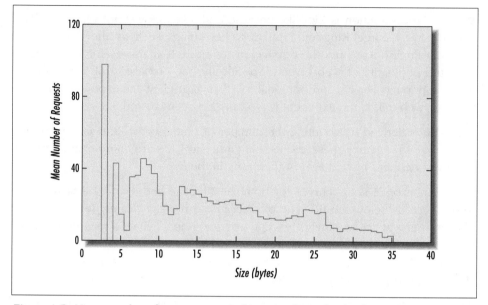

Figure A.5. Mean number of requests versus object size (IRCache data)

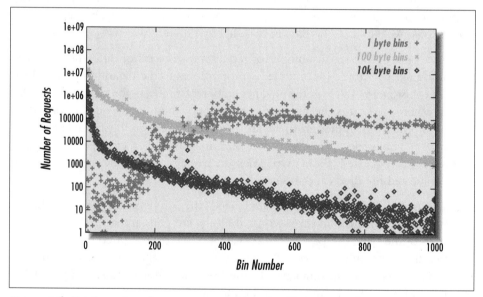

Figure A.6. Total number of requests versus object size (IRCache data)

The procedure for generating this data is similar to the one used for reply and object sizes. Unlike the object size distribution, however, I want to count each request, not each object. Unlike the reply size data, I want to count the object size, not the reply size. For this data, I take only GET requests with a status code of 200 or 304 and filter out any Squid-specific requests. For some objects, the size, as logged by Squid, may change significantly over time. To account for this, I use the average size for all requests of a particular URL. The 304 responses do not contribute to the size calculation but are counted as a request.

A.7   Cachability

Table A.10 shows the cachability percentages for different classes of responses. This data comes from an analysis of Squid's *store.log* files. Squid writes an entry in this file for every object saved to disk and every object that is released from the cache. Objects are released either because they are uncachable or to free up space for new objects. For each URL, I count the number of times it is successfully written to disk and the number of times it is not cached. Releases made by the cache replacement algorithm are ignored. If it is cached more times than not, the object is cachable. If it is not cached more times, it is uncachable. If the counters are equal, then the object's cachability is unknown.

Table A.10. Response Cachability (IRCache Data)

Type	% Cachable	% Uncachable	% Unknown
All	75.9	23.9	0.2
text/html	36.7	63.1	0.2
image/*	90.9	8.9	0.2

This analysis represents the cachability of an object rather than a response. It does not include popularity effects. The IRCache data does not lend itself to a response-based analysis of cachability because the IRCache proxies receive a higher-than-normal percentage of requests for uncachable objects. The child caches filter out most of the cache hits but not the cache misses; the misses find their way to the top of the hierarchy. I compensate for this by looking at unique URLs rather than each request.

A.8   Service Times

Table A.11 shows the mean and median service times for different types of requests. The type is taken directly from the fourth field of Squid's *access.log* file. The three-digit number following the slash is the HTTP status code. Here I show only 200 (OK) and 304 (Not Modified) replies.

Table A.11. Mean and Median Service Times by Cache Result (IRCache Data)

Type	Mean (sec)	Median (sec)
TCP_REFRESH_HIT/200	5.165	0.281
TCP_MISS/200	4.590	0.466
TCP_REFRESH_MISS/200	4.091	0.468
TCP_CLIENT_REFRESH_MISS/200	1.889	0.215
TCP_HIT/200	1.819	0.050
TCP_MISS/304	1.151	0.294
TCP_REFRESH_HIT/304	1.107	0.219
TCP_IMS_HIT/304	0.102	0.042

The string before the slash indicates how the cache handled the request. TCP_MISS means the object wasn't found in the cache at all. TCP_HIT indicates an unvalidated cache hit. TCP_IMS_HIT occurs when Squid receives an If-modified-since request and returns a 304 (Not Modified) reply immediately because the response is fresh according to the local configuration. TCP_CLIENT_REFRESH_MISS means that the user-agent sent the no-cache directive. TCP_REFRESH_HIT occurs when Squid validates its cached response and learns that the object hasn't changed. If the client's request includes an If-modified-since header, Squid returns the 304 message. Otherwise, it sends the entire object, and the status is 200. Finally, TCP_REFRESH_MISS means Squid sent a validation request to the origin server, and the cached object was out-of-date.

This data is derived from the second field of Squid's *access.log*. Squid records the elapsed time for each HTTP transaction. The timer starts when Squid accepts a new connection or when it reads the first byte of the request on a persistent connection. The timer stops when the connection is closed or when the last byte of the response is written on a persistent connection. Note that Squid's notion of service time is inaccurate for a couple of reasons:

- The operating system buffers data as it is written out to the network. It accepts data from the application, typically up to 32 KB, and then transmits it to the other end according to the TCP/IP protocols. Squid doesn't know when the client actually receives the final packet. This is especially significant for cache hits, most of which are smaller than 32 KB. TCP packets may be delayed, dropped, and retransmitted without affecting the service time.

- Similarly, when Squid closes a connection, the operating system takes care of the final handshake. The application doesn't know when the client receives the FIN packet that closes the connection.

Not too surprisingly, all the 200 (OK) status responses take longer than the 304 (Not Modified) responses. The 304 responses are smaller, consisting of HTTP headers only. Also, as we would expect, cache hits (except for TCP_REFRESH_HIT) are sent faster than cache misses. By comparing the mean and median values, we can conclude that the reply size distributions have heavy tails.

A.9 Hit Ratios

In this section, I use the Anon-U trace files in two different simulations. We'll see how the number of cache clients affects hit ratio and how the hit ratio changes as a function of the cache size.

For hit ratio versus number of clients, I used one day's access log from the Anon-U data. I am restricted to a single day because the client IP addresses are not sanitized consistently between log files. The access log I used has 1.7 million requests from 2,415 different clients. I can't tell from this data which of the objects are uncachable, so in the simulation all URLs are uniformly uncachable with a 25% probability.

Given a trace with 2,415 clients, how can we calculate the hit ratio for one, two, or any particular number of clients? My approach is to first create a random ordering of clients. Then I run a program that reports the hit ratio for requests from the first client, the first two clients, the first three clients, and so on, all the way up to the maximum. For small numbers of clients, the hit ratio varies greatly depending on the ordering of clients. In one case, the first 20 clients might have a 20% hit ratio, while another results in 90%. To improve the precision, I ran the simulation with 100 different client orderings and averaged the results. Note that, in these simulations, the cache size is infinite, and there are no If-modified-since or no-cache requests. The random seed is always the same so that the set of uncachable URLs remains consistent between runs.

Figure A.7 shows the mean hit ratios with "error bars," which represent the minimum and maximum cache hit ratio values for the 100 different runs. As the number of clients increases, the minimum-maximum spread decreases.

The linear scale of the first figure makes it difficult to see the trend for small numbers of clients. Figure A.8 is a graph of the same data but on a logarithmic scale and without error bars. Here you can see that the mean hit ratio starts at around 18% and increases in proportion to the logarithm of the number of clients.

Figure A.9 gives the results from a simulation with different cache sizes and also shows how the hit ratio increases with the number of total requests. As with Figure A.8, the hit ratio increases in proportion to the logarithm of the cache size. For

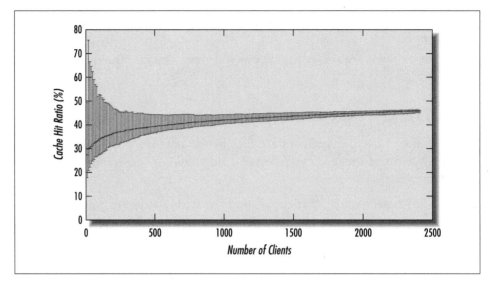

Figure A.7. Cache hit ratio versus number of cache clients (Anon-U data)

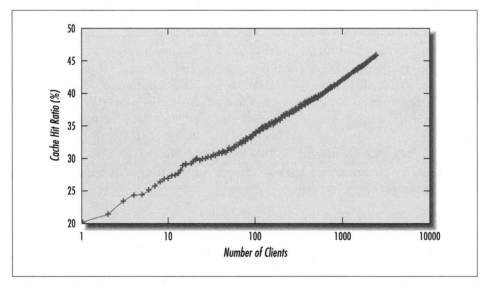

Figure A.8. Cache hit ratio versus number of cache clients, logarithmic scale (Anon-U data)

this trace, each order of magnitude increase in cache size results in an increase in hit ratio of 11%.

The different lines in Figure A.9 show the hit ratio trace after reading a certain number of requests from the log file. For example, the lowest line shows the simulation results after reading 10,000 requests. You can see that the hit ratio doesn't change once the cache size reaches 50 MB. In other words, a 50 MB cache is sufficient to store every cachable response from the first 10,000 requests. At the other

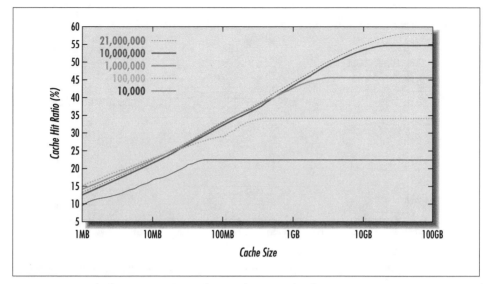

Figure A.9. Cache hit ratio versus cache size (Anon-U data)

extreme, all 21 million requests in the Anon-U logs require a 40 GB cache to achieve maximum hit ratio.

A.10   *Object Life Cycle*

In this section, I provide a few clues into the temporal characteristics of web objects. By analyzing Squid's *store.log* files, we can see how old an object is when it enters the cache, when it was last modified, and when it expires.

Age, expiration, and modification time calculations depend on the presence of certain HTTP headers. The Date header is quite common, but the Expires header is rare. If a header is missing or invalid, the response is not included in the analysis.

In Figure A.10, you'll see cumulative distribution (CDF) plots for object age, time since modification, and time until expiration. Age values are taken from the HTTP Age header or, in most cases, by subtracting the Date header value from the current time. Whenever a cache receives a response from an origin server, the object's age should be zero. However, the age may be nonzero for one or more of the following reasons:

- The origin server's clock may be wrong. Even if the response is generated at the current time, the server's Date header may be in the future or the past by a significant amount. In this analysis, negative age values are discarded.

- The response may have been served from a neighbor cache rather than the origin server. Most IRCache proxies have neighbors, so it's likely that about 5% of requests are found in those neighbors.

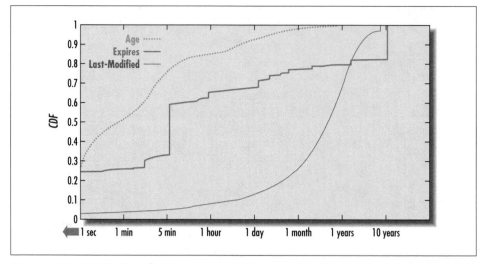

Figure A.10. Distribution of object ages, modification, and expiration times (IRCache data)

- The origin server may actually be a surrogate. The Akamai content distribution network falls into this category. When you request an object such as *http://a1.g.a.yimg.com/7/1/31/000/us.yimg.com/i/mail/mailicon.gif,* you receive a cached response, and the Date header is set to a specific time in the past.

Table A.12 shows the same data in tabular form. You can see, for example, that 28% of responses with valid Date or Age headers are less than 1 second old, and 94% are less than 1 day old.

Table A.12. Object Life Cycle Percentiles

Time	Age percentile	Expiration percentile	LMT percentile
1 second	28	25	4
1 minute	62	31	5
1 hour	86	66	9
1 day	94	73	15
1 week	98	78	24
1 month	99	80	39
1 year	100	83	86
1 decade	100	100	100

The distribution of expiration times is particularly interesting. Unlike the others, it is not very smooth. The vertical increases correspond to spikes in the histogram. For example, there is a sudden increase from 30% to 60% right at the 5-minute mark. This means that, of the responses with an expiration time, 30% were set to expire after 5 minutes. You can also see "spikes" at 1 minute, 1 hour, 1 day, 1 month, and 1 year.

The `Last-modified` distribution is shifted farther to the right, indicating that the time since modification is relatively large. As Table A.12 shows, of the responses entering the cache that have the `Last-modified` header, 60% have not changed in the previous month. In fact, 47% of those responses have a last modification time between 1 month and 1 year ago.

A.11   Request Methods

Table A.13 lists the distribution of HTTP request methods. This data is skewed because, by default, Squid does not forward non-GET method requests up to parent caches. Also, the ICP and Cache Digest protocols work for GET methods only. It is likely that most of the non-GET methods are forwarded directly to origin servers by the lower layers.

Table A.13. Distribution of Request Methods (IRCache and Anon-U Data)

Method	IRCache %	Anon-U %
GET	98.78	98.31
POST	0.881	1.634
HEAD	0.293	0.058
PROPFIND	0.041771	-
MOVE	0.002518	-
PROPPATCH	0.002076	-
CONNECT	0.001292	-
DELETE	0.000474	-
OPTIONS	0.000414	-
PUT	0.000095	0.000180
COPY	0.000015	-
MKCOL	0.000007	-
LOCK	0.000007	-
TRACE	0.000001	-

Note that the Anon-U data doesn't have any WEBDAV request methods. Most likely, these methods were not in use when the Anon-U data was generated (May 1999).

A.12 Reply Status Code

Table A.14 shows the percentage of requests for different status codes. Only the popular and possibly interesting status codes are included here.

Table A.14. Reply Status Code Breakdown (IRCache and Anon-U Data)

Status	IRCache %	Anon-U %
200 OK	59.76	71.35
304 Not Modified	19.31	17.23
302 Found	9.27	8.12
504 Gateway Time-out	5.88	0.22
404 Not Found	1.46	1.21
403 Forbidden	1.39	0.04
301 Moved Permanently	0.50	0.48
500 Internal Server Error	0.37	0.07
401 Unauthorized	0.26	0.10
206 Partial Content	0.08	0.05

Approximately 20% of all responses are for validation requests where the resource has not changed. Sadly, almost 10% of responses are HTTP redirects (302 status) for pages that have moved to a new location. The high percentage of 504 responses in the IRCache data is from sibling requests that would have resulted in a cache miss. The 206 response code is used for HTTP "range" requests whereby the client requests some subset of the object data. The small percentage of 206 replies is somewhat surprising but perhaps less so given that the data was collected in March of 2000.

B

Internet Cache Protocol

This appendix describes the message format and opcodes of the Internet Cache Protocol, Version 2. You may also want to read RFCs 2186 and 2187. The final section of this appendix describes experimental opcodes not mentioned in the RFCs. Visit *http://icp.ircache.net* for up-to-date information on the protocol.

B.1 ICPv2 Message Format

Figure B.1 shows the structure of an ICP message. The 20-byte header is the same for all messages. As with all Internet protocols, it is necessary to convert all multi-octet fields to network byte order before transmission. Each field is discussed in the following sections.

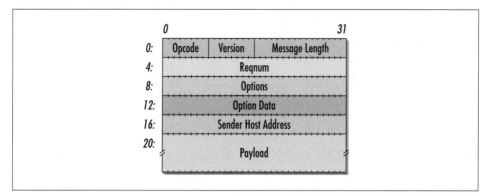

Figure B.1. ICP message format

B.1.1 Opcode

The opcode determines the type of an ICP message. There are three query opcodes: ICP_OP_QUERY, ICP_OP_SECHO, and ICP_OP_DECHO. All other opcodes are reply messages. These include ICP_OP_HIT, ICP_OP_MISS, and ICP_OP_ERR. Each opcode is explained in Section B.2, "Opcodes."

B.1.2 Version

ICP includes an 8-bit version field to indicate the protocol version. Currently, two version numbers are in use: 2 and 3. If there ever was a Version 1 specification or implementation, nothing is known about it. Harvest and Squid use Version 2 in ICP messages. Netcache/Network Appliance uses Version 3. Section 8.1.3.7, "Interoperation," describes the interoperation issues between these versions. Note that RFCs 2186 and 2187 describe only ICPv2.

B.1.3 Message Length

This 16-bit field holds the size of the entire ICP message. Its purpose is to verify that a cache receives the whole message as sent. If the number of bytes read from the network is not equal to the message length value, the received message must be ignored.

B.1.4 Reqnum

Reqnum is short for request number. This is a 32-bit identifier used to correlate queries and replies. Normally, a cache increments its request number counter for every ICP query sent. A cache that receives an ICP query must use the same request number in its reply message.

Harvest and Network Appliance fail to properly implement ICP request numbers. Both always set this field to 0 for ICP queries and ICP replies. This causes a minor incompatibility with Squid installations because it relies on matching request numbers to implement private cache keys (see Section 8.1.3.7, "Interoperation").

B.1.5 Options

The *Options* field is a 32-bit-wide bitmask of option flags. A cache can set these flags to indicate support for optional features. See Section B.3, "Option Flags," for names and descriptions of the defined flags.

B.1.6 Option Data

The *Option Data* field is four octets that can be used to support new features. Currently, only the SRC_RTT feature uses this field.

B.1.7 Sender Host Address

The *Sender Host Address* field is a historical legacy from the origins of this protocol. It is supposed to contain the IPv4 address of the host sending the message. However, this is redundant information. An application that receives a TCP or UDP packet already knows the address of the remote host. Current ICP implementations set this field to all 0's in outgoing messages and should ignore it for all incoming messages.

B.1.8 Payload

The variable-sized *Payload* field normally contains the URL string. In some cases, the payload contains other data in addition to a URL. For this reason, the URL must be null-terminated to indicate where the URL ends and where the next field begins. The median size of a URL is approximately 45 bytes, so most ICP messages are less than 100 bytes in length.

The opcodes with special payload formats are ICP_OP_QUERY and ICP_OP_HIT_OBJ. The QUERY payload includes an IPv4 address field, but it is superfluous and unused in practice. The HIT_OBJ payload includes object data in addition to the URL string.

B.2 Opcodes

This section describes the nine opcodes defined by RFC 2186. Some experimental opcodes are discussed in Section B.4, "Experimental Features." The numeric (decimal) code appears in parentheses following the opcode name.

ICP_OP_QUERY (1)

A query message that asks a neighbor cache if it has the object with the URL given in the payload. A cache that receives a QUERY must respond with one of the following reply opcodes: ICP_OP_HIT, ICP_OP_MISS, ICP_OP_ERR, ICP_OP_MISS_NOFETCH, ICP_OP_DENIED, or ICP_OP_HIT_OBJ.

The payload of a QUERY message is shown in Figure B.2. The *Requester Host Address* is an artifact from the protocol's very early design and remains only for backwards compatibility. Originally, it was meant to hold the IPv4 address of the client that initiated the (HTTP) request. Note that this is different from the *Sender Host Address*. Instead, it is the address of the sender's client. Apparently, this field was meant to be used for analyzing the flow of requests through a hierarchy. In practice, it is always filled with 0's. The variable-sized URL field should be terminated with a null byte.

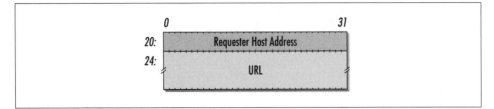

Figure B.2. ICP QUERY payload

ICP_OP_SECHO (10)

SECHO is short for Source Echo. This opcode is used for ICP queries sent to the UDP echo service (port 7) of origin servers. If enabled, the origin server simply sends the unchanged packet right back to the cache. Thus, ICP_OP_SECHO is also an ICP reply opcode. The SECHO payload is identical to the QUERY payload. The source echo feature can be used to tell if an origin server is closer than any parent caches. If so, the cache may want to forward the request directly to the origin server instead of a neighbor cache.

Unfortunately, many server administrators do not like to be probed in this manner. To them, the ICP messages appear as random UDP packets. The echo service is disabled on many hosts, and those who leave it enabled often misinterpret the ICP SECHO packets as hacker attacks. The use of source echo is now discouraged.

ICP_OP_DECHO (11)

This is also an ICP query opcode. DECHO is short for dumb echo, where *dumb* refers to a proxy cache that does not understand ICP. As with SECHO, its technique is to bounce an ICP message off the cache's UDP echo port. A DECHO reply message is treated just like a MISS. In other words, we assume the dumb proxy does not have the object cached. The primary purpose of the DECHO message is to measure network connectivity to the cache. The DECHO payload is identical to the QUERY payload.

ICP_OP_MISS (3)

The MISS reply message indicates that the neighbor cache does not have a fresh copy of the specified object. Note that the neighbor cache uses its own settings to determine whether a cached object is fresh or stale. These settings may be different from the querying cache's, and this causes problems with false hits (see Section 8.1.3.3, "False hits").

In a parent-child relationship, a MISS reply implicitly grants permission for the child to request the object from the parent. This is not true, however, for a sibling relationship. An ICP MISS from a sibling means the querying cache must not forward the request there.

The payload of an ICP_OP_MISS message includes only the URL from the query, as shown in Figure B.3. Having the URL in the reply is probably unnecessary, since the request number is also the same in a query/reply pair. If the ICP_FLAG_SRC_RTT flag is set in the query message, and the proxy supports this feature, it may include a RTT measurement for the URL host in the *Option Data* field.

Figure B.3. ICP MISS payload

ICP_OP_MISS_NOFETCH (21)

This opcode is just like a regular MISS, with one important difference: the MISS_NOFETCH message tells the querying cache that it should not request this object from the responding cache at this time. Essentially, this allows the responding cache to act like a sibling if it wants to. The MISS_NOFETCH payload is identical to the MISS payload.

The responding cache may not want to handle the request for any number of reasons, including:

- The cache may detect that upstream Internet connectivity is suboptimal. Connection timeouts and name lookup failures are good indications of this. By using the MISS_NOFETCH message, a parent cache instructs a child cache to use an alternate path, if possible.

- The cache may become overloaded with requests. Thus, the MISS_NOFETCH message tells child caches to back off a little bit, if possible.

- In a usage-based charging network, the cache may want to avoid serving cache misses during peak times.

ICP_OP_HIT (2)

The HIT reply indicates that the neighbor cache holds a fresh copy of the specified object. RFC 2187 recommends that a HIT be returned only if the object will be fresh for at least the next 30 seconds. The HIT message payload includes only the URL, just like the MISS payload.

ICP_OP_HIT_OBJ (23)

This is like a HIT reply, except that the cached HTTP response is also included in the ICP payload. The HIT_OBJ feature probably does not require its own opcode because the presence of content in the payload can be indicated with the ICP_FLAG_HIT_OBJ flag. However, the flag was invented after the opcode, as a means to indicate support for this feature.

The HIT_OBJ payload is shown in Figure B.4. Note that the object data does not necessarily begin on a four-octet boundary, as shown in the figure. In other words, the URL length is not necessarily a multiple of four octets. The object data begins immediately following the null byte that terminates the URL string.

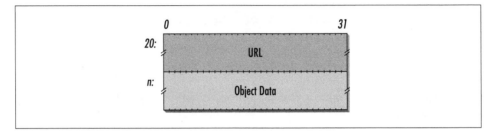

Figure B.4. ICP HIT_OBJ payload

ICP_OP_ERR (4)

An ERR response indicates that the receiver was unable to process the query because of a protocol error. ICP_OP_ERR should be sent only in response to a QUERY. Squid sends this opcode only if the URL string is not really a URL. For other types of errors, such as an unknown opcode or version, the QUERY message is silently ignored. The ERR reply payload consists of only the URL, or whatever should have been the URL, just like the MISS reply.

ICP_OP_DENIED (22)

A DENIED message is sent in response to a query that is disallowed due to access controls. The DENIED message payload consists of only the URL, just like the MISS reply.

ICP queries from unknown sources should always be denied. In theory, ICP can be used to acquire sensitive information about the contents of your cache. Unfortunately, ICP has no real security features, so we can't be sure that a message is authentic. The best we can do is allow or deny based on the source IP address and trust that our hosts and routers are correctly configured to detect address spoofing.

A large percentage of DENIED messages indicates some sort of misconfiguration between a pair of caches. A cache that sends or receives a large amount of denied messages to another should try to get the administrator's attention so the situation can be remedied. Furthermore, I recommend that an implementation should stop sending DENIED messages to a neighbor after reaching a certain threshold. It is better just to ignore the queries than to continue filling the network with DENIED messages that seem to have no effect.

B.3 Option Flags

This section describes the flags for the *Options* field, defined in RFC 2186. Some experimental option flags are discussed in Section B.4, "Experimental Features." The flag's hexadecimal value appears in parentheses following its name.

ICP_FLAG_HIT_OBJ (0x80000000)

When this flag is set in an ICP query, it indicates that the sender supports the HIT_OBJ feature (see Section 8.1.2.3, "Object data with hits").

ICP_FLAG_SRC_RTT (0x40000000)

This option is used to include network round-trip time measurements in ICP replies (see Section 8.1.2.4, "Source RTT measurements"). The ICP_FLAG_SRC_RTT bit is set in the ICP query message to indicate that the sender would like to receive the neighbor's RTT measurement to the origin server. If the recipient has a measured value, it includes the RTT in the low 16 bits of the *Option Data* field and sets the ICP_FLAG_SRC_RTT bit in the reply. The RTT value is encoded as a 16-bit integer in milliseconds.

B.4 Experimental Features

Since the publication of RFC 2186, a number of experimental opcodes and flags have been added to ICP. These were generally added so specific software developers could implement new features for their products.

B.4.1 Pointers

ICP_OP_MISS_POINTER (18)
ICP_FLAG_POINTER (0x20000000)

Mirror Image Internet designed a web caching product that operates in a cluster configuration. Each node in the cluster knows, or remembers, which objects are stored by each neighbor. Thus, instead of returning an ICP miss message, a cache may be able to say, "I don't have this object, but I know who does." In other words, a cache provides a pointer to an object located in a neighbor cache. Mirror Image has proposed some experimental ICP opcodes and features to implement these features.

To indicate its support for the pointer features, an ICP client sets the ICP_FLAG_POINTER bit (0x20000000) in the *Options* field of a query message. An ICP server then sends a MISS_POINTER message instead of a MISS if the option bit is set and it knows of a neighbor cache that holds the requested object. The payload of the MISS_POINTER message is a list of IPv4 addresses, one for each neighbor cache that has the object. The payload does not include the URL because the ICP client should be able to determine the URL from the ICP reply's *Reqnum* field.

ICP pointers and other types of distributed cache directories do not address permission and authorization issues. A directory may tell client A that cache B has a cached copy of the response. However, this does not necessarily mean that A is allowed to request it from B. If A and B have no prior agreement in place, then most likely B would deny any request from A. In the case of a MISS_POINTER reply with many addresses, it is entirely possible that the ICP client does not have permission to get the object from any of them.

Researchers at AT&T also developed a centralized directory system, which they call CRISP [Gadde, Chase and Rabinovich, 1998]. Their implementation, based on Squid, uses ICP for information exchange but does not use the opcodes described here.

B.4.2 Object Advertisement

ICP_OP_ADVERTISE (19)
ICP_OP_UNADVERTISE (20)
ICP_FLAG_PREADVERTISE (0x10000000)

A centralized directory requires some method for the group members to inform the directory when objects are added or removed. The two experimental opcodes, ICP_OP_ADVERTISE and ICP_OP_UNADVERTISE, provide this functionality. The payload of an ADVERTISE message is simply the URL, and the recipient does not generate a reply.

When a parent cache also provides a directory service, the ADVERTISE message normally follows a QUERY. For example, a child cache sends a QUERY to its parent, which sends back a MISS. The client fetches the URL from somewhere, then sends an ADVERTISE message to the parent. As an optimization, we can eliminate the advertise message by setting the ICP_FLAG_PREADVERTISE bit in the QUERY message. The flag indicates that the sender intends to have the named object in its cache soon.

B.4.3 Request Notification

ICP_OP_NOTIFY (12)

The ICP_OP_NOTIFY opcode and associated flags were added to support prefetching between Squid and the Wcol proxy.* Wcol can be used to prefetch objects through a normal (nonprefetching) proxy, as shown in Figure B.5. Instead of sending client requests through Wcol directly, the NOTIFY message is used to tell Wcol that someone requested a particular resource.

The Squid cache sends a NOTIFY message to the prefetching engine (Wcol) for every client request it receives. The prefetching engine may also elect to request the given URL and parse it for inline images and referenced links. The format of the NOTIFY message is identical to the QUERY message. However, the receiver does not send any reply message back. The following four flags are defined for the *Option Data* field to provide additional information about the requested URL:

ICP_NOTIFY_MISS (0x00000008)
   The requested URL does not exist in the cache.

ICP_NOTIFY_HIT (0x00000004)
   The requested URL exists in the cache.

ICP_NOTIFY_REFRESH (0x00000002)
   The client's request includes a no-cache directive.

ICP_NOTIFY_IMS (0x00000001)
   The request includes an If-Modified-Since header or other cache validator.

Although NOTIFY was invented to support prefetching, it is not limited to that. It can also be used for simple remote request logging, for example.

B.4.4 Object Removal and Invalidation

ICP_OP_INVALIDATE (13)
ICP_OP_PURGE (14)

In a tightly coupled cache cluster, it may be desirable to propagate object deletions and invalidations with ICP. The INVALIDATE message requests a cache to mark the named object as stale, without removing it. The next time the object is requested, it should be validated with the origin server. Similarly, the PURGE message requests that a cache remove the named object from its storage. There is no response for either of these messages. Because ICP messages are normally sent via

---

* You can find more information on Wcol at *http://shika.aist-nara.ac.jp/products/wcol/wcol.html.*

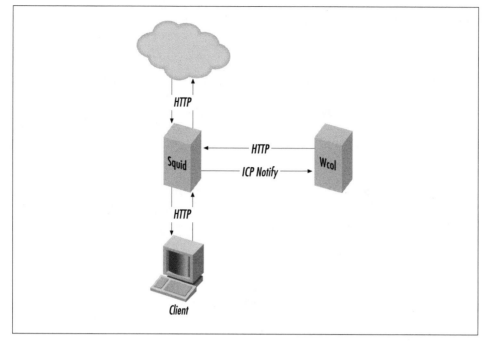

Figure B.5. ICP NOTIFY usage

UDP, there is no guarantee the message will be received. Even if the message is received, there is no guarantee the other cache will honor the request.

Remember that ICP provides no authentication mechanism. In theory, this feature could allow a third party to wipe out entirely a cache's contents. An implementation should probably accept these requests only from specific IP addresses. Even then, the address may be spoofed or the machine broken into. It may also be a good idea to limit the number or rate of delete/invalidate messages that are accepted.

B.4.5 MD5 Object Keys

ICP_FLAG_MD5_KEY (0x08000000)

At some point in time, product developers considered using MD5 checksums, instead of URLs, in ICP messages. Although nothing was ever implemented (as far as I know), the ICP_FLAG_MD5_KEY bit was reserved. Note that there is no standard for calculating an MD5 checksum for an HTTP request or response.

B.4.6   Eliminating URLs from Replies

ICP_FLAG_DONT_NEED_URL (0x04000000)

The ICP_FLAG_DONT_NEED_URL option bit informs an ICP server that it doesn't need to include the URL in its reply message. This optimization reduces the size of ICP replies by about 75%.

B.4.7   Wiretapping

ICP_OP_WIRETAP (15)

The ICP_OP_WIRETAP message is a request to receive a stream of NOTIFY, ADVERTISE, and UNADVERTISE messages from a neighbor for a certain amount of time. This opcode was added for Cidera, which uses these ICP messages in its satellite-based cache filling service. Rather than statically configuring a cache to continually transmit these messages to its collection service, it wanted something more flexible and dynamic. The WIRETAP payload holds the amount of time, in seconds, for which the recipient should send the NOTIFY and ADVERTISE messages back to the sender. The time is encoded as a single, unsigned, 8-bit value. Thus, the WIRETAP message must be sent at least every 255 seconds, or the flow of messages will stop.

B.4.8   Prefetching

ICP_FLAG_PREFETCH (0x02000000)

The ICP_FLAG_PREFETCH option, also added for Cidera, is a request for the recipient to prefetch the named URL if it is not already cached. This is a suggestion only; the recipient may refuse to prefetch the URL without giving a reason.

C

Cache Array Routing Protocol

CARP consists of two different components: a membership table format and an algorithm. The membership table is one way an agent learns about about the set of parent caches (the other is manual configuration). The algorithm is how an agent selects the appropriate parent for a given request.

The information in this appendix is taken from an expired Internet Draft. You can also find information on CARP by searching Microsoft's web site.

C.1 Membership Table

The format of the Proxy Array Membership Table is an ASCII text file. It has a global information section followed by a blank line and a list of caching proxies with various parameters.

The first line of the global information section identifies the file as a CARP table and includes the protocol version number, for example:

```
Proxy Array Information/1.0
```

The draft document describes only CARP Version 1.0.

The remainder of the global information section consists of the following headers:

ArrayEnabled
> The draft states, "This field allows proxies to advertise their implementation of CARP v1 even if they are not members of a Proxy Array." Valid values are 0 and 1. Presumably, a caching proxy sets this field to 0 if it supports CARP but is not a member of an array.

ConfigID

This is a 32-bit integer identifier for a particular instance of a table. This is not a version number—you can't use *ConfigID* to tell if one version of a table is newer than another. You can use it to find out if two members have the same table. Perhaps the designers intended it to be something like a cache validator.

ArrayName

This is a purely informational name for the table to help administrators figure out where it came from.

ListTTL

This header specifies the number of seconds for which the table is valid. After this amount of time, the agent should update its copy of the table.

Following the global information and a blank line, the table includes one line for each member of the cache array. These lines have the following nine fields:

Name

The fully qualified domain name of the caching proxy. Downstream agents (i.e., those that treat this proxy as a parent) should resolve this name when opening a connection.

IP address

The IP address that other array members should use when opening a connection. This may be different from the address derived by resolving the hostname in the first field. Some caching proxies have multiple IP addresses. This field allows the member to specify which address should be used.

Port

The TCP port where the proxy accepts HTTP connections.

Table URL

A URL where agents can find a current copy of the array table. In most cases, it is the same URL used to get the table in the first place.

Agent

A string that identifies the vendor and version number of the caching proxy. Its not clear why the protocol designers think this is useful information. The agent string is not used by the algorithm; it appears to be purely informational.

State time

The amount of time, in seconds, that the caching proxy has been a member of the array in its current state. This field also appears to be informational. It is not used in the algorithm to select an array member.

Status

>   Describes the cache's current state and its ability to accept requests. Legal values are UP and DOWN.

Load factor

>   An integer value that defines how much of the total load this cache should receive, relative to the whole array. The relative load factor is calculated by dividing a cache's load factor by the sum of all load factors in the array.

Cache size

>   The maximum size, in megabytes, of this cache. Cache size is purely informational and not used in the routing function calculations.

C.2 Routing Function

The routing function is an algorithm that calculates a score for each member of the cache array. In other words, when forwarding a request, an agent calculates a score for each parent, then routes the request to the cache with the highest score.

A score is calculated from three values: a hash of the URI, a hash of the proxy name, and a load factor multiplier. The proxy name hashes and multipliers don't change over time, so they are calculated just once. The URI hash is computed for each request that needs to be routed.

I will use a simple implementation of CARP in C to explain how the algorithm works. This is a complete program, but I'll explain it in chunks. The program consists of the following functions:

*   *CalcHostHash* calculates a hash value for a proxy host name.

*   *CalcMultipliers* calculates the load factor multipliers for all members of the array.

*   *CalcURIHash* calculates a hash value for a URI request.

*   *CalcScore* calculates a score for a (URI, cache) tuple.

*   The *main* function reads URIs and finds the cache with the highest score.

The program begins with some basic header files:

```
#include <stdio.h>
#include <unistd.h>
#include <stdlib.h>
#include <string.h>
#include <math.h>
```

We also need to define a data structure and an array that holds information about the proxy caches:

```
/* a structure to hold information about the parent caches */
struct _peer {
    char *name;
    unsigned int LF;        /* integer load factor */
    unsigned int hash;
    double RLF;             /* relative load factor */
    double LFM;             /* load factor multiplier */
    int reqs;
};

/* a hardcoded list of parents */
#define N_MEMBERS 4
static struct _peer Peers[N_MEMBERS] =
{
    {"cache1.carp.net", 1},
    {"cache2.carp.net", 2},
    {"cache3.carp.net", 3},
    {"cache4.carp.net", 4}
};
```

Note that this code initializes the array with proxy names and integer load factors. In this case, all the load factors add up to 10, so *cache1* should get $1/10$ of all requests, *cache2* $2/10$, *cache3* $3/10$, and *cache4* $4/10$. We'll need to convert these integer load factors into floating point values later.

The algorithm uses bitwise left rotation when computing hash values. This operation rotates the set of bits from right to left by a certain number of positions. Bits that fall off the left side are wrapped back around to the right side. The following C macro implements left rotation for 32-bit integers:

```
#define ROTATE_LEFT(x, n) (((x) << (n)) | ((x) >> (32-(n))))
```

The following is the function that calculates a hash value for a proxy hostname:

```
unsigned int
CalcHostHash(const char *hostname)
{
    unsigned int HostHash = 0;
    char *c;
    for (c = hostname; *c != 0; c++)
        HostHash += ROTATE_LEFT(HostHash, 19) + (unsigned int) *c;
    HostHash += (HostHash * 0x62531965);
    HostHash = ROTATE_LEFT(HostHash, 21);
    return HostHash;
}
```

We also need to calculate a load factor multiplier for each member of the cache array. The load factor multiplier is based on the integer load factor values specified previously. The first step is to convert the integer load factors into floating point relative load factors (RLF) so they all add up to 1. In other words, divide each factor by the sum of all factors:

```
void
CalcMultipliers(void)
{
    int i;
    unsigned int load_sum = 0;      /* sum of all integer load factors */
    double ProdLFM;

    for (i = 0; i < N_MEMBERS; i++)
        load_sum += Peers[i].LF;
    for (i = 0; i < N_MEMBERS; i++)
        Peers[i].RLF = (double) Peers[i].LF / (double) load_sum;
```

Next comes the trickiest part of the algorithm. The load factor multipliers (LFM) are calculated iteratively. For this reason, they must be calculated in order from the smallest to the largest RLF. I cheated here by initializing the array with ascending load factors. Here's the rest of the function:

```
    Peers[0].LFM = pow((Peers[0].RLF * N_MEMBERS), (1.0 / N_MEMBERS));
    ProdLFM = Peers[0].LFM;
    for (i = 1; i < N_MEMBERS; i++) {
        double j = N_MEMBERS - i;
        Peers[i].LFM = (j * (Peers[i].RLF - Peers[i - 1].RLF)) / ProdLFM;
        Peers[i].LFM += pow(Peers[i - 1].LFM, j);
        Peers[i].LFM = pow(Peers[i].LFM, 1.0 / j);
        ProdLFM *= Peers[i].LFM;
    }
}
```

The URI hash function is similar to the proxy name hash function, but simpler:

```
unsigned int
CalcURIHash(const char *uri)
{
    unsigned int URIHash = 0;
    const char *c;
    for (c = uri; *c != 0; c++)
        URIHash += ROTATE_LEFT(URIHash, 19) + (unsigned int) *c;
    return URIHash;
}
```

Now that we know how to calculate each value, we can write the function that combines them to calculate a score:

```
double
CalcScore(unsigned int URIHash, unsigned int HostHash, double multiplier)
{
    /* multiplier is a peer->LFM */
    unsigned int CombinedHash = (URIHash ^ HostHash);
    CombinedHash += (CombinedHash * 0x62531965);
```

```
        CombinedHash = ROTATE_LEFT(CombinedHash, 21);
        return (multiplier * CombinedHash);
    }
```

Now we have everything needed to actually implement CARP. The following *main* function reads URIs from standard input and determines the best proxy cache for each. Before exiting, it prints the distribution of requests among the array members:

```
int
main(int argc, char *argv[])
{
    char uri[512];
    int n = 0;
    int i;

    for (i = 0; i < N_MEMBERS; i++)
        Peers[i].hash = CalcHostHash(Peers[i].name);
    CalcMultipliers();

    while (NULL != fgets(uri, 512, stdin)) {
        unsigned int URIHash;
        double score;
        double high_score = 0.0;
        int high_index = 0;
        strtok(uri, "\r\n");     /* truncate end-of-line characters */
        URIHash = CalcURIHash(uri);
        for (i = 0; i < N_MEMBERS; i++) {
            score = CalcScore(URIHash, Peers[i].hash, Peers[i].LFM);
            if (score > high_score) {
                high_score = score;
                high_index = i;
            }
        }
        Peers[high_index].reqs++;
        n++;
    }
    for (i = 0; i < N_MEMBERS; i++) {
        printf("%20.20s %d reqs, %f%%\n",
            Peers[i].name,
            Peers[i].reqs,
            (double) Peers[i].reqs / (double) n);
    }
    return 0;
}
```

C.3 Examples

The following is a fictitious CARP membership table that shows the global information section followed by the list of array members. The three array members should each appear on one line. These lines are too long to fit on the page, so they are wrapped around and indented:

```
Proxy Array Information/1.0
ArrayEnabled: 1
ConfigID: 12345
ArrayName: My-Array
ListTTL: 3600

proxy1.isp.net 10.2.3.4 3128 http://proxy.isp.net/carp.txt
    SmartCache-v1 21600 UP 1 2048
proxy2.isp.net 10.2.3.5 3128 http://proxy.isp.net/carp.txt
    SmartCache-v1 20127 UP 1 2048
proxy3.isp.net 10.2.3.6 3128 http://proxy.isp.net/carp.txt
    SmartCache-v1 22928 UP 1 2048
```

The following tables may be useful to developers who want to verify their implementation. Table C.1 is a list of proxy names and load factors. I took the program described previously and added **printf** statements to print the hash values, RLF, and LFM.

Table C.1. Proxy Array Values

Hostname	Hash Value	Load Factor	RLF	LFM
test1.ircache.net	0x96010320	1	0.142857	0.869442
test2.web-cache.com	0x84965f0f	1	0.142857	0.869442
test3.squid-cache.org	0x4f5d7332	2	0.285714	1.064844
test4.packet-pushers.com	0xa79af670	3	0.428571	1.242318

Table C.2 consists of hash values and Table C.3 shows CARP scores for five different URIs. The four scores correspond to the four proxy names given earlier. The score values are truncated (not rounded) after the decimal point to improve the readability of this table.

Table C.2. URI Hash Values

URI	Hash Value
http://www.squid-cache.org	0x16073a01
http://www.ircache.net	0xae0af388
http://www.web-cache.com	0xd6b2152d
http://www.oreilly.com	0x31952fdd
ftp://ftp.microsoft.com	0x50cc09bf

Table C.3. URI Scores

URI	Score 1	Score 2	Score 3	Score 4
http://www.squid-cache.org	1937807807	737946946	3043043329	4019296969
http://www.ircache.net	1372682590	2237060277	2349863321	543856355
http://www.web-cache.com	2885259455	1656192339	4204309062	2705367480
http://www.oreilly.com	843623848	2648286094	3561199409	5289183760
ftp://ftp.microsoft.com	1098649645	993566466	675513163	2319331913

D

Hypertext Caching Protocol

I introduced you to HTCP in Section 8.3, "HTCP." That section mostly talked about how HTCP compares to ICP, as well as some of its other characteristics. The information in this appendix is primarily written for developers who want to implement HTCP in their own products. It might also be useful to someone trying to debug an HTCP-related problem. In the following sections, we'll look at the structure of HTCP messages and values for all the fields. RFC 2756 is the authoritative specification of HTCP Version 0.0.

D.1 Message Format and Magic Constants

An HTCP message consists of three sections: HEADER, DATA, and AUTH. All multioctet fields are encoded in network byte order.

D.1.1 HEADER

Figure D.1 shows the four-octet, fixed-size HTCP HEADER section. The LENGTH field specifies the size of the UDP message, and it should be equal to the number of octets written to and read from the network. MAJOR and MINOR specify the protocol version the sender is using. A change in the minor version number must not affect compatibility. In particular, when a reserved field is placed into service, the minor version number is incremented. When new fields or identifiers are added, the major version number is incremented.

D.1.2 DATA

The DATA section, shown in Figure D.2, is where all the interesting stuff happens. It consists of eight fixed-format octets followed by a variable-sized OP-DATA field.

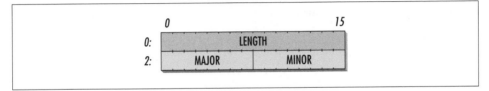

Figure D.1. HTCP HEADER format

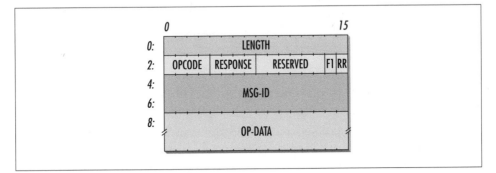

Figure D.2. HTCP DATA format

These are the DATA section fields:

LENGTH

>   This LENGTH field, not to be confused with the HEADER section LENGTH
>   field, specifies the number of octets comprising the DATA section. This is
>   needed, of course, because the OP-DATA field varies in size.

OPCODE

>   HTCP Version 0.0 defines five opcodes: NOP, TST, MON, SET, and CLR. These
>   are fully discussed in Section D.3, "HTCP Opcodes." Note that the OPCODE
>   field is only 4 bits wide, which allows for up to 16 opcodes.

RESPONSE

>   RESPONSE is a numeric error code set for response messages only. Further-
>   more, this field is only meaningful when the F1 flag is set. This field must be
>   ignored for query messages (RR=0) and when F1 equals 0.

>   When F1 is set, RESPONSE codes are interpreted as given in Table D.1. When
>   F1 is not set, the RESPONSE code has an opcode-specific meaning, as
>   described in Section D.3, "HTCP Opcodes."

Table D.1. HTCP Overall Response Codes

Code	Description
0	AUTHENTICATION wasn't used but is required.
1	AUTHENTICATION was used but unsatisfactorily.
2	OPCODE not implemented.
3	MAJOR version not supported.
4	MINOR version not supported (MAJOR version is okay).
5	Inappropriate, disallowed, or undesirable OPCODE.

RESERVED

In HTCP/0.0, these 6 bits are reserved for future use.

F1

F1 is a single-bit flag whose meaning is different for requests and responses. In a request, F1 indicates whether a response is desired. Certain opcodes, such as TST, are meaningless unless F1 is set. For other opcodes, such as CLR, the response is optional.

When F1 is set in a response message, the RESPONSE code refers to the overall message. F1 is set only when an error occurs. If the operation succeeds, F1 is not set and RESPONSE takes on an opcode-specific meaning, which may indicate some other kind of error.

RR

The RR bit simply indicates whether a particular message is a request or a response. The bit is not set for requests and set for responses.

MSG-ID

This is a 32-bit identifier that uniquely identifies an HTCP transaction. The MSG-ID value must be copied from a request message into the corresponding response. Usually, there is a one-to-one pairing between requests and responses. The MON request, however, may result in numerous MON responses. Thus, many MON responses may have the same MSG-ID.

OP-DATA

The content of the OP-DATA field is opcode-specific and usually different for requests and responses. These are fully explained in Section D.3, "HTCP Opcodes."

D.1.3 AUTH

Figure D.3 shows the AUTH section, which is optional in HTCP/0.x. Its purpose is to provide some level of assurance that a particular message has not been spoofed by a third party.

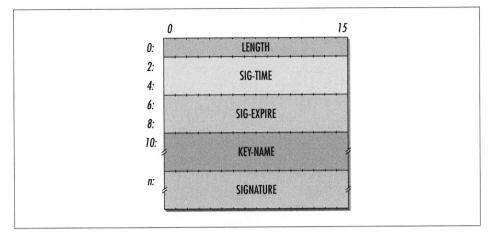

Figure D.3. HTCP AUTH format

The following list describes the AUTH section fields:

LENGTH

> The LENGTH field specifies the number of octets in the entire AUTH section. If authentication is not to be used for a particular message, then the LENGTH field is set to 2, and the remaining fields are dropped.

SIG-TIME

> SIG-TIME is the time at which the SIGNATURE is generated. The time is expressed as the number of seconds since midnight on January 1, 1970 UTC (also known as "Unix time").

SIG-EXPIRE

> This is the time at which the SIGNATURE expires. It is also expressed as the number of seconds since midnight on January 1, 1970.

KEY-NAME

> This field is the name of a shared secret key. It is only a name used to identify a key and not the key itself. The secret key named by this field is used in the HMAC-MD5 algorithm.

SIGNATURE

> The SIGNATURE is an HMAC-MD5 digest [Krawczyk, Bellare and Canetti, 1997] of the concatenation of the ten fields shown in Figure D.4.

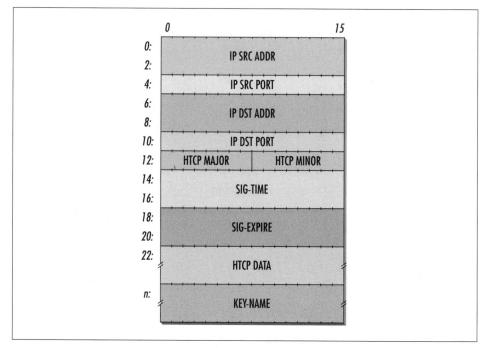

Figure D.4. HTCP SIGNATURE format

D.2 HTCP Data Types

HTCP messages are built on a simple hierarchy of data types. I'll start with the most simple and finish with the complex ones.

D.2.1 COUNTSTR

A COUNTSTR is a string of ISO8859-1 (Latin-1) characters preceded by the length of the string. The string length is encoded (in network byte order) using two octets. The string is not necessarily null-terminated. For example, the following hexadecimal values encode the string "Cache" as a COUNTSTR:

```
00 05 43 61 63 68 65
   5  C  a  c  h  e
```

D.2.2 SPECIFIER

A SPECIFIER, shown in Figure D.5, encodes an HTTP request using four COUNTSTRs. It is used in TST, SET, and CLR requests, and in MON responses. METHOD, URL, and VERSION are all taken from the first line of an HTTP request. REQ-HDRS consists of all the remaining request headers.

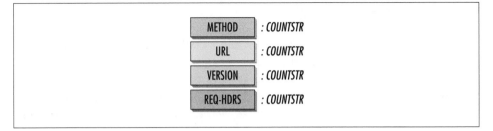

Figure D.5. HTCP SPECIFIER format

D.2.3 DETAIL

Figure D.6 shows the DETAIL type, which is used in TST response messages. It provides the information about a cached response. These are all HTTP-style headers with CRLF line termination. RESP-HDRS is the set of HTTP response headers, as defined in Section 6.2 of RFC 2616. These include Etag, Age, and others. ENTITY-HDRS is the set of HTTP headers defined in Section 7.1 of RFC 2616. These include Expires, Last-modified, and others. CACHE-HDRS, on the other hand, are defined by HTCP, rather than HTTP. They are used to convey additional information about a resource that may prove to be useful. For example, the Cache-Location header is a list of other proxy caches that are likely to hold a copy of the object. Refer to Section 4 of RFC 2756 for the full details.

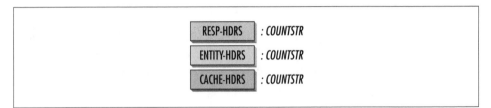

Figure D.6. HTCP DETAIL format

D.2.4 IDENTITY

As you can see in Figure D.7, IDENTITY is just a combination of SPECIFIER and DETAIL. It is used for the MON and SET opcodes.

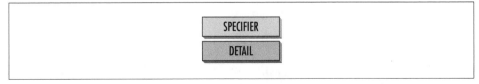

Figure D.7. HTCP IDENTITY format

D.3 HTCP Opcodes

HTCP/0.0 defines five opcodes: NOP, TST, MON, SET, and CLR. Note that ICP has different opcodes for queries and replies—for example, ICP_OP_QUERY and ICP_OP_MISS. HTCP, however, uses the same opcode for both messages. The previously described RR flag indicates whether a given message is a request or a response. The following sections describe each opcode, including how each one uses the OP-DATA field.

D.3.1 NOP

The NOP (null operation) opcode is similar to an ICMP echo or a "ping" message. It can be used to measure network delays between caches, as well as simply to find out if they are alive.

There is no OP-DATA for either NOP queries or responses, and the RESPONSE code is always zero.

D.3.2 TST

The TST (test) opcode is similar to the ICP query operation. It tests for the existence of a cached response in a neighbor cache.

D.3.2.1 TST request

For a TST request, the OP-DATA is a SPECIFIER. Recall that a SPECIFIER includes the HTTP request method, URI, HTTP version, and the client's request headers. The request headers are important because the client may have certain freshness requirements (`Cache-control: max-age` or `max-stale`).

D.3.2.2 TST response

Table D.2 shows the RESPONSE codes defined for a TST response when F1 is not set.

Table D.2. HTCP TST Response Codes

Code	Description
0	Entity is present in responder's cache.
1	Entity is not present in responder's cache.

Note that the RESPONSE code indicates only the presence or absence of the object and says nothing about its freshness. If the cached object is stale, the server may set the RESPONSE code to either 1 or 0. Setting RESPONSE to 1 forces the client to predict a cache miss for the request. Setting it to 0, however, causes the client to make its own hit/miss prediction based on the HTTP reply headers included in the TST response. In other words, the client cannot predict a cache hit simply because the RESPONSE code is 0.

When the RESPONSE code is 0, the TST response OP-DATA is a DETAIL that describes the cached response. In particular, it includes the HTTP entity headers (Expires, Last-modified, Content-length, etc.) and the HTTP response headers (Age, Vary, etc.). The HTCP client must check the entity headers for freshness information. It may want to collect a number of responses and then choose the cache that has the most recent copy of the object. The DETAIL may also include various cache headers, which are potentially useful bits of information a cache has learned about the resource.

When the RESPONSE code is 1, the TST response OP-DATA consists of CACHE-HDRS (a COUNTSTR) only. Even though the other cache doesn't have a copy of the resource, it might have information that can help to minimize the time to fetch the object.

D.3.3 MON

The MON (monitor) opcode allows caches to inform each other about the objects they add, delete, and update. It is similar to the WIRETAP, ADVERTISE, and UNADVERTISE opcodes of ICP. With the MON opcode, a cache knows which objects its neighbor has stored and therefore may be able to avoid per-request delays caused by TST messages.

The monitoring feature has the potential to expose private information about a cache to third parties. Imagine a clever person being able to find out which web sites the cache users visit. Although authentication is optional with HTCP/0.0, implementations should require authentication for the MON opcode, or at least support address-based access controls.

D.3.3.1 MON request

The MON request message initiates a monitoring session with another cache. That is, the sender asks the receiver to send back a stream of MON responses for some amount of time.

The MON request OP-DATA is simply a one-octet (8 bits) time field. It specifies the duration, in seconds, for the monitoring session. Given the size of this field, the maximum possible value is 255 seconds.

D.3.3.2 MON response

Table D.3 lists the two possible RESPONSE codes for a MON response.

Table D.3. HTCP MON Response Codes

Code	Description
0	Request accepted; the OP-DATA field contains useful data.
1	Request refused because too many MON sessions are already active.

When the RESPONSE code is 0, the OP-DATA field has the structure shown in Figure D.8.

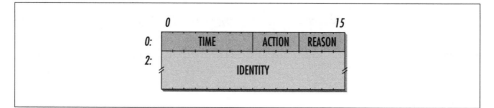

Figure D.8. HTCP MON OP-DATA format

These are the parts of the OP-DATA field:

TIME

> TIME is the number of seconds remaining for the current monitoring session (identified by the MSG-ID field).

ACTION

> ACTION is a numeric code that indicates the action taken on the given object. The valid ACTION codes are given in Table D.4.

Table D.4. HTCP ACTION Values

Code	Description
0	The object has been added to the cache.
1	The object in the cache has been refreshed. This corresponds to receiving a 304 Not Modified reply from a validation request.
2	The object in the cache has been replaced. This corresponds to receiving a full response for a cached object. The new response may or may not be different that the cached response. This can occur from a no-cache reload, or from a validation request that returns 200 (OK).
3	An entity in the cache has been deleted.

REASON

> A numeric code that indicates the reason for the ACTION taking place. The valid reason codes are shown in Table D.5.

Table D.5. HTCP MON Reason Codes

Code	Description
0	A reason not covered by any of the other REASON codes.
1	A proxy client requested this resource.
2	A proxy client requested this resource, but caching is disallowed.
3	The proxy prefetched this resource.
4	The resource expired, per the reply headers.
5	The resource was purged because of the cache's storage limits.

D.3.4 SET

The SET opcode allows one cache to push certain updates to another. For example, when a cache issues a validation request and receives a 304 (Not Modified) response, some of the reply headers (Age, Expires) are updated. Pushing these updated headers to neighbor caches with a SET message obviates the need for the neighbors to issue validation requests.

SET requests must be handled carefully because they may modify the information stored by a cache. A SET request that incorrectly extends a response's expiration time may cause users to receive a stale page for a long time. Therefore, trust is very important for SET messages. An HTCP server is free to ignore any SET request, for any reason whatsoever. Although not required, an HTCP implementation really should ignore any SET request that does not have a valid AUTH section.

D.3.4.1 SET request

The OP-DATA for a SET request is an IDENTITY structure, which is simply a SPECIFIER and a DETAIL. The SPECIFIER holds information such as the request method, URI, and request headers. The DETAIL contains the updated reply headers.

If the F1 flag is not set, the receiver must not send back a response.

SET requests should be generated due to HTTP transactions only. Caches should not pass SET requests on to their own neighbors due to the strong possibility of flooding a hierarchy with HTCP messages.

D.3.4.2 SET response

A SET response is very simple since it does not include any OP-DATA. Only the RESPONSE code is significant. Table D.6 lists the defined SET response codes.

Table D.6. HTCP SET Response Codes

Code	Description
0	IDENTITY was accepted.
1	IDENTITY was ignored; no reason given.

D.3.5 CLR

The CLR (clear) opcode is used to suggest that a neighbor remove an object from its cache storage. This feature may be useful if one cache determines that an object has been updated or removed at the origin server.

As with SET, the CLR opcode is dangerous because it modifies the cache storage. In the worst case, a malicious person could delete most or all of the objects stored in a cache. An HTCP agent may choose to ignore any CLR request for any reason. CLR requests without valid AUTH sections should definitely be ignored.

D.3.5.1 CLR request

A CLR request has the OP-DATA structure shown in Figure D.9. REASON is a 4-bit numeric code that explains why the sender wants the object (specified by the SPECIFIER) to be removed. The allowed reason codes are shown in Table D.7.

Table D.7. HTCP CLR Reasons

Code	Description
0	Some reason not better specified by another code.
1	The origin server says the object no longer exists.

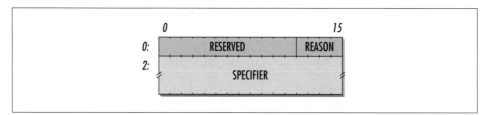

Figure D.9. HTCP CLR OP-DATA format

D.3.5.2 CLR response

The CLR response also does not include an OP-DATA section. Only the RESPONSE code is important. Table D.8 describes the defined values and their meanings.

Table D.8. HTCP CLR Response Codes

Code	Description
0	I had the object, and I just deleted it.
1	I have the object, and I'm not deleting it.
2	I don't have the object.

E

Cache Digests

We talked about Cache Digests and Bloom filters in Section 8.4, "Cache Digests." This appendix provides further information on the implementation. The discussion here is targeted towards developers and gets a little technical at times. Since interoperation is important, I include an example that developers can use to verify their implementations.

E.1 The Cache Digest Implementation

Since digests are designed to be shared between cooperating caches, all implementations must agree on (or have some way to determine) how many and which hash functions to use, the format of the digest key, and the size of the Bloom filter. This section describes Cache Digests Version 5, as implemented in Squid. Currently, there is no other formal documentation for Cache Digests, apart from some pages on the Squid web site.

E.1.1 Keys

Let's start with the digest key. This is the chunk of data to which we apply the hash functions. The key is simply a unique identifier for each object in the cache. The URI alone is not a good cache key. Cached responses are identified by a request method, a URI, and possibly additional request fields. A Cache Digest key consists of the request method, encoded as an 8-bit value, followed by the URI string (see Figure E.1). The null byte that terminates the URI string is not included in the key. The values used to encode the request method are listed in Table E.1.

Table E.1. Cache Digest Request Method Encodings

Value	Method
0	NONE
1	GET
2	POST
3	PUT
4	HEAD
5	CONNECT
6	TRACE
7	PURGE
8	OPTIONS

Not all of these request methods are cachable, and thus not all are appropriate for a Cache Digest, but the full list is included here for completeness. This encoding scheme leaves much to be desired. New request methods cannot be supported in a Cache Digest until they are assigned a value.

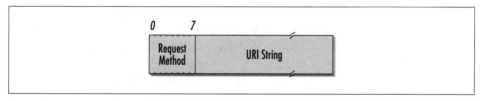

Figure E.1. Cache Digest key

Strictly speaking, there are numerous other attributes that should probably be included in a cache key. For example, the client may specify a language preference. If a resource (HTML page) is available in different languages, the response can vary on the client's Accept-language request header.

E.1.2 Hash Functions

Recall that the Bloom filter design uses K independent hash functions to produce K bit locations. The Cache Digest implementation uses four hash functions. Intuitively four feels like about the right number, but the decision is somewhat arbitrary. As computer scientists, we like powers of two. Two hash functions are probably not enough, and eight are probably too many.

The number four works well because it evenly divides 128—the number of bits in an MD5 hash. The four Cache Digest hash functions are really just four chunks of the MD5 checksum. That is, we take the 128 bits and chop them into four 32-bit pieces. The first hash function is bits 1–32, the second is bits 33–64, etc.

When converting a 32-bit MD5 chunk into an integer, the result depends on the byte ordering of the CPU architecture. Since Cache Digests are exchanged between all types of systems, we must enforce a consistent conversion for this step. We use the `htonl()` function to interpret the MD5 chunk in network byte order. This code snippet from Squid demonstrates the necessary conversion:

```
unsigned int *
cacheDigestHashKey(const CacheDigest * cd, const MD5 * md5)
{
    const unsigned int nbits = cd->mask_size * 8;
    unsigned int tmp_vals[4];
    static unsigned int hashed_vals[4];
    memcpy(tmp_vals, md5, sizeof(tmp_vals));
    hashed_vals[0] = htonl(tmp_vals[0]) % nbits;
    hashed_vals[1] = htonl(tmp_vals[1]) % nbits;
    hashed_vals[2] = htonl(tmp_vals[2]) % nbits;
    hashed_vals[3] = htonl(tmp_vals[3]) % nbits;
    return hashed_vals;
}
```

E.1.3 Sizing the Filter

Determining the optimal filter size is an interesting problem. If the filter is too small, there are too many false positives. If it's too large, most of the bits will be 0, which results in wasted space. Bloom says that the filter has an optimal size when exactly half the bits are on. Recall from Section 8.4.1, "Bloom Filters," that M is the number of bits in the filter, N is the number of objects in the cache, and K is the number of hash functions. Now we can calculate the optimal number of bits per item that should turn on half of the bits.

$$-e^{\frac{-KN}{M}} = \frac{1}{2}$$

$$\frac{-KN}{M} = \ln 2$$

$$\frac{KN}{M} = -\ln 2$$

$$\frac{M}{N} = \frac{K}{\ln 2}$$

According to these formulas, we should use 5.77 bits per entry with four hash functions. The ratio of M/N is a local decision only. A digest user does not need to know what the ratio is; it only needs to know M, the number of bits in the digest. Thus, the digest creator determines the false-hit probability for his own digest.

The previous formulas are for the so-called optimal digest size, which, according to Bloom, is when exactly half the bits are on. This requirement determines the ratio of *M/N* and the false-hit probability. We might like to specify the false-hit probability first and then determine the bits per entry ratio. Solving the previous equation for *M/N* in terms of the probability, *p*, and *K*, we have:

$$p = \left[1 - e^{\frac{-KN}{M}} \right]^{K}$$

$$\frac{M}{N} = \frac{-K}{\ln(1 - p^{1/K})}$$

For example, if we want a false-hit probability of 1%, then we need 10.5 bits per entry. Figure E.2 is a graph of all probabilities.

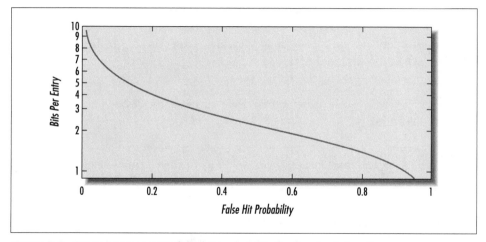

Figure E.2. Bits per entry versus false hit probability for four hash functions

E.1.4 Selecting Objects for the Digest

A cache need not, and probably should not, add every cached object to its digest. Any object that, when requested, would result in a cache miss should not be added. Obviously this includes uncachable objects, which might temporarily be in the cache. It also includes objects that are likely to become stale, or even removed in the near future. We'll talk more about these objects in the following section.

Generally, there are no rules for determining which objects should be put in the digest. The digest essentially advertises the objects that a cache is willing to serve to its neighbors. The cache may choose to advertise only a subset of its cache. For example, we may want to serve only small objects to our neighbors. Thus, objects that are larger than a certain threshold should not be added to the digest. In theory, a cache can have more than one digest it gives to neighbors. One digest could be given to child caches and a different one to parents.

E.1.5 False Hits and Digest Freshness

When using cache digests, a false hit can occur for one of two reasons: when a digest lookup is a false positive or when an object added to the digest becomes stale or is removed from the cache. As described previously, the false-hit probability can be controlled by adjusting the Bloom filter parameters (increasing the filter size, for example). Limiting false hits due to the second factor requires a little more work.

A Cache Digest represents a cache's contents at a single point in time. Obviously, the contents change with time, so the digest must be updated. The current implementation does not support incremental updates because we cannot remove entries from a Bloom filter. Instead, the cache rebuilds its own digest from scratch at regular intervals. In Squid, the rebuild interval defaults to one hour. In addition, a cache must update its copies of its neighbor's digests. A neighbor's digest is refreshed when its expiration time is reached. Thus, a copy of a neighbor's digest represents the state of the cache within the last hour.

In conjunction with the update interval, we can use the following heuristics to minimize false hits:

* Do not add objects that will become stale before the next digest update, according to response headers or the local freshness rules. Unfortunately, a client's Cache-control request header may still cause freshness-based cache misses.

* Do not add objects that are likely to be removed quickly due to the cache replacement policy. For example, with an LRU replacement policy, we can identify objects that will be removed if they are not accessed before the next digest update.

E.1.6 Exchanging Digests

Digests are transferred using HTTP. A cache periodically requests its neighbor's digest with a well-known URL. The Cache Digest protocol does not specify how or under what URL a digest is requested. Thus, each product must currently choose its own naming scheme. In Squid, the digest URL consists of the cache's hostname and port number followed by */squid-internal-periodic/store_digest*, for example:

> *http://squid.ircache.net:3128/squid-internal-periodic/store_digest*

The digest's response header includes valid Expires and Last-modified values. As you would expect, the Last-modified value indicates when the digest was created.

Similarly, the `Expires` value indicates when the digest becomes stale and a new version is available. The update period is set by local policy. In Squid, the default value is one hour. A digest must not be used after it becomes stale. Instead, the digest user (i.e., a neighbor cache) should fetch a fresh digest.

E.2 Message Format

A Cache Digest message consists of a fixed 128-octet header (see Figure E.3 followed by a variable-sized Bloom filter. The header definitions are as follows:

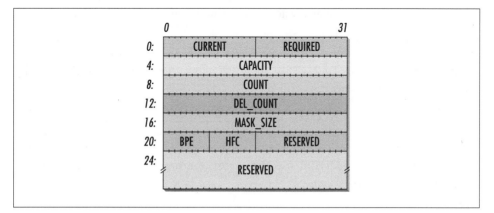

Figure E.3. Cache Digest header

CURRENT

> This is the version number of the digest. The CURRENT version number is incremented whenever a significant feature is added to the Cache Digest protocol. When the digest recipient decodes a message, the CURRENT value indicates which protocol features are included.

REQUIRED

> This is the minimum version number required to correctly interpret the digest message. In other words, this specifies the last version this message is backward-compatible with. It can also be used to "eliminate" serious bugs. If a bug is found with the Version X implementation, a sender can set the REQUIRED value to X+1. Then, all buggy implementations that support only Version X are forced to ignore the cache digest message.

CAPACITY

> This is an estimate of the number of objects for which the digest was built. It is in the header for informational purposes only. A digest user does not need to know the CAPACITY to decode the digest.

COUNT

This is the actual number of objects encoded by this digest. It may be larger or smaller than CAPACITY. This value also is not needed to decode the digest.

DEL_COUNT

This is a counter that tracks the number of objects removed from the cache since the digest was last created. Deletions are not supported in the current implementation, so this value is always 0.

MASK_SIZE

This is the number of octets comprising the Bloom filter. In other words, the message includes this many octets immediately following the header.

BPE

BPE is an abbreviation for bits-per-entry. This value is used to size the Bloom filter, based on the CAPACITY. In any Cache Digest header, the following equation must be true:

$$MASK\_SIZE = \frac{CAPACITY \times BPE}{8}$$

The bits-per-entry value really doesn't belong in the Cache Digest header because it is not needed to use the digest. Furthermore, bits-per-entry is not necessarily an integer value.

HFC

HFC is an abbreviation for hash function count. It specifies the number of hash functions used by the Bloom filter. Note, however, that it does not specify *which* hash functions are used. In the current implementation, HFC is always set to 4.

RESERVED

The remaining 106 octets are currently unused and reserved for future growth. All RESERVED areas must be zero-filled.

E.3 An Example

If you find yourself in the position of implementing Cache Digests, you can use the following two tables to verify your code. Table E.2 shows three sample URIs and their MD5 hash values. Table E.3 lists the same three URIs with the bit positions for four hash functions based on the MD5 column in Table E.2. This example uses a MASK_SIZE of 625,000 bytes, or 5,000,000 bits.

Table E.2.   Cache Digest Example: URIs and Hash Values

Method	URI	MD5
GET	*http://www.squid-cache.org*	69677C33244C8D776D1ED1210E07C120
GET	*http://www.oreilly.com*	4DC8FAFB9B5B0A4C08D992E453059333
GET	*ftp://ftp.ircache.net*	F36FB917F5D687629A6E2BEB6BB569FF

Table E.3.   Cache Digest Example: URIs and Bit Positions

Method	URI	B1	B2	B3	B4
GET	*http://www.squid-cache.org*	3,389,683	3,996,727	736,161	389,216
GET	*http://www.oreilly.com*	17,083	1,434,892	3,476,644	2,874,291
GET	*ftp://ftp.ircache.net*	4,185,367	4,477,282	911,467	2,051,263

F

HTTP Status Codes

This list of HTTP status codes is meant to be a quick, albeit incomplete, reference. Many of these codes are not mentioned elsewhere in this book. However, you may encounter them when examining log files or debugging HTTP problems. Refer to Section 10 of RFC 2616 for complete and official definitions.

F.1 1xx Intermediate Status

100 Continue
> This code informs the client that it should proceed with its request. This is useful when the client is sending a large message body. After sending the headers, the client waits for the 100 response and then sends the message body.

101 Switching Protocols
> This code allows clients and servers to negotiate the use of an alternate transfer protocol or a different version of HTTP.

F.2 2xx Successful Response

200 OK
> This code indicates the request was successful. For GET requests, the body of a 200 response contains the entire object requested.

201 Created
> This code informs the client that its request resulted in the successful creation of a new resource, which can now be referenced.

202 Accepted

> This code means that the client's request was accepted and scheduled for further processing. The request may or may not be successful when eventually acted upon.

203 Non-Authoritative Information

> This code may be used in place of 200 when the sender has reason to believe the information in the response's entity headers is different from what the origin server would send.

204 No Content

> This code is used in cases where the request was successfully processed, but the response doesn't have a message body.

205 Reset Content

> This code is similar to 204. The request was successful and the response doesn't include a message body. Furthermore, this code instructs the client to reset the document view—for example, by clearing the fields of an HTML form.

206 Partial Content

> This code may be used in response to a range request (a.k.a. partial GET), whereby the client requests only a subset of the object data.

F.3 *3xx Redirects*

300 Multiple Choices

> This code informs users and user agents that the resource is available at multiple locations, perhaps in different representations.

301 Moved Permanently

> This code redirects clients to a new location for the requested resource. This happens often when people relocate files on their servers or when content is moved from one server to another. Because the redirection is permanent, clients and caches can remember the new location and automatically redirect future requests.

302 Moved Temporarily

> This code is a temporary redirect to a new location. Apparently, many user agents always issue GET requests for the new URI, regardless of the original request method. This action violates even the older HTTP RFCs (1945 and 2068) but has become the expected behavior. RFC 2616 added two new status codes, 303 and 307, to "fix" this problem.

303 See Other

This code is the same as 302, except that the client should make a GET request for the new URI, regardless of the original request method.

304 Not Modified

This code is used when the client makes a conditional GET request (e.g., If-modified-since) and the resource has not changed.

305 Use Proxy

This code allows origin servers to redirect requests through a caching proxy. The proxy's address is given in the Location header.

306 (Unused)

A search of the HTTP working group archives reveals that, at one time, this code was named *Switch Proxy*.

307 Temporary Redirect

This code is similar to 302, indicating a temporary new location for the resource. However, clients must not use a different request method when requesting the new URI.

F.4 4xx Request Errors

400 Bad Request

This code indicates that the server could not understand the client's request or found it to be incorrect in some way.

401 Unauthorized

This code is used when access to a resource is protected and the client did not provide valid authentication credentials. Often, the 401 response includes information that causes the user agent to prompt the user for a username and password.

402 Payment Required

This code is reserved but not yet described in the HTTP/1.1 specifications.

403 Forbidden

This code indicates that the resource cannot be accessed, regardless of any authentication credentials. For example, this happens if a directory or file is unreadable due to file permissions.

404 Not Found

This code indicates that the requested resource does not exist on the server. It may also be used in place of 403 if the server doesn't want to acknowledge that the resource exists but cannot be accessed.

405 Method Not Allowed

This code indicates that the request method is inappropriate for the given URI. The response should include a list of methods that are allowed.

406 Not Acceptable

This code is used when the client's requirements, as given in the `Accept` header, conflict with the server's capabilities. For example, the client may indicate it will accept a GIF image, but the server is only able to generate JPEG images.

407 Proxy Authentication Required

This code is similar to 401 but is only returned by proxies. A proxy returns a 407 message upon receipt of a client request that doesn't have valid authentication credentials.

408 Request Time-out

This code is used when a server times out waiting for the client's request.

409 Conflict

This code indicates that the server's resource is in a state of conflict, such that it cannot satisfy the request. Presumably, the user will be able to resolve the conflict after receiving this response.

410 Gone

This code is used when an origin server knows that the requested resource has been permanently removed.

411 Length Required

This code is used when the server requires, but did not receive, a `Content-length` header in the client's request. Requests for some methods, such as POST and PUT, have message bodies by default and therefore require `Content-length` headers.

412 Precondition Failed

This code indicates that the request was unsuccessful because one of the client's conditions was not met. For example, the client can tell the server, "Only update this resource if the current version is X." If the current version is not X, the server returns a 412 response.

413 Request Entity Too Large

This code is used when a client's request is larger than the server is willing to accept.

414 Request-URI Too Large

This code indicates that the requested URI exceeds the server's limits. Although servers should accept URIs of any length, practical considerations may require actual limits.

415 Unsupported Media Type

This code is returned when a server refuses a request because the message body is in an inappropriate format.

416 Requested Range Not Satisfiable

This code indicates that the server could not process the client's partial GET request.

417 Expectation Failed

This code indicates that the client's expectation, given in an Expect header, cannot be met. HTTP/1.1 clients typically use the Expect header to tell the server they expect to receive a 100 (Continue) status line.

F.5 5xx Server Errors

500 Internal Server Error

This code is the default for an error condition when none of the other 5xx codes apply.

501 Not Implemented

This code indicates that the server does not implement the necessary features to satisfy the request.

502 Bad Gateway

This code indicates that the server received an invalid response from an upstream server.

503 Service Unavailable

This code indicates that the server is temporarily unable to process the client's request. A server that becomes overloaded may use this code to let the client know that it can retry the request later.

504 Gateway Time-out

This code is used by proxies and some servers to indicate a timeout when forwarding the client's request. It's also used when a request with the only-if-cached directive would result in a cache miss.

505 HTTP Version Not Supported

This code indicates that the server refuses to handle this request because of the HTTP version in the request line.

G

U.S.C. 17 Sec. 512.
Limitations on Liability
Relating to Material Online

Below is the text of the United States Code, title 17, Section 512, subsections (a) and (b). These regulations relate to a service provider's liability for copyright infringement due to network transmission and caching.

(a) Transitory Digital Network Communications.

A service provider shall not be liable for monetary relief, or, except as provided in subsection (j), for injunctive or other equitable relief, for infringement of copyright by reason of the provider's transmitting, routing, or providing connections for, material through a system or network controlled or operated by or for the service provider, or by reason of the intermediate and transient storage of that material in the course of such transmitting, routing, or providing connections, if—

(1) the transmission of the material was initiated by or at the direction of a person other than the service provider;

(2) the transmission, routing, provision of connections, or storage is carried out through an automatic technical process without selection of the material by the service provider;

(3) the service provider does not select the recipients of the material except as an automatic response to the request of another person;

(4) no copy of the material made by the service provider in the course of such intermediate or transient storage is maintained on the system or network in a manner ordinarily accessible to anyone other than anticipated recipients, and no such copy is maintained on the system or network in a manner ordinarily accessible to such anticipated recipients for

a longer period than is reasonably necessary for the transmission, routing, or provision of connections; and

(5)   the material is transmitted through the system or network without modification of its content.

(b)   System Caching.

(1)   Limitation on liability.

A service provider shall not be liable for monetary relief, or, except as provided in subsection (j), for injunctive or other equitable relief, for infringement of copyright by reason of the intermediate and temporary storage of material on a system or network controlled or operated by or for the service provider in a case in which—

(A)   the material is made available online by a person other than the service provider;

(B)   the material is transmitted from the person described in subparagraph (A) through the system or network to a person other than the person described in subparagraph (A) at the direction of that other person; and

(C)   the storage is carried out through an automatic technical process for the purpose of making the material available to users of the system or network who, after the material is transmitted as described in subparagraph (B), request access to the material from the person described in subparagraph (A), if the conditions set forth in paragraph (2) are met.

(2)   Conditions.

The conditions referred to in paragraph (1) are that—

(A)   the material described in paragraph (1) is transmitted to the subsequent users described in paragraph (1)(C) without modification to its content from the manner in which the material was transmitted from the person described in paragraph (1)(A);

(B)   the service provider described in paragraph (1) complies with rules concerning the refreshing, reloading, or other updating of the material when specified by the person making the material available online in accordance with a generally accepted industry standard data communications protocol for the system or network through which that person makes the material available, except that this subparagraph applies only if those rules are not used by the person described in paragraph (1)(A) to prevent or unreasonably impair the intermediate storage to which this subsection applies;

(C) the service provider does not interfere with the ability of technology associated with the material to return to the person described in paragraph (1)(A) the information that would have been available to that person if the material had been obtained by the subsequent users described in paragraph (1)(C) directly from that person, except that this subparagraph applies only if that technology—

   (i) does not significantly interfere with the performance of the provider's system or network or with the intermediate storage of the material;

   (ii) is consistent with generally accepted industry standard communications protocols; and

   (iii) does not extract information from the provider's system or network other than the information that would have been available to the person described in paragraph (1)(A) if the subsequent users had gained access to the material directly from that person;

(D) if the person described in paragraph (1)(A) has in effect a condition that a person must meet prior to having access to the material, such as a condition based on payment of a fee or provision of a password or other information, the service provider permits access to the stored material in significant part only to users of its system or network that have met those conditions and only in accordance with those conditions; and

(E) if the person described in paragraph (1)(A) makes that material available online without the authorization of the copyright owner of the material, the service provider responds expeditiously to remove, or disable access to, the material that is claimed to be infringing upon notification of claimed infringement as described in subsection (c)(3), except that this subparagraph applies only if—

   (i) the material has previously been removed from the originating site or access to it has been disabled, or a court has ordered that the material be removed from the originating site or that access to the material on the originating site be disabled; and

   (ii) the party giving the notification includes in the notification a statement confirming that the material has been removed from the originating site or access to it has been disabled or that a court has ordered that the material be removed from the originating site or that access to the material on the originating site be disabled.

H

List of Acronyms

I've used many acronyms throughout this book, in some cases without explanation. This glossary provides brief descriptions for acronyms only. Although the definitions aren't very detailed, they should be enough to get you started in the right direction on your search for more information.

ACK
> An acknowledgment packet in TCP, used to guarantee delivery and for connection establishment.

AFS
> The Andrew Filesystem. A distributed/network filesystem similar to NFS.

ARP
> Address Resolution Protocol. Used to find out the layer two (Ethernet) address associated with an IP address.

ASP
> Active Server Pages. A technique for dynamically generating HTML pages, developed by Microsoft and similar to CGI.

ATM
> Asynchronous Transfer Mode. A layer two data transmission protocol, typically used on high-speed fiber links.

BIND
> Berkeley Internet Name Daemon. The de facto standard DNS server and client library software package. For more information, visit *http://www.isc.org/products/BIND/*.

CARP
> Cache Array Routing Protocol. A technique for distributing requests to an array of caching proxies.

CDA
> Communications Decency Act. A U.S. law passed in 1996 intended to criminalize the transmission of pornography. Largely struck down as unconstitutional in 1997.

CDF
> Cumulative Distribution Function. A certain way of presenting probability distribution data.

CDN

Content Distribution Network. A service, available from companies such as Akamai and Digital Island, that replicates origin server content at different Internet locations.

CGI

Common Gateway Interface. An interface between a web server and external programs, mostly used for generating dynamic HTTP responses. For more information, visit *http://hoohoo.ncsa.uiuc.edu/cgi/ overview.html.*

DHCP

Dynamic Host Configuration Protocol. A broadcast protocol that enables hosts to discover their network configuration, such as IP addresses and host names. One of the discovery methods supported by WPAD.

DMCA

Digital Millennium Copyright Act. A law passed in 1998 that brings the U.S. into compliance with international treaties and also addresses issues raised by the so-called "Information Age."

DMZ

Demilitarized Zone. A term borrowed from military battlefields to describe a small network that separates internal networks from the hostile Internet.

DNS

Domain Name System. A distributed database that contains different types of records for Internet domain names. Most often used to translate host names into IP addresses. Documented in RFCs 1034, 1035, and others.

FDDI

Fiber Distributed Data Interface. A local area network data transmission standard that uses optical fibers and runs at 100 Mbps.

FTP

File Transfer Protocol. The Internet's original bulk data transfer protocol. Documented in RFC 959.

GDS

GreedyDual-Size. A cache replacement algorithm.

GMT

Greenwich Mean Time. The time zone located at 0° longitude, named after Greenwich, England. Equivalent to UTC.

HMAC

Hashed Message Authentication Code. A technique for generating codes that verify message authenticity. Uses a hash function, such as MD5, and a shared secret key.

HTCP

Hypertext Caching Protocol. A second-generation intercache protocol, similar to ICP. Documented in RFC 2756.

HTML

Hypertext Markup Language. A de facto standard markup language for writing web pages.

HTTP

Hypertext Transfer Protocol. An application-level protocol used to transfer most of the content available on the Web. Also the most popular application protocol in use on the Internet today. Documented in RFC 2616.

HTTPS

HTTP over TLS. A method for secure transmission of data using HTTP. Documented in RFCs 2817 and 2818.

IANA

Internet Assigned Numbers Authority. The group tasked with maintaining and delegating certain name and numeric spaces, such as IP addresses, DNS domains, and TCP/UDP port

numbers. For more information, visit
http://www.iana.org.

ICP

Internet Cache Protocol. The first
intercache protocol, ICP allows caches
to locate specific URLs in neighbors.
Documented in RFCs 2186 and 2187.

ICMP

Internet Control Message Protocol.
The *ping* application uses ICMP to
test network connectivity and show
round-trip times. ICMP has other, less
well known functions as well. Documented in RFC 792.

IDE

Integrated Drive Electronics. A generic
term that describes a class of hard
drives with a particular interface.
These drive interfaces are more correctly called ATA, or AT Attachment.

IETF

Internet Engineering Task Force. The
loosely organized body that develops
and documents Internet standards.
For more information, visit
http://www.ietf.org.

IOS

The operating system for Cisco's
router products.

ISP

Internet Service Provider. A general
term for any company providing
Internet services, such as user dialup
accounts, large backbone networks,
and server hosting.

LFU

Least Frequently Used. A relatively
simple cache replacement algorithm.

LRU

Least Recently Used. Another simple
cache replacement algorithm.

LVD

Low Voltage Differential. A type of
SCSI interface that supports high data
transfer rates with reasonably long
cable lengths.

MD5

A Message Digest algorithm used to
create a unique "fingerprint" of a
message. Documented in RFC 1321.

MIB

Management Information Base.
Describes the SNMP capabilities of a
device or application.

MRTG

Multi-Router Traffic Grapher. A popular application that collects and displays SNMP counters from routers and
other devices. For more information,
visit *http://www.mrtg.org.*

MSIE

Microsoft Internet Explorer. A popular
web browser application.

MSL

Maximum Segment Lifetime. The maximum amount of time that TCP
assumes a segment (packet) can exist
in the network. Typical values are 30,
60, and 120 seconds.

MTU

Maximum Transmission Unit. The
largest cell or frame that a particular
network link can transmit.

NFS

Network File System. A distributed/
network filesystem, popularized by
Sun Microsystems.

NIC

Network Interface Card. A generic
term for a computer's network interface, which may or may not actually
be a card.

NLANR

National Laboratory for Applied Network Research. A virtual research organization, headquartered at the San Diego Supercomputer Center. Home of the Squid and IRCache projects from 1996–2000. For more information, visit *http://www.nlanr.net*.

NNTP

Network News Transfer Protocol. The application-layer protocol used for distributing Usenet newsgroup messages. Documented in RFC 977.

NTFS

Microsoft's Windows NT Filesystem.

NTP

Network Time Protocol. Used to keep system clocks synchronized with an accurate, reference source. For more information, visit *http://www.ntp.org*.

OC-3

Optical Carrier 3. A layer two transmission standard that operates at 155 Mbps. Typically used for wide-area network connections rather than for local area networks.

OSI

Open Systems Interconnect. Usually refers to the OSI Reference Model, which defines the seven networking layers.

PAC

Proxy Auto-Configuration. A technique developed by Netscape that uses a JavaScript function to select a caching proxy. User-agents execute the function for each request. The function returns a list of proxies or tells the client to connect directly to the origin server.

PGP

Pretty Good Privacy. An application that uses strong encryption to protect the privacy of email and files.

PICS

Platform for Internet Content Selection. A standard way of labeling content such as web pages. PICS-aware applications can filter content based on user or administrative preferences.

POP

Point of Presence. Generally refers to the places where an ISP has equipment located.

RAID

Redundant Array of Inexpensive Disks. A number of different techniques for providing reliable storage with multiple disk drives.

RRD

Round-Robin Database. Refers to the RRDTool package, which is a general-purpose version of MRTG.

RFC

Request For Comments. These are the Internet's standards documents, generally written by the working groups of the IETF. For more information, visit *http://www.rfc-editor.org*.

RTT

Round-Trip Time. The time it takes for something, such as a data packet, to get from one place to another and back.

RUP

Resource Update Protocol. This is new work within the IETF's WEBI working group that would allow origin servers to expire and update objects from caches.

SCSI

Small Computer System Interface. A standard for connecting disk drives, tape drives, and other I/O devices to a computer system.

SLP

Service Location Protocol. A protocol and framework that allows user-agents to discover the network addresses of particular services without the need to assume well-known names and ports. Documented in RFC 2608.

SNMP

Simple Network Monitoring Protocol. A standard for monitoring and managing various types of network devices and applications. Most people do not find it simple.

SOAP

Simple Object Access Protocol. An open protocol based on HTTP and XML for invoking methods on servers, services, components, and objects. For more information, visit *http://www.develop.com/soap/*.

SSH

Secure Shell. An application that uses encryption to provide secure remote access to hosts and devices.

SSI

Server-Side Includes. A feature of the NCSA and Apache HTTP servers for generating dynamic HTML pages.

SSL

Secure Sockets Layer. A standard that uses encryption to provide a secure communication channel between two applications. More correctly known as TLS.

SYN

A type of TCP packet used to initiate connection establishment.

T1

A layer two data transmission standard that operates at 1.5 Mbps. Also known as DS1.

T3

A layer two data transmission standard that operates at 45 Mbps. Also known as DS3.

TCP

Transmission Control Protocol. The most popular layer four protocol in use on the Internet. TCP provides reliable delivery of data streams with acknowledgments and retransmission. Contrast with UDP. Documented in RFC 793.

TLS

Transport Layer Security. The new, correct name for SSL. TLS provides security to applications by running between layer four protocols such as TCP and application-layer protocols such as HTTP.

TPC

Transaction Processing Performance Council. A nonprofit corporation that oversees development and presentation of database benchmarks. For more information, visit *http://www.tpc.org*.

TTL

Time-To-Live. In the context of an IP packet, the maximum number of remaining router hops a packet may make before it is discarded. In other contexts, such as the DNS, refers to the amount of time until some piece of information expires.

UDP

User Datagram Protocol. A simple, but unreliable, layer four transport protocol. Contrast with TCP. Documented in RFC 768.

UFS

Unix File System.

UPS

Uninterruptible Power Supply. Provides backup power in the event of an outage.

URI

Uniform Resource Identifier. A standard naming scheme for web resources. Documented in RFC 2396.

URL

Uniform Resource Locator. A subset of URIs, URL resources are tied to specific locations (hostnames).

URN

Uniform Resource Name. A subset of URIs, URN resources are not tied to specific locations.

UTC

Universal Time Coordinated. Equivalent to GMT.

WAIS

Wide Area Information Service. A protocol for searching databases and retrieving results. Popular around 1994–1995 but not used much today.

WCCP

Web Cache Coordination Protocol. Cisco's formerly proprietary protocol for communication between network devices (routers, switches) and caching proxies.

WEBDAV

Distributed Authoring and Versioning extensions to HTTP. Used for certain applications such as remote file editing and email.

WEBI

Web Intermediaries. A working group of the IETF chartered to address issues related to caching proxies and other types of web intermediaries.

WPAD

Web Proxy Auto-Discovery. A protocol that user-agents can use to discover caching proxies.

WREC

Web Replication and Caching. A now defunct working group of the IETF. For more information, visit *http://www.wrec.org.*

XML-RPC

A protocol specification for making remote procedure calls using HTTP as the transport and XML as the encoding. For more information, visit *http://www.xmlrpc.co.*

Bibliography

Books and Articles

Banga, Gaurav and Peter Druschel, "Measuring the Capacity of a Web Server," *USENIX Symposium on Internet Technologies and Systems*, December 1997.

Bloom, Burton, "Space/time Trade-offs in Hash Coding with Allowable Errors," *Communications of the ACM, v13, n7, pp 422–426*, July 1970.

Bowman, C. Mic, Peter B. Danzig, Darren R. Hardy, Udi Manber, and Michael F. Schwartz, "Harvest: A Scalable, Customizable Discovery and Access System," *University of Coloardo Tech Report CU-CS-732-94*, 1994.

Breslau, Lee, Pei Cao, Li Fan, Graham Phillips, and Scott Shenker, "Web Caching and Zipf-like Distributions: Evidence and Implications," *Proceedings of Infocomm'99*, April 1999.

Cao, Pei and Sandy Irani, "Cost-Aware WWW Proxy Caching Algorithms," *Proceedings of the USENIX Symposium on Internet Technologies and Systems*, December 8–11, 1997.

Duska, Bradley, David Marwood, and Michael Feely, "The Measured Access Characteristics of World-Wide-Web Client Proxy Caches," *USENIX Symposium on Internet Technologies and Systems*, December 1997.

Friedl, Jeffrey E. F., *Mastering Regular Expressions,* January 1997.

Friedman, Johnathan A. and Francis M. Buono, "Using the Digital Millennium Copyright Act to Limit Potential Copyright Liability Online," *The Richmond Journal of Law & Technology, v6, n4*, Winter 1999–2000. (*http://www.richmond.edu/jolt/v6i4/article1.html*)

Gadde, Syam, Jeff Chase, and Michael Rabinovich, "A Taste of Crispy Squid," *Proceedings of the Workshop on Internet Server Performance (WISP98)*, June 1998.

Kent, Christopher A. and Jeffrey C. Mogul, *Fragmentation Considered Harmful,* December 1987.

Lessig, Lawrence, *Code and Other Laws of Cyberspace,* December 1999.

Pool, Martin, *meantime: non-consensual http user tracking using caches,* 2000. (*http://sourcefrog.net/front/mbp/meantime/*)

Rousskov, Alex and Duane Wessels, *The Third Cache-off,* October 2000. (*http://www.measurement-factory.com/results/*)

Schlachter, Eric, "System Operator Liability: What have we learned?," *Boardwatch Magazine,* April 1997.

Siever, Ellen, Stephen Spainhour, Jessica P. Hekman, and Stephen Figgins, *Linux in a Nutshell,* 3rd ed. 2000.

Stevens, W. Richard, *TCP/IP Illustrated, Volume 1,* 1994.

Tewksbury, Russell Baird, "Is the Internet Heading for a Cache Crunch?," *On The Internet,* 1998.

Williams, S., M. Abrams, C.R. Standridge, G. Abdulla, and E.A. Fox, "Removal Policies in Network Caches for World-Wide Web Documents," *Proceedings of ACM Sigcomm'96,* August 26–30, 1996.

Zona Research, *The Economic Impacts of Unacceptable Web Site Download Speeds,* June 1999. (*http://www.zonaresearch.com/deliverables/white_papers/wp17/*)

Zwicky, Elizabeth D., Simon Cooper, and D. Brent Chapman, *Building Internet Firewalls,* 2nd ed. June 2000.

Request For Comments

Bhushan, Abhay and others , *RFC 172 The File Transfer Protocol,* June 1971.

Clark, David D., *RFC 813 Window and Acknowledgement Strategy in TCP,* July 1982.

Postel, Jon and Joyce Reynolds, *RFC 959 File Transfer Protocol (FTP),* October 1985.

IETF, *RFC 1122 Requirements for Internet Hosts—Communication Layers,* Robert Braden, Ed. October 1989.

Rivest, Ronald L., *RFC 1321 The MD5 Message-Digest Algorithm,* April 1992.

Berners-Lee, Tim, *RFC 1630 Universal Resource Identifiers in WWW,* June 1994.

Hanks, S., Tony Li, D. Farinacci, and P. Traina, *RFC 1701 Generic Routing Encapsulation (GRE),* October 1994.

Berners-Lee, Tim, Larry Masinter, and Mark McCahill, *RFC 1736 Uniform Resource Locators (URL),* December 1994.

—, Roy Fielding, and Henrik Frystyk, *RFC 1945 Hypertext Transfer Protocol—HTTP/1.0,* May 1996.

Krawczyk, H., M. Bellare, and R. Canetti, *RFC 2104 HMAC: Keyed-Hashing for Message Authentication,* February 1997.

Moats, Ryan, *RFC 2141 URN Syntax,* May 1997.

Mogul, Jeffrey C., Roy Fielding, Jim Gettys, and Henrik Frystyk, *RFC 2145 Use and Interpretation of HTTP Version Numbers,* May 1997.

Mogul, Jeffrey and Paul Leach, *RFC 2227 Simple Hit-Metering and Usage-Limiting for HTTP,* October 1997.

Dierks, Tim and Christopher Allen, *RFC 2246 The TLS Protocol Version 1.0,* January 1999.

Berners-Lee, Tim, Roy Fielding, and Larry Masinter, *RFC 2396 Uniform Resource Identifiers (URI): Generic Syntax,* August 1998.

Goland, Y. Y., E. J. Whitehead, A. Faizi, S. R. Carter, and D. Jensen, *RFC 2518 HTTP Extensions for Distributed Authoring— WEBDAV,* February 1999.

Eastlake, Donald, *RFC 2535 Domain Name System Security Extensions,* March 1999.

Fielding, Roy, Jim Gettys, Jeffrey Mogul, Henrik Frystyk, Larry Masinter, Paul Leach, and Tim Berners-Lee, *RFC 2616 Hypertext Transfer Protocol — HTTP/1.1,* June 1999.

Vixie, Paul and Duane Wessels, *RFC 2756 Hyper Text Caching Protocol (HTCP/0.0),* January 2000.

Kristol, David and Lou Montulli, *RFC 2965 HTTP State Management Mechanism,* October 2000.

Cooper, Ian, Ingrid Melve, and Gary Tomlinson, *RFC 3040 Internet Web Replication and Caching Taxonomy,* January 2001.

Index

We'd like to hear your suggestions for improving our indexes. Send email to *index@oreilly.com*.

About the Author

Duane Wessels discovered Unix and the Internet as an undergraduate student studying physics at Washington State University. After playing system administrator for a few years, he moved to Boulder, Colorado, to attend graduate school. In late 1994, he joined the Harvest project, where he worked on searching, indexing, and caching. From 1996 until 2000, he was co-principal investigator of the NLANR Information Resource Caching project (IRCache). During this time, he and others developed and supported the Squid caching proxy. In 1999, his team organized the first "Cache-Off," a performance benchmarking event for caching proxies. Currently, he is co-owner and president of The Measurement Factory, Inc., a company that specializes in evaluating the performance and behavior of HTTP-aware devices. Like many other Colorado residents, he enjoys hiking, bicycling, and snowboarding.

Colophon

Our look is the result of reader comments, our own experimentation, and feedback from distribution channels. Distinctive covers complement our distinctive approach to technical topics, breathing personality and life into potentially dry subjects.

The animal on the cover of *Web Caching* is a rock thrush. Rock thrushes belong to the order Passeriformes, the largest order of birds, containing 5,700 species, or over half of all living birds. Passerines, as birds of this order are called, are perching birds with four toes on each foot, three that point forward and one larger one that points backward. Rock thrushes belong to either the genus *Monticola* or the genus *Petrocossyphus*, such as *Monticola solitarius*, the blue rock thrush, and *Petrocossyphus imerinus*, the littoral rock thrush.

Leanne Soylemez was the production editor and copyeditor for *Web Caching*. Matt Hutchinson was the proofreader, and Jeff Holcomb provided quality control. Brenda Miller wrote the index.

Edie Freedman designed the cover of this book. The cover image is a 19th-century engraving from the Dover Pictorial Archive. Emma Colby produced the cover layout with QuarkXPress 4.1 using Adobe's ITC Garamond font.

Melanie Wang designed the interior layout based on a series design by Nancy Priest. The print version of this book was created by translating the DocBook XML markup of its source files into a set of gtroff macros using a filter developed at O'Reilly & Associates by Norman Walsh. Steve Talbott designed and wrote the underlying macro set on the basis of the GNU *troff –gs* macros; Lenny Muellner adapted them to XML and implemented the book design. The GNU groff text formatter version 1.11.1 was used to generate PostScript output. The text and heading fonts are ITC Garamond Light and Garamond Book; the code font is Constant Willison. The illustrations that appear in the book were produced by Robert Romano and Jessamyn Read using Macromedia FreeHand 9 and Adobe Photoshop 6. This colophon was written by Leanne Soylemez.

Whenever possible, our books use a durable and flexible lay-flat binding. If the page count exceeds this binding's limit, perfect binding is used.

How to stay in touch with O'Reilly

1. Visit Our Award-Winning Web Site
http://www.oreilly.com/

★ "Top 100 Sites on the Web" —*PC Magazine*
★ "Top 5% Web sites" —*Point Communications*
★ "3-Star site" —*The McKinley Group*

Our web site contains a library of comprehensive product information (including book excerpts and tables of contents), downloadable software, background articles, interviews with technology leaders, links to relevant sites, book cover art, and more. File us in your Bookmarks or Hotlist!

2. Join Our Email Mailing Lists
New Product Releases
To receive automatic email with brief descriptions of all new O'Reilly products as they are released, send email to:
ora-news-subscribe@lists.oreilly.com
Put the following information in the first line of your message (*not* in the Subject field):
subscribe ora-news

O'Reilly Events
If you'd also like us to send information about trade show events, special promotions, and other O'Reilly events, send email to:
ora-news-subscribe@lists.oreilly.com
Put the following information in the first line of your message (*not* in the Subject field):
subscribe ora-events

3. Get Examples from Our Books via FTP
There are two ways to access an archive of example files from our books:

Regular FTP
- ftp to:
  ftp.oreilly.com
  (login: anonymous
  password: your email address)
- Point your web browser to:
  ftp://ftp.oreilly.com/

FTPMAIL
- Send an email message to:
  ftpmail@online.oreilly.com
  (Write "help" in the message body)

4. Contact Us via Email
order@oreilly.com
To place a book or software order online. Good for North American and international customers.

subscriptions@oreilly.com
To place an order for any of our newsletters or periodicals.

books@oreilly.com
General questions about any of our books.

software@oreilly.com
For general questions and product information about our software. Check out O'Reilly Software Online at **http://software.oreilly.com/** for software and technical support information. Registered O'Reilly software users send your questions to: **website-support@oreilly.com**

cs@oreilly.com
For answers to problems regarding your order or our products.

booktech@oreilly.com
For book content technical questions or corrections.

proposals@oreilly.com
To submit new book or software proposals to our editors and product managers.

international@oreilly.com
For information about our international distributors or translation queries. For a list of our distributors outside of North America check out:
http://www.oreilly.com/distributors.html

5. Work with Us
Check out our website for current employment opportunites:
http://jobs.oreilly.com/

O'Reilly & Associates, Inc.
101 Morris Street, Sebastopol, CA 95472 USA
TEL 707-829-0515 or 800-998-9938
      (6am to 5pm PST)
FAX 707-829-0104

International Distributors

UK, EUROPE, MIDDLE EAST AND AFRICA (EXCEPT FRANCE, GERMANY, AUSTRIA, SWITZERLAND, LUXEMBOURG, AND LIECHTENSTEIN)

INQUIRIES
O'Reilly UK Limited
4 Castle Street
Farnham
Surrey, GU9 7HS
United Kingdom
Telephone: 44-1252-711776
Fax: 44-1252-734211
Email: information@oreilly.co.uk

ORDERS
Wiley Distribution Services Ltd.
1 Oldlands Way
Bognor Regis
West Sussex PO22 9SA
United Kingdom
Telephone: 44-1243-843294
UK Freephone: 0800-243207
Fax: 44-1243-843302 (Europe/EU orders)
or 44-1243-843274 (Middle East/Africa)
Email: cs-books@wiley.co.uk

FRANCE

INQUIRIES & ORDERS
Éditions O'Reilly
18 rue Séguier
75006 Paris, France
Tel: 1-40-51-71-89
Fax: 1-40-51-72-26
Email: france@oreilly.fr

GERMANY, SWITZERLAND, AUSTRIA, LUXEMBOURG, AND LIECHTENSTEIN

INQUIRIES & ORDERS
O'Reilly Verlag
Balthasarstr. 81
D-50670 Köln, Germany
Telephone: 49-221-973160-91
Fax: 49-221-973160-8
Email: anfragen@oreilly.de (inquiries)
Email: order@oreilly.de (orders)

CANADA (FRENCH LANGUAGE BOOKS)

Les Éditions Flammarion ltée
375, Avenue Laurier Ouest
Montréal (Québec) H2V 2K3
Tel: 00-1-514-277-8807
Fax: 00-1-514-278-2085
Email: info@flammarion.qc.ca

HONG KONG

City Discount Subscription Service, Ltd.
Unit A, 6th Floor, Yan's Tower
27 Wong Chuk Hang Road
Aberdeen, Hong Kong
Tel: 852-2580-3539
Fax: 852-2580-6463
Email: citydis@ppn.com.hk

KOREA

Hanbit Media, Inc.
Chungmu Bldg. 210
Yonnam-dong 568-33
Mapo-gu
Seoul, Korea
Tel: 822-325-0397
Fax: 822-325-9697
Email: hant93@chollian.dacom.co.kr

PHILIPPINES

Global Publishing
G/F Benavides Garden
1186 Benavides Street
Manila, Philippines
Tel: 632-254-8949/632-252-2582
Fax: 632-734-5060/632-252-2733
Email: globalp@pacific.net.ph

TAIWAN

O'Reilly Taiwan
1st Floor, No. 21, Lane 295
Section 1, Fu-Shing South Road
Taipei, 106 Taiwan
Tel: 886-2-27099669
Fax: 886-2-27038802
Email: mori@oreilly.com

INDIA

Shroff Publishers & Distributors Pvt. Ltd.
12, "Roseland", 2nd Floor
180, Waterfield Road, Bandra (West)
Mumbai 400 050
Tel: 91-22-641-1800/643-9910
Fax: 91-22-643-2422
Email: spd@vsnl.com

CHINA

O'Reilly Beijing
SIGMA Building, Suite B809
No. 49 Zhichun Road
Haidian District
Beijing, China PR 100080
Tel: 86-10-8809-7475
Fax: 86-10-8809-7463
Email: beijing@oreilly.com

JAPAN

O'Reilly Japan, Inc.
Yotsuya Y's Building
7 Banch 6, Honshio-cho
Shinjuku-ku
Tokyo 160-0003 Japan
Tel: 81-3-3356-5227
Fax: 81-3-3356-5261
Email: japan@oreilly.com

SINGAPORE, INDONESIA, MALAYSIA AND THAILAND

TransQuest Publishers Pte Ltd
30 Old Toh Tuck Road #05-02
Sembawang Kimtrans Logistics Centre
Singapore 597654
Tel: 65-4623112
Fax: 65-4625761
Email: wendiw@transquest.com.sg

ALL OTHER ASIAN COUNTRIES

O'Reilly & Associates, Inc.
101 Morris Street
Sebastopol, CA 95472 USA
Tel: 707-829-0515
Fax: 707-829-0104
Email: order@oreilly.com

AUSTRALIA

Woodslane Pty., Ltd.
7/5 Vuko Place
Warriewood NSW 2102
Australia
Tel: 61-2-9970-5111
Fax: 61-2-9970-5002
Email: info@woodslane.com.au

NEW ZEALAND

Woodslane New Zealand, Ltd.
21 Cooks Street (P.O. Box 575)
Waganui, New Zealand
Tel: 64-6-347-6543
Fax: 64-6-345-4840
Email: info@woodslane.com.au

ARGENTINA

Distribuidora Cuspide
Suipacha 764
1008 Buenos Aires
Argentina
Phone: 5411-4322-8868
Fax: 5411-4322-3456
Email: libros@cuspide.com